Shattered Dreams

BETTE PRATT

Copyright © 2020 by Bette Pratt.

ISBN   Softcover   978-1-953537-13-3

All Scripture Quoted is taken from the New International Version of the Bible.

All rights reserved. No part of this book may be reproduced or transmitted in any form or by any means, electronic or mechanical, including photocopying, recording, or by any information storage and retrieval system without express written permission from the author, except in the case of brief quotations embodied in critical reviews and certain other non-commercial uses permitted by copyright law.

Printed in the United States of America.

To order additional copies of this book, contact:
Bookwhip
1-855-339-3589
https://www.bookwhip.com

ONE

November was busy in the little town of Vansville, Georgia. Several of the best cooks in the town got together to fix the best dinner ever before the rehearsal of Duncan Roads and Nancy Southerland's wedding. Isabel was their landlady and she was determined to do it up right, everyone knew she was a stickler for perfection, but then, she had Sandy DeLord as her helper. What could go wrong with a combination like that? Several friends in town had decorated the large waiting room in the clinic next door to Isabel's cabins so it was beautiful for both the rehearsal dinner and the reception.

Nancy's family came from south Georgia bringing a delicious catered dinner with them for the rehearsal dinner. Duncan's mom was barely speaking to him, so everyone wondered if she would even come to see her only son married. Of course, she had been invited along with her daughter's family and Duncan's sister had made it happen. Still, Duncan was surprised.

The wedding itself, held in the little community church, was lovely, since both Duncan and Nancy were members there. The sanctuary was decorated beautifully in fall colors. Sandy DeLord, of course, played and sang. After the reception, Duncan took his bride on a lovely, memorable Caribbean cruise for six days. Nancy couldn't remember having such a perfect week, she couldn't remember ever being so happy in all her life. As far as she was concerned, life couldn't be better. Duncan was the love of her life, they'd had a rough start, but Duncan was the best man there was.

Duncan had been busy on his days off and especially since the hiking season ended; building their home mostly himself on a parcel of land he'd bought from Brad Thomas that was behind Isabel's cabins. No one had really known who owned that land, but now that Brad was coming regularly to church, people found he was much easier to approach and Duncan had done it. Now most of the town knew who'd been behind getting a clinic in Vansville as well. Business had picked up a bit in the hardware store, too. Brad was much more pleasant to his customers than he'd been in many, many years.

Isabel was happy for her two renters she'd watched their romance bloom and flourish even before the two of them would admit any attraction. However, she became discouraged in December when her bills started coming in because Duncan had rented one of her cabins for more than a year and his rent had supplemented Isabel's income so she could afford the higher cost of fuel to keep her home warm during the winter. Nancy had rented another cabin when she started working at the Vansville clinic in July. Now they were both gone from her cabins and winter was coming. Because of the water lines, Isabel had to keep minimal heat in her six cabins through the winter, even if there wasn't anyone living in them or renting for a night or two.

Pastor Roger performed the wedding, but in the audience his pregnant wife sat wondering when their baby would be born. The first due date her doctor gave them was close to Thanksgiving, but later, he told them he'd miscalculated. Perhaps some time in December was a better date. The wedding happened on the Saturday before Thanksgiving and here she sat, watching her friend get married and she as big as a house! Would this baby ever decide to come outside so she could put him down once in a while? Being the pastor's wife, she gave the happy couple a smile as they went down the aisle, but her heart wasn't in it at all. She was really waiting for that first horrendous backache to happen. Roger, being the town pastor performed his obligations, however, he watched his wife like a hawk he would whisk her away to the hospital at the first twinge of a contraction.

The morning of December fifth, Isabel, Raylyn's grandmother, received a frantic call from Roger that they were on the way to Blairsville Hospital, because Raylyn's water had broken. Ruth insisted they stop for her and drop off Heidi to stay with Isabel while Raylyn was in labor. Roger decided that was a simple request he would gladly comply with. Several hours later, little Roger Allen Jr. was born and weighed a strapping eight pounds, four ounces. Raylyn finally got her wish, she could now hold Lenny in her arms, on the *outside* of her body and praises be – she could put him down every so often!

The Vansville Community Church planned on the second annual Christmas concert on the Sunday before Christmas. The major performer again this year would be Sandy DeLord. Even though she was becoming uncomfortable in her pregnancy, Sandy insisted that the concert be performed. Last year, Ramon was the MC, Sandy played and sang and Roger ran the over-head projector displaying words to some of the pieces.

The program this year was completely different, but still using words projected on the wall. However, because Sandy was pregnant and because Ramon could tell she was very uncomfortable trying to sing, he called Sandy's family and asked them to come early. Without Sandy knowing it, he asked Marcy to sing the songs. Reluctantly, she agreed but only if they could come early so Marcy could practice with her sister, since she wasn't an accomplished musician and didn't read music as Sandy did. Marcy and her parents came a week before the program and stayed with them through Christmas. Sandy was happy to have her family, but Ramon was glad for the help they were to Sandy.

Dr. Stan, from the Vansville Clinic, had consulted with his OBGYN doctor friend from Blairsville Hospital almost as soon as he'd learned of Sandy's pregnancy, since he had only graduated from his medical studies in ER medicine and didn't feel comfortable taking a pregnant paraplegic through nine months of her pregnancy. They were following her very closely, neither of them had ever had a pregnant patient who also had the problems of a long time paraplegic.

When he learned that Sandy and Ramon usually went to Philadelphia for Christmas, he nearly demanded that Sandy not travel due to her pregnancy, even though she wasn't due until March. The baby was healthy and doing well, but Sandy, because of her disability, was having a hard time. Ramon was glad not to go he knew the trip would be very hard for Sandy. Not that it would happen, but he knew Sandy's mom would try everything to keep her daughter in Philadelphia. Never mind that they'd been married for over a year, Mama tried each time they saw her to keep her precious, 'cripple' daughter from going back.

Charlie and Ramon both shook their heads when Colleen was saying a tearful goodbye to her daughter the Wednesday after Christmas, when she said, "Sandy, you really need to come home, I can't stay here, but your room is still waiting and I can take care of you there. You know, Dear, how much I miss you."

Sandy looked at her mom for a long minute, before she said, "Mom, I'm almost thirty years old, Ramon and I have made our home here. Our doctors are here. You can come back after the baby's born to help me, if you want, but our home is not in Philadelphia, it's here." To everyone's amazement, Colleen took two steps to the car and sat down, closed the door and fastened her seatbelt, then looked ahead until Marcy and Charlie stepped in. Charlie started up and pulled away. As she had done another time, Colleen did not wave.

Marcy's mouth dropped open, as she watched her mom's actions. She'd known how her mom had treated Sandy when she left for Vansville, but hadn't spoken about it at the time. After waving to her sister, as they pulled away, she turned back and said angrily, "Mom! That was the cruelest thing I've ever seen you do! Why did you treat my sister like that!"

Charlie looked at his daughter in the rearview mirror, but didn't speak. What could he say? For so many months he and Colleen had been over this same territory. Colleen pulled in a loud gasp, but didn't answer her daughter. Finally, when there was silence in the car for several minutes, Marcy looked daggers at the back of her mom's head and said, "Well?"

Barely above a whisper, Colleen said, "She's a *cripple*, I need her home to care for her!"

They were barely on the two lane highway outside of Vansville when Marcy said, "Dad, please stop the car!"

Charlie looked as his younger daughter's fierce expression and pulled to the side of the road. The instant he stopped, Marcy was out and grabbed the door handle of her mom's door. She flung it open then got in her mom's face. Making sure the woman was looking at her. She said, in a soft and deadly voice, "Mom, I don't want to **ever, EVER** hear you call my sister a cripple again! She hates that word and so do the rest of us. Sandy has a severe handicap, but she is living with it and has overcome it so much, hardly anyone notices. You heard what she said, she and Ramon make their home here they have for quite a while. It is despicable that you treat her as you do! You didn't wave goodbye to her when she left to come here, you don't ever wave to her when she leaves to come back and you didn't wave now. EVERY time you see her you tell her she needs to come home! How do you think that makes Ramon feel? How do you think that makes her feel? I **know** how I'd feel…!"

Colleen's mouth had dropped open when Marcy started talking. When she asked her question, Colleen's mouth closed, but when she opened it again, nothing came out. Charlie and Marcy both saw her swallow, but still no words or sound left the woman's mouth. Marcy had said her peace she slammed her mom's door, climbed in the back seat and slammed hers too. As she buckled her seatbelt, Charlie pulled the stick into drive and pulled back on the highway. No one spoke until long after they'd reached the interstate outside of Blairsville.

Also right before the concert, Roger's family surprised them and came for a week's visit. Because Lenny was so small, Roger's family, his sister and brother-in-law stayed in two of Isabel's cabins for over a week. The younger Clemens' were shocked when Roger's sister stepped from the rental car sporting maternity clothes. After all, she'd been married for over five years. Roger knew his brother-in-law had wanted a family for several of those years.

Isabel was glad for the added income Roger's family gave her. However, they all went home before New Year's Day, but Isabel filled her propane tank for the winter with that added income. She knew that the full tank would see her through the winter if she only rented her cabins occasionally the rest of the winter.

Isabel's daughter, Ruth, had been in Vansville for an extra long visit. She'd come in plenty of time to be there for Lenny's birth then stayed for the holidays. Some time after cold weather came, Ruth watched the weather, not only for Vansville, but also Detroit and decided not to go back to Detroit, but sell her house in Michigan and move permanently to Vansville. After all, Ruth had no family left in Michigan, her mom, daughter and grandchildren were all in Vansville. With the sale of her home and her husband's monthly pension, she took over the short fall in Isabel's income. Things seemed to be working out well for them.

Pastor Roger hosted a New Year's Eve game night and a midnight service to bring in the new year at the community church and most of the community came. However, Ramon and Sandy didn't come. She was too uncomfortable she'd had to give up sitting long days in her chair, so Roger's praise team supplied the music. Isabel wasn't too crazy about that. Maybe some people praised the Lord that way, but to her, it was just noise. Noise didn't praise the Lord, not to her way of thinking.

It was New Year's Day, people were sleeping in after attending the late night service at the church, but at the Clemens house, Cow didn't know it was to be a day of rest. She decided it was time for breakfast, even though it was barely light. Reluctantly, Roger quietly slipped from the bed, hoping to leave his exhausted wife to sleep a few more minutes until her tiny alarm clock decided it was time for his breakfast.

By the time Roger came in with the milk and eggs everyone was up. Heidi was 'helping' her mommy, Raylyn held Lenny since he'd just finished his breakfast, but before Roger could strain the milk, the phone rang. Raylyn still held Lenny, but she answered then handed the handset to Roger. It seemed another family who lived in Vansville had urgent need of their pastor, on this dreary, cold first day of the new year. Before he hung up Roger asked Joyce if she'd called the ambulance.

Roger arrived at the Thomas home about ten minutes after he received the call from Joyce Thomas about her husband. Brad was lying in bed, he hadn't been able to move from the time it got light, he had a feeling he'd been in the same position since long before that, but what really frustrated him, he couldn't tell her, he couldn't make the words come out he wanted to say, it was only noise.

Roger barely got inside the front door before Joyce quickly ushered him into the bedroom. Roger immediately made his own silent assessment, but then took Brad's good hand and put his other arm around Joyce and said, "Let's pray for Brad, shall we, Joyce?"

"Yes, Pastor, I'll be glad for you to."

Roger was still praying when they heard the wail of the ambulance siren on the clear morning air as it came into town. Roger ended his prayer,

"Father, we hear the ambulance coming and we pray that as they take Brad to the hospital that You will give the doctors wisdom and gentle hands as they work with our friend. We know You are the Great Physician, bless we pray in Your Son's Name, amen."

"Thank you, Pastor," Joyce murmured. "I'm so glad you got here so quick! When Nathan said he'd call the ambulance I was worried they'd get here first."

Around a lump in his throat, Roger said, "Joyce, I'm your pastor, it's what I must do."

Only moments later Nathan Thomas opened the door to the paramedics with their stretcher and said, "He's in the bedroom, I'll show you the way."

The men nodded and followed closely behind Nathan. "Thanks, we really appreciate that. Sometimes people get caught up in the stress and just assume we know where to go."

Roger kept his arm around Joyce and stepped back from the side of the bed so that the men with their stretcher had plenty of room. The men quickly and efficiently lifted Brad from the low bed onto their stretcher and strapped him down. As they began to wheel him from the room, Joyce asked, "Can I go with him in the ambulance?"

The older man smiled at Joyce, then started pulling the gurney from the room, while the younger man followed along behind and said, "Of course, Ma'am, we're always happy to have a family member go with the patient in the ambulance, as I'm sure you know, he feels more secure that way." Looking at the lady still in bare feet, the paramedic said, "But we'll be leaving in only a few minutes. It is quite cold out there, you know. In fact, on our way from Blairsville, we saw a few flakes of snow."

Stepping out of Roger's arm, Joyce nodded and said, "Good, I'll grab my purse and coat and I'll be with you."

"That'll be fine, Ma'am." He didn't add, but he did look at her feet again.

As she left Roger's arm, she said to him, "Roger, thanks for coming and praying with Brad. I know he heard you and it quieted him, I could tell."

Wondering how she could tell how it quieted him, he really hadn't moved, other than to close his eyes and then open them when Roger finished praying, he said, "Joyce, it was the least I could do. We'll be praying for him."

"Thanks," she said, meaning it.

Brad's stretcher was already out the door when Joyce stuffed her feet into some loafers close by, grabbed her purse and coat and also vanished from sight. Nathan and Maryann and their spouses were hurrying to get their coats. They planned to drive behind the ambulance so they could be with their parents at the hospital. This was not the way any of them had planned to spend their holiday vacation.

Since Natt was old enough to stay with the kids, Roger followed Nathan and his wife and Maryann and her husband as they hurried to follow the ambulance, then he went to his car. As the ambulance went screaming out of town and Nathan's car rushed after it, his flashers going, Roger slid into his Jeep and turned toward Isabel's house. His stomach rumbled, reminding him he hadn't eaten yet, even though he felt like he'd done a full day's work. However, he knew what waited at the small house on the next street over, across the gravel parking lot, some melt-in-your-mouth cinnamon buns and the finest brewed coffee in Vansville. These southern ladies sure knew how to cook! He was glad he was now related to one of them.

People were sleeping in on New Year's Day when the stillness was shattered by an ambulance siren. Isabel was making her famous cinnamon buns because she and Ruth had invited the Clemens for brunch when she heard the wail of the siren. She wished she had a scanner, but they'd have to wait for the village grapevine to find out who and what had happened. However, they didn't have too long to wait, Raylyn and Heidi and the baby came at the time they'd agreed on, but Roger wasn't with them.

Heidi didn't knock on Isabel's door, she rarely did instead, she burst through the door at Isabel's house and exclaimed, "Gamaw! Daddy had to go watch Mr. Brad and Ms Joyce go in the ambulance this morning! He told Mommy we come without him, he come later for buns, 'cause Ms Joyce was crying real bad on the phone."

Looking at Raylyn, Isabel asked Heidi, "What happened, little one?"

Heidi shrugged. "Dunno, Gamaw, ask Mommy, maybe she does."

Raylyn sank into a chair at the table and sighed, still holding Lenny. The diaper bag slipped off her arm onto the floor and she let it. The baby wasn't sleeping through the night yet and the dark circles under her eyes easily showed how exhausted she was. Ruth poured a mug of fresh coffee and set it in front of her, then happily took the baby for a few minutes, blowing bubbles at the infant, hoping to be the first to see him smile.

As she doctored her coffee, Raylyn answered, "Grandma, Roger had just come in from milking when Joyce Thomas called, nearly frantic. Brad couldn't move when she tried to wake him. Roger took the call and said he'd come pray with them then stay until the ambulance came. Their children and grandchildren are there, but she wanted Roger to come pray for him."

Hearing Raylyn's words reminded Isabel how far Roger had come in little over a year. A year ago Thanksgiving, Roger had preached his first sermon ever in Vansville Community Church, even though he'd stood in the pulpit nearly every Sunday for five years. Until then, he'd never prayed with anyone going to the hospital, even though people called him to come before the ambulance, but now, he was a real pastor and the community loved him. All of that was thanks to one persistent lady, Sandy DeLord.

"I'm glad, Missy," Isabel said, that's all she could say around the lump in her throat. However, there were unshed tears sparkling in her eyes.

Ruth and Isabel had finished one carafe full of coffee before Raylyn and the children came, so Ruth had started another through the coffeemaker for breakfast. Once Raylyn finished doctoring her coffee, Ruth gave the baby back and now she stood at the sink washing and fixing a big dish of fresh fruit for their brunch and Isabel had a mitt on her hand to take her cinnamon buns from the oven. Heidi climbed up in her chair and watched all three ladies. Lenny, of course, waved his arms around, but only cooed his delight.

Isabel pulled the buns from the oven and said, "It's already gone, so we'll wait for him."

"Sure, Grandma, I'm sure he'll be here soon."

"Yeah, Gamaw, Daddy be here quick! He likes your buns." Heidi added.

Moments later there was a tap on the front door, then it opened and a man's voice said, "Mmm, do I smell Isabel's cinnamon buns?"

Heidi jumped from the chair and flew from the kitchen, barreling into Roger's legs. Hugging his legs, she exclaimed, "Daddy! Yes, Gamaw's buns are ready now. Grandma has lotsa fruit and there's coffee for you grownups and chocolate for me. Come on, they don't wanna wait too long, you know. We're all hungry!"

Swinging Heidi up in his arms, Roger kissed the little girl's cheek and said, "Okay, I'm with you, Munchkin, let's go put away some of Gamaw's buns."

Heidi leaned back in Roger's arms, put a very perturbed look on her face, then put her hands on his cheeks and seriously looked into his eyes. "Daddy, you know, I told you zillions of times, I **not** munchin, I Heidi!"

Roger clicked his tongue, his eyes twinkling. "You mean I started the new year off wrong and called you munchkin, Munchkin?"

Heidi let out a big sigh, but leaned forward and rested her head on his shoulder. "Yes, Daddy, you done it *again!*"

Roger leaned forward and kissed the little girl's cheek. "It's okay, it's my special name for you," he whispered, as he made his way to the kitchen. "You know, I'd never call any other boy or girl Munchkin, that's your special name."

Heidi put a slobbery kiss on Roger's cheek, rubbed it in and said, "Daddy, I'm not mad."

When everything was on the table, people took their seats and after Roger said a blessing, Isabel asked, "So what happened to old Brad? Raylyn told us a bit, but she said you'd have to tell us all about it."

Roger picked up a cinnamon bun, put it on Heidi's plate, cut it in half; then took one for himself. "Classic stroke symptoms, Isabel. His left side was effected and his speech was slurred enough it was impossible to understand him. The ambulance arrived just after I prayed. Their children drove behind them. The paramedics who came thought he'd make a good recovery. It was good their children were still here. It was a real comfort to them both."

"I'm sure that's true and since you prayed, I'm sure that made Joyce happy. So what happens to the store and all that business? Thank goodness it's New Year's Day and everything's closed today, but what happens tomorrow when it's supposed to be open again?" Shaking her head, Isabel said, "It's always such a shock when something like this happens. That store's been run by Thomases for generations!"

"For the time being, Natt and his dad'll cover things; at least I assume that's what'll happen. Natt's on Christmas vacation and semester break from the university, so he's available. I think it depends on what Brad's prognosis is. They'll be most of today getting him stabilized. I'm sure there'll have to be some kind of therapy, too."

"Natt is their grandson, isn't he?"

Stuffing the last mouthful of his first cinnamon bun in his mouth, Roger nodded and said, "That he is, Isabel. He's supposed to be entering the second semester of his junior year after vacation. I know his dad can't leave his job in Atlanta, since he's CEO of the newspaper there in the city, but he'll do all he can, I'm sure. I think Natt was taking courses to become a journalist like his dad. Maybe that'll have to go on hold for a while. Like I say, I think it all depends on what kind of recovery Brad makes." After another sip of his coffee, Roger reached for another of the enormous cinnamon buns on the platter.

"Well," Isabel said, "if it's like all those I know who had strokes, Brad won't be doing too much for a good long time."

With his second bun in his hand, Roger took a bite, then set the bun back on his plate and licked his fingers, before he agreed, "That's probably true, Isabel; but they have medication that can bring a person out of those stroke symptoms quite well. They usually only need therapy and a change in their diet."

"Well, he is an old man, you know." *Like you're not an old lady?* Several around the table thought but didn't voice out loud.

Roger nodded. "That's true, Isabel."

Ruth finished her bun, left the table and brought back the coffee carafe. As she filled the empty mugs, she asked, "How's Sandy doing since her family left? Her sister has a nice voice I was impressed that she could sing all those songs at the concert so well."

Raylyn put the baby on her shoulder and said, "Yes, Marcy has a nice voice and she sings well, but she doesn't read music. I guess Ramon had to talk loud and long over the phone to convince her. That's why they came well before the concert so she could practice with Sandy. Nancy, Heidi and I get together each week with her. Sometimes I get away a bit early for Heidi's piano lesson and do some cleaning.

"Still, I can't do much with this baby. I was so big when I was carrying him and now… but I do bring a casserole when I can and it's fun to get together for the day. I know Sandy is so grateful for Nancy's help. I guess she's always had a bit of trouble with personal hygiene, but now it's even worse and since Nancy's a nurse she's been a big help to her. She also does a lot of her cleaning, at least stuff that Ramon doesn't." Raylyn shook her head. "That man is awesome! He's great with her."

"But I thought Ramon did the cleaning," Ruth said.

"Yes, he does, but there are a few things Sandy would rather have a woman do." Raylyn shook her head and sighed, "I've gotten disgusted with Sandy several times. There she is, sitting in that chair, trying to do everything she's ever done with that baby pushing on her bladder and her lungs! She is really struggling and both her doctors keep telling her to slow down. In fact, they've threatened to put her in the hospital early, just so she can't do so much. She says she has so much to do, she has some commissions to paint for people around here she wants to get finished before the baby's born and that gallery in Philadelphia is always running out! I think she's afraid the baby'll take so much more of her time, but real soon she'll have to stop sending stuff up to Philadelphia, it's too much for her. Even now, she's still teaching her piano students! Fifty of them! Ramon does all he can, he's a good cook and he does the cleaning, but he sure can't paint her pictures or teach her students, for crying out loud! And then, beside all that, the phone keeps ringing off the hook for the hiking service; it's awful!"

"Ramon's helping her, though, isn't he?"

Lenny chose that moment to let some moisture come through onto Raylyn's arm, so she reached for the diaper bag, then stood up and said, "Of course! He's a great help. He's been by her side nearly every minute since the hiking season ended in October. I know he wishes he could carry the baby for her."

Heidi looked at her own mommy and giggled. "Mommy, Mr. Ramon couldn't do that! He's a man and them can't do babies."

Raylyn grinned at Roger and said, "Heidi, don't I know that! I'd have given this baby to Daddy in a heartbeat if I could have a long time ago."

Heidi gave her baby brother an adoring big sister look and said, "Bucha couldn't. Mommy, he's good. He's the bestest baby ever!"

"Yes, Pumpkin, he's good."

"We hadda wait for God's time, but it was long, you know."

"Yes, but he's here now and he definitely needs a change!" Raylyn wrinkled her nose and headed for the bathroom.

Heidi clapped her hands. "Yes! Yes! Daddy and me help you lots now. He says we help lots once the baby come."

Before Raylyn could answer, Isabel, looking shocked, said, "He did?" Heidi nodded to Isabel. "I'll have to see that." Isabel grinned at Roger. "You change diapers, too?"

Roger grinned, leaning back holding his coffee mug close to his lips. "But of course! Thanks, Isabel, thanks a lot! I knew you were part of my fan club, even back when you sent me home to change clothes at Sandy's first concert."

"Well, of course!" she huffed.

Knowing her husband quite well, Raylyn called from the bathroom where she was changing Lenny, "Roger Clemens, don't you dare finish up my cinnamon bun! As soon as I get this son of yours changed, I shall return to finish my brunch." There was a short silence, then Raylyn continued, "You, young man, can take your turn holding your son."

Roger chuckled, as he set down his mug and took another bite of his own cinnamon bun. "Yes, Sweetheart, it's still here waiting."

Heidi called out, "Mommy, he's drinkin' his coffee, but I guard your bun." The little girl giggled. "But Grandma looks kinda hungry, maybe I gotta guard it from her. She work hard with breakfast, maybe she's extra hungry."

Ruth chuckled, but as sternly as she could, with a grin on her face, she said, "Why you little scamp! I wouldn't swipe your mommy's cinnamon bun! Whatever gave you that idea? I'm your grandma, for goodness sake!"

A grin covering her whole face, Heidi said, "Mommy told us you play tricks lots of times when she was growing up, Grandma. She even told us you'd hide stuff on her! Mommy says she couldn't find it lotsa times!"

Scowling at the little girl, but with eyes that twinkled, Ruth said, "What! She's telling stories out of class?"

Heidi shrugged. "I guess, Grandma."

"Why, I'll have to get after that girl! My goodness, after all, I'm her mom, she's telling you *I* hid stuff on her?"

"Uh huh, she did."

Brad and Joyce's grandchildren stayed at the house in Vansville after their parents and grandparents left. The youngest was seven, but Natt Thomas was the oldest of the five and attended the university. He worked hard at ignoring his pesky brother and younger cousins, but those three also worked hard at being the bane of his existence whenever the two families got together. Of course, it wasn't hard to ignore his sixteen year old sister she was enthroned, sitting in the most uncomfortable-looking way, in her grandad's recliner with her novel. The only noise she made, blowing and bursting the biggest bubbles she could with her bubblegum.

He answered the phone when it rang later that afternoon. "This is the Thomas residence, Natt speaking, could I help you?" he said, importantly.

"Natt, this is Gramma Joyce." He could hear her sniff and knew she was trying not to cry. "Is everything okay there?"

"Gramma," Natt sighed dramatically, wanting to cheer her a little, "everything's fine, except these rag-a-muffins… You know what I mean?"

She chuckled her two young grandsons were always after each other. Maryann's son was seven and Natt's younger brother was nine. They lived about a hundred miles apart, so they really got after each other when they came to their gramma's house. Someone always tried to keep them apart, because Brad didn't like all the racket, but usually they found a way to get into mischief together anyway. What one didn't think of to do, the other did. Of course, Natt's other cousin was right between the two boys. She didn't think of too much of the mischief, but when it was happening she was in the middle and egging the boys on. With Christmas toys to play with, they were making more noise than a classroom of third graders, it seemed. Grandmother toys at grandmother's house….

"Yes, they are a trial, aren't they? But boys will be boys, you know." Of course, Gramma Joyce was sure her younger granddaughter could do no wrong!

After Joyce took another breath, she said, "Natt, what I called about, the doctors want to keep your grandad for several days here at the hospital after he's stabilized start therapy. I guess they must work with getting his speech back and a therapist knows how to do that best. Your dad can't give up his work in Atlanta at the paper, of course and since you're on vacation now could you run the store and gas station until I can bring Grandad home? They tell me it'll probably only be a few weeks."

Natt pulled in a long breath; this was something he'd never thought about. He was on vacation! Running his grandad's store had never even appeared on his radar! All he'd ever thought about was finishing college to become that world renowned journalist. He'd not only be managing a hardware store, which he knew little about, but a gas station and Laundromat. What a responsibility! It was the biggest operation in Vansville! After a deep breath, he swallowed and said, "Let me give it some thought, Gramma. I guess I'd stay here with you if I did?"

"Of course! There isn't another place!" Of course there was another place to stay in town, but obviously his gramma didn't want to think about it.

They chatted for several minutes, but Natt wasn't in the conversation. He felt like Joyce's request was a hurdle of mammoth proportions. Finally Joyce hung up and Natt thoughtfully replaced the receiver. Just as he did, something hit the floor in the living room with a loud thud. Natt hurried to the living room, wondering what could have caused the noise, but only saw total chaos from three young children playing. He shook his head surely he hadn't been like that when he was that age! Well, no, he hadn't had cousins his age to play with.

He put his fingers between his teeth and gave an ear splitting whistle. When the children were motionless and silent, he said, "Guys, it's not a bad day. The sun's shining and the branches aren't moving, so it can't be windy. That was Gramma Joyce on the phone and she wants me to think about something really important. Believe me, I can't think of much of anything with all the noise you're making! You guys take yourselves and your new Christmas stuff out to the backyard and wear yourselves out. I gotta think and I can't with your noise. It's like a jet engine warming up in here with all this racket."

His younger brother sighed and whined, "Aw, come on, Natt, we're bein' good. Do we gotta go outside?"

"Yup! Be gone!" He flashed an imaginary wand and the younger children laughed, but they reluctantly found some toys to keep them occupied outside. Of course, Natt had to supervise coats, hats and mittens before the exodus. After all, it was the first day of January and in the foothills where Vansville was located, it was cold.

Natt was an aspiring journalist, taking a full load at the university in Atlanta. Although he was on semester break, he had his courses arranged for the next semester. He wanted to follow in his dad's steps and be employed by the newspaper where his dad was the CEO. His goal was to be a world traveling journalist for the Atlanta paper, of course, being the very best in his field. He studied constantly and got excellent grades, his friends said he was a studyholic, whatever that was. He was on the university newspaper staff and had written several features. His profs held out great hopes for him. His dad was a great encouragement, telling him he had a spot at the paper with his name on it. He was chafing at the bit, wishing this was his final year, rather than only his junior year of school. He couldn't wait for the new semester to start, one of his classes had him doing some field work and he was excited about doing it. Running a hardware store-gas station-Laundromat in the back side of beyond? Not so much!

Right now, he'd come with his family to Vansville for Christmas and he was planning to leave for Atlanta with his family tomorrow to spend the rest of his vacation at home. He planned to vegetate; TV, Video games, texting his friends, stuff like that. After vacation, he'd planned to start the second semester of his junior year, sixteen hours of hard labor in the stacks, newsroom, library, classroom…. After all, he was young, virile….

His gramma's request wouldn't change much he still had two weeks of vacation. From the way she talked, Grandad would be up and about, ready to take back his business before Natt had to get back to school. Still it was a big undertaking, managing both the hardware store and the gas station and overseeing the Laundromat. Surely, his grandad would be back to his former self by the time his vacation ended in two and a half weeks so he could go back to school. After all, they'd given him medication to reverse the stroke. Hadn't they? Of course they had! Piece of cake! With two weeks of therapy, he'd be as good as new. Modern medicine could work wonders, he was sure of it.

When the house was quiet, he closed the back door, stood and watched his kid brother and cousins romp around the backyard for a minute, glad that he'd made that happen, then trudged into the living room, where his sister sat curled up in contortionist fashion in their grandad's recliner, cracking her gum and reading her newest book. He sank onto the couch, looked at her for a moment, wondering how she could possibly be comfortable, then leaned back into the cushions, planted his feet on the coffee table, laced his hands behind his head, stared at the ceiling and muttered. "Do I gotta?"

Natt's sister, Joylyn, dressed in ratty jean shorts and a cutoff, holey T-shirt, looked up from her novel, snapped her gum and said, "Do you gotta do what, old man?"

Natt sighed, then turned his head and looked at his sister. The girl hardly ever left a comfortable chair and always had a paperback in her hands. "Should have sent you out with them, too! Joylyn, I'm a Junior at the university. I'm no old man! Anyway, Gramma Joyce wants me to run Grandad's store and gas station until he's better. It's a big job it's not something I've ever done!"

Joylyn put her finger to mark the page, shrugged, as any sixteen year old would, blew a huge bubble and snapped it before she pulled her novel back in position to read. "So, do it!" She shrugged. "What's so hard about that? I know you're not a math major, but still, how hard can running some store in this spot in the road be?"

Natt leaned forward, his feet hitting the floor and looked at his sister intently. "Joylyn, it's the only store that doesn't sell groceries in town or had you forgotten how small this town is! He does a lot of business and it's the only gas station in town, too. He has the place open from eight to eight six days a week! And that doesn't count the Laundromat! Give me a break!"

Joylyn shrugged again, snapped her gun opened her book again, as if she'd start reading before answering, but she said, "So you got a girlfriend back home you gotta spend lots of time with? How come you didn't bring her with? You run the store Gramma has to pay you something. Get real, Bro, think how rich you'd get!"

"Rich! Rich! I'd be so washed up I'd crash before supper." He scowled at his sister. "And no, I don't have a girlfriend. What's that got to do with anything?"

She shrugged again. "You could buy her a diamond with all that money."

Getting more exasperated by the second, he looked at her intently and hollered, "A diamond! I don't even have a girl! Do you know something I don't know, woman? Give me a break! Good grief!"

Joylyn snapped her gum, shrugged and said, "So find one! You're not a *bad* looker."

Under his breath, he said, "Thanks, Joylyn."

"Sure."

Natt brought his feet back to the coffee table, slumped back into the cushions again and said, "Woman, hast thou looked around this metropolis that is called Vansville, to see how many prospects there are for a fair maiden to bestow a diamond on? As far as I know, there is no such critter to find here! From what I've heard, the last three weddings the men had to find their women some other place besides Vansville."

"Where's that wand of yours? You were flinging it around at those kids. Maybe Cinderella's scrubbing floors somewhere," Joylyn said, not taking her eyes from her book.

"Yeah, maybe she is," he grumbled. "But Vansville? Not so much."

"Bro, I know you could find one somewhere, if you'd quit studying so hard at the university. Dad says you're a workaholic, just like him." The girl flashed her hand around and said, "Lighten up, Bro, get a life!"

"Sure!" His feet back on the coffee table, he looked at his sister and grumbled, "It won't happen if I do what Gramma wants me to do."

"Nope, probably not."

Joyce Thomas didn't come home that night she slept in a recliner at the hospital beside Brad's bed. Late in the evening Natt's parents and aunt and uncle came back to Vansville, but Natt waited for them to find out how his grandad was doing. Of course, as long as Natt was up, Joylyn still sat in her grandpa's chair with her novel.

Before they all went to bed, they had a long talk, since they knew better how Brad was and their perspective wasn't as clouded by love as much as Joyce's. Natt was their only option free enough to do the job. They knew it was a big responsibility, but they were sure Natt could do the job in the crisis. The four who'd been with their parents all day felt that Brad would probably be able to run the Thomas enterprise when he was discharged.

Reluctantly, in the morning, as his family left for the hospital, then Atlanta, Natt took the keys from beside the front door and left for the Thomas Hardware Store & Gas Station in the heart of the village of Vansville. The store wasn't overly busy, but people always came and went. Of course, the day after Brad had gone to the hospital, many more came in just to find out how he was. Small town Georgia grapevine was alive and well in Vansville. Several who came in brought a casserole they'd heard that Joyce planned to stay at the hospital, so Natt had plenty of food on hand. He also realized that since many of the meals he only had himself to serve, there were many leftovers, too. Since his forte wasn't cooking, he was happy for the handouts.

At first, for about a week, Joyce spent most of the day at the hospital with Brad, so Natt stayed at his gramma's house when the store wasn't open. It seemed the thing to do, the room and board seemed good enough, but during the off hours, which weren't many, he had time to look around town and discovered Isabel's cabins weren't far from the store complex. He'd lived away from home for two and a half years now, he liked his independence.

His parents drove up the next weekend and brought his car and the rest of his belongings from home. They went to see Brad during the day on Saturday then had another long talk with Natt before they went home, but Brad's long-term prognosis was still rather nebulous. Brad didn't seem to be getting back a hundred percent as quickly as Joyce seemed to think he would. The doctors weren't really giving much of an opinion. After all, the man was in his late seventies, he wasn't some spring chicken. The doctors now said he was doing as well as could be expected. Whatever that was…

TWO

By Tuesday of the second week Natt found out why for so many years his grandad had been such a grouchy man, Gramma drove him to it! Joyce spent several more hours a day at home, including over nights and by Tuesday night of the second week Natt knew he'd go bananas if he stayed in the same house. If she wasn't sleeping, she was... well... talking! Wednesday morning, he quickly packed his things and before bedtime he'd rented one of Isabel's cabins and moved in, deciding that Gramma Joyce could talk the wallpaper off the wall. He sighed with relief in the quietness. He must pay rent and buy groceries, but it was well worth it not to be with Joyce so much.

So, by the middle of January, when Joyce brought Brad home, Isabel had a long term renter that took Duncan's place in cabin number two. Natt found it suited him much better than putting up with his gramma's many whims and her constant chatter. He could even tolerate her coming by the store occasionally to ask his advice better that way. By the end of January, Natt had reluctantly withdrawn from the university completely and brought all his things from Atlanta to Isabel's cabin, planning on staying for the long haul. Isabel couldn't have been more pleased. She liked the young man and it gave her some much needed income.

Although the doctors had regulated Brad's blood pressure and given him medication to reverse the stroke symptoms and sent him through speech therapy for two weeks, Brad was not the same. At least not physically. He seemed to speak well and all his extremities worked well enough. At least physically he seemed to have recovered, but other things dragged him down.

When the doctor released him for normal activity, Nathan and Maryann saw it immediately. Almost the same day the siblings scheduled a long session with the doctor to convince Joyce that Brad couldn't handle running the store, gas station and Laundromat alone again. Joyce was not the type of person to manage the store, either. She had been a stay-at-home lady all her life and she'd left all the hard stuff to her husband.

Even before Joyce brought Brad home, Natt found that she brought lots of her problems to him, even at the store, when he was supposed to be working. He didn't mind too much, he wasn't that busy. Natt, of course, realized as soon as his grandad entered the living room and slumped into his chair when he came from the hospital that the old man wouldn't be handling the store alone, at least any time soon, maybe not ever.

Another thing Natt found upsetting when he entered the store the day after New Year's, Brad didn't own a computer. All of his accounts were kept in ledgers in the den at home, not even at the store. Natt didn't even ask Joyce or Brad for permission, before his dad and mom left for Atlanta he asked his dad to get him a laptop. The first day he was officially in charge of the store, he called his dad to purchase a machine to keep at the store. Being the kind of person he was, Natt had it installed in the little workroom before the day was over and soon had accounts changed over and updated. Inventory and ordering were much easier and quicker that way. Brad seemed happy enough to let Natt take care of things like that. Natt couldn't believe how much more laid back Grandad was this year than ever before.

For years, Brad had kept the store open long hours every day, saying that people depended on the gas station being open and since that was, he had to keep the store open so they could pay for their gas. His pumps couldn't take credit cards; customers had to come inside to pay. He stayed open, even though the grocery store had always closed at five o'clock and was closed on Sunday. Only recently Brad had started closing on Sunday. However, once he came home from the hospital everyone knew he couldn't do it any more, he didn't have the stamina he'd had before his stroke. It wasn't anything therapy could give him.

Brad came home on Monday and was back in the store with his grandson on Tuesday, but on Wednesday, when he came in after twelve hours at the store, he flopped in his chair and said, "Can't do it no more!"

"What can't you do, Dear?" Joyce asked.

Natt kept quiet as he followed his grandad in. Normally he would have gone to his cabin, but Brad had asked him to come home with him while he talked with Joyce. He knew what the old man couldn't do, but he wanted his grandad to say it himself and Joyce, ever the optimist, had to be convinced. Joyce had one of the casseroles heated up that Natt hadn't eaten when they walked in the door, so the men sat down at the table to eat it and share some conversation.

After supper and dishes, Brad wandered to his chair in the living room. As it creaked back and the other two found seats nearby, he said, "Joyce, I can't do this eight to eight stuff no more. It wears me out."

"But Nathaniel's there!"

Brad raised his coffee cup to his lips, but before he drank, he said, "Joyce, it ain't right! Big city stores stay open that late, they got two shifts. Alex closes the grocery at five 'cept on Friday. People want gas, they come when we're open. They got laundry, they do it when we're open. This here little town can get along with Thomas place closin' at five o'clock."

Joyce patted her husband on the shoulder and said, "Whatever you say, Dear. You know better what to do with all those things."

"I say we close the door at five o'clock ever' day but Friday just like Alex does. He makes enough to keep the place open. Ain't that right, Natt?"

"Yeah, Grandad, he closes at five o'clock, except on Friday."

Brad nodded. "That's what I said! So, startin' next week, that's what we'll be doin'. Natt needs a bit of time for hisself and I cain't do no more. We'll post signs tomorra."

"Whatever you say, Dear."

That first week Brad opened the hardware store at eight o'clock each morning, but Natt learned right away that he must be there very shortly after that, because Grandad forgot to turn the gas pumps on or unlock and turn the lights on in the Laundromat, so Natt hurried to be there by eight o'clock. Not only that, Brad fell asleep soon after opening and dozed most of the day. On Tuesday, just after he unlocked the door he brought the desk chair from the back and set it behind the counter. The first customer hadn't even showed up before he plopped into it, appearing totally exhausted. From that day, as soon as Natt appeared he sat there, only ringing up what people bought and giving them their receipts.

On Tuesday Brad wanted Natt to come for supper. He told Joyce life wasn't the same. Once Joyce served the last casserole and Natt had cleaned the bowl, he left, but Brad took himself off to bed. He didn't even sit in his recliner to watch TV with Joyce. That was when she knew for sure Brad would never be the same again.

Starting the last week of January and for the first two weeks of February they had the nastiest weather in the mountains of north Georgia that the old timers could remember in a very long time. When it didn't snow, the precipitation that came down was either freezing rain or sleet, making travel treacherous and walking was very bad on the sidewalks. Natt was glad he'd gone to Atlanta the Sunday before to clean out his dorm room and done everything he needed to withdraw from the university. He finally admitted that he was no longer a student, but a store manager in a tiny town. Sometimes life didn't go quite the way you'd envisioned it.

Dreams of being a world traveler died a reluctant death. Wishing he could keep that dream alive, Natt brought his huge world map from his dorm room and hung it on the empty wall in his walk-in closet. It was hard not to sigh each time he looked at it. There were the huge continents nestled in the blue oceans, he dreamed about writing about somewhere on each one, but he'd never left the United States. He was stuck in Vansville and it was so tiny he could only guess where it was on his map, Georgia was barely a spot in the United states. One good thing, it was colorful and added just the right touch to his closet.

Smart people in Vansville and in the country around stayed off the roads and sidewalks during the bad weather and Nancy Roads was glad that Duncan had built their house close enough she could walk to the clinic each day. The temperature never rose above freezing for those three weeks. People had to bundle up if they planned to be outside for long. The clinic in Vansville found itself busy with traffic and pedestrian related injuries day after day, because it was so wet and the county didn't get to their roads and walks all that quickly to clear the snow and slush or to put down sand and salt on the ice. The town itself was so small, they didn't have their own road crew and equipment.

They had some precipitation nearly every day. Sometimes it was snow, but much of the time it was a glare of ice when people woke up. The sun never came out to melt anything, only the gunmetal gray clouds, so there was a build up from day to day. Still many people had jobs they needed to get to and usually they tried to get to work, whether they lived in Vansville and worked in Blairsville or some other place. The clinic had to be open there were too many injuries to close. The sheriff's department even purchased an SUV with four wheel drive.

Isabel was unhappy, like all the other permanent residents of Vansville, with the weather, but she found that her cabins were full much more this year than any other, because the clinic staff couldn't drive away each night even the half hour drive to Blairsville. Since her cabins were the only place to stay in Vansville, they were full most nights. Dr. Stan missed several days at the Blairsville Hospital ER because he couldn't get away from Vansville after his shift was finished. However, as in many tiny communities, the grocery store and the hardware store opened for business each day because Alex, Brad and Natt all lived within walking distance of their stores, so it was business as usual. Natt found himself ordering icemelt several times to sell to Vansville citizens, but also to keep his own parking lot and gas pump area cleared.

It was February, the new quarter had been going for several weeks, when Marcy and her two nursing student friends sat down for morning report in the nurse's office on the men's surgical ward in the huge medical center teaching hospital in Philadelphia. The three of them were assigned to one of the busy surgical units.

Marcy loved nursing, every aspect of it was challenging and interesting. They were always busy, someone was always going or coming from surgery, but that was just fine with Marcy. After report, the instructor kept them in the office for a few minutes and gave out assignments, then sent them to complete their tasks, including baths, treatments and medications. As with most teaching hospitals, they didn't staff their hospital with students, but just. Of course, Marcy was just fine with that. Their instructors were challenging and Marcy loved every minute of the classes and the ward work.

Marcy had her arms full when she entered the room of her first patient and said, "Good morning, Mr. Hain, how are you this cold morning? Did you have a restful night? I'm Marcy and I'm here to get you cleaned up for the day and also change your dressing." She smiled at the man and continued, "I even brought a pain pill with me so you won't hurt so badly when you roll over so we can change your bed and dressing."

Mr. Hain groaned, as he looked up at the pretty girl and the armload she carried. "All of that? We have to do it all now? I can't rest in-between? You gotta remember I had this surgery only the other day!"

Marcy put her armload in the chair close by, only keeping the tiny medicine cup in her hand. She chuckled, holding out the medicine and his water glass. "Mr. Hain, just think, when we get this all done you'll be set until lunch time. You had a good breakfast, when I'm finished, you can rest for all those hours."

The man sighed and held out his hand. "Well, little miss, let's have the pain pill and get on with it. I guess I'm as ready as I'll ever be."

Still chuckling, Marcy put the pill cup in his hand and said, "Here you go, Mr. Hain! I was hoping you'd see it my way."

"Mmm, well…"

Giving the man a sunny smile, Marcy said, "That's the spirit!"

About fifteen minutes later, Marcy had Mr. Hain's bed in the highest position and the man himself on his left side. She planned to change his bottom sheet and give him a backrub while she talked to him. Moments later, the man realized Marcy wasn't talking and nothing was happening behind him. However, there was still a lump behind him, holding him in place.

He looked over his shoulder and when he didn't see his nurse, he wondered why she'd left, but he hadn't seen her go by the bed, so he carefully rolled over the hump of sheets to his other side. The bedrail was down, but much to his astonishment, he saw the girl's legs sprawled on the floor, the rest of her was hidden. Fortunately for her, his bed was in the highest position.

"Miss, Miss Marcy?" Marcy didn't respond, she didn't even move.

He frowned, but immediately, fumbled for his call button, searching for several seconds, since Marcy had moved it to work on the bed and pressed it frantically. The instant someone answered, he yelled, "Hurry! Hurry! My nurse is on the floor! She's not getting up and she won't answer! Something's really wrong with her!"

No one answered, but the charge nurse and the nursing instructor who were both at the nurse's desk, looked at each other, then flew down the hall to the room and jostled each other through the doorway. The man lay on his side, but his bed was at its highest setting and one bedrail was down. In the center, behind him, the clean and dirty sheets were bunched into quite a wad, but his nurse was no where to be seen. The nurses looked at each other, the charge nurse went to the bed to finish making it, while the instructor moved around the bed, intent on raising the bedrail, but stumbled over Marcy who was face down on the floor, her head under the bed.

Miss Tallman squatted down, Marcy's color was a bit ashen, but not terribly abnormal. However even when she shook her, Marcy didn't respond. She then reached for Marcy's wrist and found a fairly strong pulse, but even with that movement the girl didn't respond. Nothing changed, not even her breathing. Perplexed, the nurse took her pulse again.

The nurse straightened up and said to the other nurse, "Call for a stretcher and some help! We need to get her out of here. Something's happened to Marcy, I can't rouse her at all!"

"Oh, of course!" the charge nurse said and reached for the call button. The minute she made the request, she came running around the bed to stare down at the fallen young woman. The nursing instructor had managed to pull Marcy out from under the bed, but that was all. Scowling, the charge nurse exclaimed, "What in the world...!" She looked at the young woman on the floor, back to the instructor and repeated, "What is going on?"

"I don't know!" Miss Tallman exclaimed. "She's never sick, she wasn't sick this morning in report – I can't imagine!"

Only moments later, both of Marcy's fellow students came rushing in pushing a stretcher. "Miss Tallman, you wanted a stretcher?" one of them asked. Since Marcy was still on the floor and on the opposite side from the door, they couldn't see her.

"Yes, actually, we need a man, go find one."

"Why?" one student asked.

"Where's Marcy?" the other asked.

A bit flustered, she wasn't one to broadcast staff problems in the presence of patients, Miss Tallman said, "Angela, Marcy's here on the floor, unresponsive and she's here at my feet. We'll need a man to pick her up and put her on that stretcher. Would you please go find a male CNA so he can help us get her out of this room?"

"Oh!" Angela turned and fled from the room. Soon, she came back with a male attendant and breathlessly said, "I found Manny, he'll help us."

"That's good, thank you." Soon they had Marcy on the stretcher and the instructor said, "I guess we'd better send her down to the ER and call Dr. Wright."

"He's in class now, Miss Tallman," Angela reminded her.

The instructor shrugged. "It doesn't matter; he's who we have to call. He's head of staff and supposed to be called with things like this, whether it's staff or students."

"Dr. Wright! Extension 4620 Stat!" the voice proclaimed over every speaker in the huge teaching hospital in downtown Philadelphia.

Jason Wright was in the second floor class room teaching a class of fourth year med students, when the page came on in the hallway outside the closed door. He scowled; everyone knew he was teaching, they also knew he always carried a pager. Why would the operator page him during class? A stat page? Yes, he was Chief of Staff, but he had no patients of his own, only used different ones on different floors to teach his students. Leaning on his teaching notes, he reached for the hospital extension on the desk, dialed the numbers and said, "Jason Wright…"

Before he could say more, the frantic voice on the other end said, "Doctor! One of our third year student nurses has collapsed in a patient's room! We can't rouse her so we put her on a stretcher and sent her down to the ER! She should be there now!"

The doctor cleared his throat, not flustered by the frantic voice and said, "Perhaps, Miss Tallman, you'd page your staff member to bring her back and put her in a private room. I'll be along in a few minutes as soon as I dismiss my class, but I don't wish to see her in the ER. Could you take care of that, please?"

Much more subdued, the voice answered, "Yes, Doctor, we'll make that call. There is a private room open we'll put her in room 1220."

"Thank you, I'll be there soon." Now he did have a patient. Anyone on staff who became ill became his patient. It also didn't surprise him that Nurse Tallman had become frantic when one of her students became ill.

Hands were in the air when Jason replaced the phone. Another young man blurted out, "What is it? What happened?"

Dr. Jason closed his folder on his notes and said, "A student nurse collapsed in a patient's room. Our illustrious nursing instructor didn't go into detail, but I guess we'd better dismiss class. You know your assignment for next session. You three who were to follow me this morning meet me on twelfth floor as soon as you put away books and change into proper attire."

"Yes, Doctor," a tall young man said, as he scooped up his text and headed for the door. Others quickly followed him. The three residents had to leave their books in their lockers and hunt for clean lab jackets to wear in patients' rooms.

Moments later, Dr. Wright left the elevator on twelfth floor. He had to go to his office to retrieve his lab coat as well. He pushed the door open onto the ward and walked to the desk just as three younger men came barreling onto the ward from the back elevator. Right behind them came a stretcher, two people maneuvering the stretcher through the doorway onto the ward.

"Oh, good!" the charge nurse let out a long sigh. "Here she is back. They were about to put her in a room downstairs when we reached Manny."

Leaning his elbow on the high counter, Dr. Wright watched the stretcher go by and said, "I guess I need to put out a directive again, but if this ever happens again, when a staff member needs such attention, put them in a room on the ward, don't send them to the ER. Another thing, call my pager, don't put a stat page throughout the whole hospital!"

The charge nurse cleared her throat, knowing that the nursing instructor had become frantic and hadn't done anything like that. "Yes, Doctor, we'll make a note of that in my office. Thank you for coming so quickly."

The doctor nodded then he and his students followed the stretcher down the hall and waited outside the room until the staff brought the stretcher out. "Mindy, has the patient responded yet?" Dr. Wright asked.

As the CNA took the stretcher away, the nurse let go and stopped by the door. Shaking her head, she said, "No, Doctor! She's breathing normally, maybe it's a little moist, we took her pulse and blood pressure right away and they are a little depressed, but she doesn't respond when we speak to her. She did flinch when we accidentally hit her hand when Manny raised the bedrail just now, but that's all we've seen."

"Thanks. Send your charge nurse down with her information as soon as you reach the desk. I'll have lots of orders for her to record immediately." He took a step toward the open door, then turned back and asked, "By the way, do you know her name?"

"Yes, it's Marcy Bernard, Doctor."

The man who had been so laid back a second before, exclaimed, "Marcy! Marcy is never sick! She just collapsed? I can't believe that!"

Nodding, the nurse said, "Yes, Doctor. She was fine this morning. She and her friends were even joking when they came in for report. She got her assignment and was doing everything. She was in 1201 doing a treatment and changing the bed. The man frantically pushed his call button three or four times and then told us his nurse was on the floor. When we went and asked, he said, she'd been working and talking with him. The next thing he knew, she was on the floor."

Shaking his head, Jason muttered, "I can't imagine what's caused this!"

"It does seem bazaar. That girl is never sick! I mean, she was just about the only one in her class who didn't come down with the flu!"

"Mmm, I'm well aware of that."

Dr. Wright entered the room and stared for several minutes at the still form in the bed. What he saw was a young woman with hardly any color in her face. Her breathing seemed normal, he watched her chest move up and down. Marcy Bernard was one of the most intelligent, dedicated nursing students he'd ever met. That was why he knew her personally, she was always asking questions in class, or she'd come to him after class to get clarification. She was never sick, hadn't succumbed to any bug or disease to strike anywhere in the building all winter or any other time since she'd started her training.

The three medical students around him were quiet, waiting for the doctor's first words. They also knew Marcy, not as well as Dr. Wright. However, he said nothing, but took three steps to her bedside and grasped her wrist. He looked down at the young woman, watching her breathe and wondering what could be the matter. As he held her wrist a frown spread across his face, but he said nothing, just kept holding her wrist.

Finally, the charge nurse entered with the portable computer chart and breathlessly said, as she pushed the door closed, "Dr. Wright, we had to wait for admissions to send information on her. Believe it or not, it took them this long!"

He turned back to Marcy, then turned again to the nurse and asked, "Has anyone thought to change her into a hospital gown so we can run tests, draw blood, all that… without getting her uniform dirty?" It was a rhetorical question, anyone could see she was still in her uniform. Her feet holding the covers up showed she still had her shoes on.

Dr. Wright refrained from shaking his head in front of his students, but this was just another indication of Miss Tallman's incompetency. When she was flustered it showed in everything she did. Jason was tempted to recommend Marcy for her job even now, even before she graduated in another year.

Also looking at Marcy, perhaps for the first time, the woman gasped and said, "I guess not! As soon as you're finished giving orders I'll see that it's done."

Dr. Wright nodded and the nurse scrolled through pages of preliminaries to an order sheet. Dr. Wright watched Marcy for any change, but nothing did. He was stumped; the only thing unusual was a slight difference in her pulse, even that wasn't a constant irregularity. He started immediately giving orders. Since he had no idea what the problem was, he must order a battery of tests to determine what could be wrong. He started to speak and the charge nurse began typing frantically to keep up with the doctor's orders. As she typed, the orders went into the central hospital system so they could be carried out immediately. Soon another nurse came with equipment to start an IV, but realized she must wait, being wintertime, Marcy's uniform had long sleeves. It would be impossible to change her with the IV going.

When Dr. Wright finished with his orders, the charge nurse left with her computer, then Dr. Wright and his crew also left. Melinda returned with a hospital gown and a bag, quickly changed her, started the IV and momentarily, a lab tech came with his tray full of needles and vials to take blood samples to try and find the cause of her collapse as soon as possible. Everyone was puzzled, Marcy was never sick. No one could remember when Marcy had been sick, not even last winter when so many staff had been out sick.

During the entire time Dr. Wright gave his orders, his students stood behind him, listening quietly. Two of them knew Marcy and wondered what could cause her to lapse into a coma for no apparent reason. While Melinda changed Marcy into a hospital gown and started the IV, Dr. Wright and his students discussed what could be happening behind the closed door of the nurse's office.

After Melinda left with her soiled IV tray, the doctor and the students returned. Another nurse wrapped a blood pressure cuff, attached to a machine on the wall that gave a read-out every five minutes, to Marcy's arm. Marcy seemed to be in a deep sleep, she never woke up. Her breathing, pulse and color never varied. She flinched several times, when a needle punctured her skin, either for a blood draw or starting the IV, but she never woke, even when someone called her name. Her behavior puzzled everyone. Every staff member on the ward said she'd showed no signs of illness until she collapsed.

Finally, Dr. Wright looked at Melinda and asked, "Has anyone called the Bernard's to let them know that Marcy is seriously ill and is now a patient here?"

Mindy looked at Melinda, who looked back at her, then at the doctor. Shaking their heads, the charge nurse said, "I guess we were so caught up in all that's happened this morning that we never thought to call her home, Dr. Wright. Melinda, you'd better run back to the desk and find her home phone number and see if anyone answers." The woman looked at her watch. "If her parents work…"

Melinda whirled around, put her hand on the door handle, yanked the door open and exclaimed, "I'll do that right now!"

Nodding, Jason said, "Yes, that would be good."

Silently, Jason shook his head. It seemed none of the staff knew or remembered what the procedure was when staff became sick. If he remembered right, it hadn't been that long. Of course, the last staff person wasn't one of Miss Tallman's student nurses, either. That woman was strangely absent at the bedside of her own student. Dr. Wright silently wondered if perhaps Miss Tallman hadn't out-stayed her usefulness as a nursing instructor. Of course, he wouldn't voice his concern out loud; he was Chief of Staff of the hospital, not Director of Nurses or dean of the nursing school. He was thankful for small favors.

Bustling around her kitchen after eating her lunch, Colleen answered the phone and immediately a voice said, "Mrs. Bernard, this is General Hospital…"

Colleen collapsed into her chair at the kitchen table, clutching the cordless phone to her ear. On a gasp, she said, "Yes, what …what is it? Is there something about Marcy?"

"Yes, Mrs. Bernard, your daughter was working on the ward and suddenly collapsed while she was working. She has been admitted for observation and tests…"

Around the huge ball of cotton in her mouth, Colleen exclaimed, "Oh, my! Oh, my! She's very sick? What could be wrong?"

"I would say she's stable right now, but several doctors have been working with her for several hours now and they will be running a number of tests that will probably take at least two days to get all the results back." After a pause, the woman said, "Ah, she hasn't woken as yet, but she does flinch when something painful happens."

Her mouth completely dry, Colleen tried to swallow, then finally whispered, "What a shock! Miss, we'll come as soon as possible."

"Thank you, that will be good, Mrs. Bernard. Please come to the information desk just inside the front doors, we'll keep them informed."

"Yes, thank you," she barely whispered.

Colleen barely heard the woman's final statement. When the dial tone hummed in her ear, she lowered the phone to her lap and looked at the far wall of her kitchen. Finally, she whispered, "My baby is so sick, she collapsed, she's a patient. Oh, my!"

Colleen was alone at home she'd finished her lunch and was cleaning up. Dear Charlie was at work, probably on his mail delivery route, it took most of his shift to complete the route. Ed's classes and studies took him away from home for most of the day and she had no way to reach him at the university. Sandy, of course, was gone. Gone to far off Georgia and eight months pregnant. She'd been gone for nearly two years, but Colleen couldn't seem to believe that her precious crippled daughter wasn't coming back to live at home where her mom could take care of her. But Marcy! Marcy was never sick! How could this be? Tears ran unchecked down Colleen's cheeks.

When the hospital person hung up, Colleen only had strength to slide the hand holding the phone from her ear to her lap. She forgot to disconnect. Fortunately, she was sitting down. She sat for several minutes staring at the empty wall across the kitchen, tears silently sliding down her cheeks, she never thought to wipe them away. Marcy was sick, very sick, according to the person who'd called. Why would she collapse without a cause?

Marcy was like her other children, she never got sick, didn't even have sniffles in the winter. When others in her classes were sick, Marcy was fine. She'd keep on going to classes and doing her work on the wards, even when no one else could. Colleen shook her head, and tried to think of the last time she knew her youngest had been sick. She couldn't remember.

Since she'd left for nurse's training, she'd never complained of being sick. All she ever talked about were her patients, even then she rarely said they were hard to care for, but how much she was learning about their illnesses. Now she was sick! Colleen could hardly put her mind around that colossal thought.

Tears streaming down her cheeks, she whimpered, "She's not only sick, she's unconscious! What has happened to my baby?"

Probably ten minutes later, Colleen remembered to disconnect when she tried to dial the local substation of the post office and nothing happened. She finally thought to push the disconnect button, then was able to press the right buttons and by the third ring when someone answered she had swallowed enough times her voice sounded fairly normal, when she said, "Would Charlie Bernard be in yet from his route?"

The man who answered knew Colleen quite well, since Charlie had been working from that substation so long and could hear the anxiety in her voice, so he said, "Colleen, he should be in momentarily. Should I have him call you?"

"Yes, yes, right away, please!"

"I'll be sure to pass on the word, he'll call soon."

"Thank you so much," she murmured. "I'll be waiting for his call."

"Ma'am, I'll get his number and he'll call you, Colleen. Hang tight, I'll get right on it." Of course, the man had Charlie's cell phone number and called it immediately.

Colleen sat holding the phone, but this time, she remembered to disconnect. A few minutes later it rang in her hand. She jumped, then activated the phone and said, "Charlie?"

"Yes, my love, what is troubling you?" asked the dear voice that had its own distinctive accent that Colleen loved.

The tears in Colleen's eyes spilled down her cheeks, and she had to swallow before she said, "Ch-Charlie, someone called a few minutes ago from General and said that Marcy collapsed on the ward two hours before. When they called she hadn't woken up and they're running tests! I told them we'd come soon. I…I didn't know what else to say, can you come home now or do you need to do something else there?"

Charlie had to swallow. Marcy hadn't been sick in years, he couldn't remember when the last time was. Keeping his voice as calm as he could, knowing how upset his wife could get, Charlie said, "Sweetheart, I'll be right home and we'll go."

"Yes, yes!" The line went dead in her ear, so she pulled the phone from her ear and sat holding it for a few minutes, but she did push the disconnect button.

Glancing at the clock, she jumped up, dropped the phone on the table, swiped at her nose with the back of her hand and raced to the bedroom for her purse. "Dear me! Charlie will be here before I have my stuff!" She sighed, "It takes so long to get to General on the train. Marcy may be…" Colleen hiccoughed, she couldn't bring herself to say the word.

When Charlie came home, he didn't leave the car, since Colleen was on the back porch with her coat on and her purse strap on her shoulder. She ran down the ramp and quickly slid in the passenger seat. As she sat down, Charlie asked, "Colleen, did you reach Ed? I'm sure he'll want to know about Marcy. It's not too far, perhaps he'll want to come see her later on. I'm sure he'll want to know there won't be any supper here when he gets home."

She turned with a perplexed look on her face, still with her purse strap over her shoulder and scowled. "Why, no, he's at the university, you know."

Charlie stifled a sigh, knowing his wife still hadn't grasped the full impact of cell phones, obviously, since she hadn't called him on his. "My dear, he's recently gotten a cell phone, I put the number in the front of the phone book for you. You know he carries it with him everywhere, just as I carry mine. Really, we can call him so he knows no one will be here when he gets home at supper time."

"My goodness! I forgot all about that!"

Charlie pulled his phone from the waist carrier and hit Ed's speed-dial number. He was upset when he heard the news, but Charlie told him he didn't need to come to the hospital, because Marcy had not yet responded, but they'd keep him informed. Ed was relieved, he had planned to stay late to study for an exam scheduled in one of his classes in the morning. As soon as he hung up, Charlie replaced his phone, pulled the stick into reverse and they left immediately for the big hospital downtown. Colleen sat in her bucket seat whimpering as Charlie drove. They didn't go to the El as Colleen thought they would.

Taking her hand, Charlie squeezed her fingers and said, "It's okay, my love, I'm sure she's in good hands and will soon be well again. Take heart, General is the best hospital in the city, they'll find what's wrong very soon, I'm sure."

Wringing her hands, with tears sliding down her cheeks, she said, "Yes, I know you're right, Charlie. It's just that…well, she's never sick!"

"I know, Love, but we'll get through this, I'm sure it's not life threatening, the doctor would surely have said so."

Fresh tears welled in Colleen's eyes, as she exclaimed, "Oh, my! Don't even think it!" Charlie didn't comment, but he was sure, since Colleen was such a pessimist, that she had certainly thought the worst already.

Some time later, Charlie parked his car in the massive parking garage, took Colleen into the huge teaching hospital and walked into the main lobby. Charlie was glad he'd been there before, it was overwhelming. Inside, he looked both ways and saw an information desk close by. With his arm around his wife, he walked up and before he could ask, the lady said, "Hello, could I help you folks?"

Charlie took a deep breath, blew it out, hoping with all the stress that his accent wouldn't be so obvious the woman wouldn't understand him. He said, "Ma'am, my wife received a call maybe two hours ago that our daughter, a student nurse, had collapsed on the ward where she was working and has been admitted for tests and such. Could you find out where we should go, please? Her name is Marcy Bernard."

The woman smiled kindly at him, picked up a piece of paper and said, "Yes, sir. I received word some time ago about her. My instructions say that you are to go to the Director of Nurses office here on first floor. She will give you all the information she has and direct you where you should go from there. Her office is down this hallway to the end, then turn left and it's the fourth door on your right."

"Thank you, Ma'am. I appreciate your help so much," Charlie said.

Colleen's tears hadn't stopped since Charlie came home. They had been falling, silently, since she had talked to him. Charlie kept her in his arm and moved away from the information desk, down the hall as he had been directed. He pulled his large handkerchief from his pocket and handed it to Colleen. She wiped her eyes and blew her nose, then took a deep breath, willing herself to stop the tears. They slowed a bit, but they still leaked from her eyes. Charlie didn't say anything, he was used to his wife's tears.

Finally, after passing many offices and large classrooms, they found the door that had 'Director of Nurses - Miss Alana Stewart'. Charlie knocked and a woman said, "Come in."

Charlie opened the door and took Colleen in with him. He smiled at the woman about their age and said, "Good afternoon, Ma'am. The lady at the information desk directed us to your office. We are Marcy Bernard's parents."

The lady was starched and prim in her white uniform. She even had a cap on the back of her head. Nurses rarely wore caps anymore, but her voice was kind, as she said, "Have a seat, Mr. and Mrs. Bernard. Thank you for coming so quickly. I'm so sorry about Marcy. Right now, she is a very sick young lady. She collapsed without warning on the ward earlier while she was caring for a patient. Our Dr. Wright and several of his residents have been working with her ever since then, examining her and doing blood tests trying to find what caused her collapse. She has finally roused, but he feels she needs as much rest as she can get, so he has her sedated and she's been sleeping for some time. I want to make it quite clear, though, that Marcy isn't out of the woods just because she's roused, she is still very sick."

"Wh-what is it?" Colleen gasped, hardly above a whisper. "Marcy's never sick. We couldn't imagine…"

The other lady smiled and shook her head. Picking up the receiver from the phone on her desk, she said, kindly, "Mrs. Bernard, I'm really not allowed to give out that information. I think Dr. Wright could get away, why don't I see if he can come here to talk with you?"

"Thank you, Miss Stewart," Charlie said, graciously, giving the lady a smile. "We would really appreciate that very much. Marcy isn't one to get sick, so we're totally in the dark about this. The whole time we were coming, we tried to imagine." Nodding at Colleen, he said, "As you can see, my wife is quite upset from the news."

The woman smiled. "Yes, I understand, Mr. Bernard. Yes, in all my dealings with her, Marcy seemed to be one of the healthiest young women I've met. Believe me, I was as shocked as you when the ward she is on informed me of what happened."

Colleen swiped at her eyes and blew her nose while Alana made her call. Charlie looked around the small office that obviously had been the Director of Nurses Office for some time. There were pictures of women wearing the same uniform as Miss Stewart wore lining the walls. They all looked starched and prim, just like Miss Stewart.

Alana only said a few words and listened for several minutes, then hung up and said, "Dr. Wright is still in her room and asked that I send you folks up. You need to go back the way you came from the information desk. Right across the hall from that desk is a bank of elevators. Take any of them to twelfth floor. When you step off, make a right, to the small waiting room, Dr. Wright will meet you there. He'll be able to answer your questions and tell you what he's ordered for her treatment."

Charlie nodded and as he helped Colleen to her feet, he said, "Thank you very much, Miss Stewart, we appreciate all the hospital's done for Marcy. It was definitely a shock to find out that Marcy was sick. She's been a very healthy person all her life." The lady could tell, even though Charlie seemed calm that he was upset, his accent was heavier than when they arrived.

The lady smiled and said, "You're welcome, Mr. Bernard. I hope Dr. Wright's news is good news. Best of everything."

"Thank you, Miss Stewart." Colleen only nodded.

On the way back to the elevators, Colleen murmured, "What in the world? What could be wrong with my baby? Why couldn't the nurse tell us? Is she that bad?"

Charlie cringed at her words, but shook his head. "I can't imagine, my dear."

Several minutes later, they reached the small waiting room. A man with silver threaded through his hair stood outside the elevator with his hand out. He smiled at the couple and said, "You'd be the Bernard's?" When they nodded, he continued, "The young lady I've been working over much of the day looks exactly like her mother. I'm Jason Wright, I'm pleased to meet you. Come sit down in the lounge and let's talk about what has happened to Marcy. As yet, we still haven't found exactly what is going on in her body."

Charlie took Colleen to a small vinyl couch and sat down with her, before he said, "Yes, Dr. Wright, Colleen and I want very much to know what has happened. Marcy is normally a very healthy person. On our way here we tried to remember when the last time she was sick and we couldn't. She hasn't even had a cold over the winter!"

Colleen nodded and whispered, "Yes, that's right."

The doctor scowled, as he slowly slid into a chair opposite the couple. "Really? She didn't have the sniffles or anything all winter? Are you sure?"

Charlie looked at Colleen whose tears had slowed, but not stopped, before he shook his head. "Not that we were aware of, Doctor. She comes home about twice a month for her days off and she rarely tells us about herself, but how great her patients are or how well she's done on a test or paper, but she's never been sick when she comes home or while she's there."

Dr. Wright put his elbows on the arms of his chair, put his fingertips together and rested his chin on them. Then he asked, "When was the last time she was home?"

"A week tomorrow, Doctor," Colleen whispered, wiping her nose with the handkerchief.

"She wasn't sick or have a cold?"

Charlie shook his head. "I don't recall that she did, why?"

THREE

The doctor studied his notebook for several minutes, before he looked up at the couple and said, "I'm surprised that you noticed nothing, no symptoms that she might feel bad, because she has the classic symptoms of Rheumatic Fever. Of course, we are still running tests to make sure of our diagnosis. Usually the precursor for someone to contract something so serious are a cold dragging on or sniffles that don't go away after a few days. So she didn't have any such symptoms that you were aware of all weekend? No sneezing, no coughing, nothing?"

Colleen shook her head. "Unless she masked how she felt, we didn't notice anything. She wasn't even sluggish, she only complained of this course she's taking being a hard one and that she has lots of class work along with it. In fact, she played down the class work and the papers and talked about how much she loved the ward she's on," Charlie said.

"I am amazed!" Dr. Wright finally said.

"When can we see her?" Charlie asked.

Looking at his watch, Jason said, "She only roused a little while ago, but she's sleeping now, I ordered a sedative given regularly to keep her drowsy. We have her on IVs at least for another twelve hours, perhaps longer. You can see her, but she probably won't wake up. We've drawn several blood samples, when those results come back we'll have a clearer picture of where we stand. I am truly astonished that she's had no cold or cough. Her instructor and student friends agree with you."

Finally, Colleen's tears stopped and she asked, "They told me on the phone these tests will take two days. No one mentioned a sedative. Will she be released to come home or can she go back to her work and classes?"

Shaking his head, Jason said, "Mrs. Bernard, she definitely won't go to work and classes! She'll probably be discharged tomorrow evening, maybe as late as the day after that, but she must go home so she can rest. There is too much risk that she'll have residual heart damage if she doesn't rest. That is why the sedative. Perhaps I need to emphasize that Rheumatic Fever is a virus that affects the heart. If she rests, does nothing until the virus runs its course, there may be no residual damage, but we can never be sure of this for several days. You can care for her?"

Colleen gasped and covered her mouth, but Charlie nodded and answered, "Colleen doesn't work outside the home, Doctor. That'll be no problem for us at all. I'm sure we can make whatever arrangements need to be made."

Jason nodded, looking intently at the couple. "I'm very glad to hear that. Marcy will recover faster at home, I'm sure. As I see the problem, Marcy will not like being forced to stay in bed. I understand she's a very active person."

"That is for sure, Doctor," Charlie said, emphatically. "Also very stubborn, very determined and expecting to succeed."

Jason nodded. "However, unless she rests in bed, only up for bathroom breaks and meals, for a week, she'll find herself nearly an invalid the rest of her life. She should not be expected to make long trips to the table for meals and definitely not going upstairs to bed."

Colleen's eyes were huge as she stared at the doctor, but Charlie had to swallow several times, before he said, "Yes, Doctor, we'll have the house ready for her when you release her." Obviously until that moment neither Charlie nor Colleen understood how very sick Marcy was.

Jason smiled at the unhappy couple and stood, then headed for the ward. "Come with me, I'll take you to see Marcy."

"Yes, Doctor, thank you very much."

Colleen didn't seem able to stand up by herself, so Charlie put his arm back around her and drew her up with him. The doctor led Charlie and Colleen onto a bustling ward. Nurses were everywhere, but speaking in quiet tones. The doctor led them down one hallway into a private room.

The light in the private bath that was just inside the door from the hallway was the only light for the whole room. There were blinds in the window and they were closed. The only noise they heard in the room was the labored breathing of the young woman in the bed. The sound intensified as Jason closed the door behind Charlie.

Jason stopped at the foot of the bed and motioned for the Bernard's to step up beside the bed. Charlie had his hand on Colleen's back and with some pressure pushed her ahead of him. Immediately she covered her mouth as it flew open with a gasp. "Doctor!" she whispered. "How could she look so awful? We only saw her less than a week ago! My goodness, her color… well, it's gray! Why? What is the matter?"

Jason nodded. "She is very ill. It's obvious she had little warning of anything being wrong with her body. We talked with the instructor and charge nurse who supervised her work today. Actually, they said she was quite normal, kidding around with the other students when they came for report. According to them, Marcy was only a little sluggish, if at all, when she took report this morning. She wasn't behind in her work and she was doing a procedure when she collapsed. In fact it was the patient who called to report that Marcy had fallen to the floor. This all seems very unusual, because Rheumatic Fever has such a long list of precursors and she seems to have had none of them. It's only by her blood work that we have made the diagnosis."

Fearfully, looking at the still person, who was her daughter, Colleen asked, "When should she wake up?"

Looking at the IV drip hanging over Marcy's bed, Jason said, "My orders say to keep her sedated until breakfast time tomorrow. Her nourishment until breakfast will be the liquid from the IV that's running now."

"My goodness!" Charlie murmured, shaking his head. He still had his arm around Colleen and could feel her trembling against him. "I had no idea she could become so ill so quickly! Her breathing… It doesn't seem normal."

Jason nodded and turned the valve to speed the IV a little more. "Yes, it is labored, but that's typical. Because of the virus, her heart has to work harder and that's causing her lungs to have to work harder."

"I see," Charlie murmured. A tear glistened in his eye, but didn't fall as he looked at his younger daughter. "So your tests will be finished tomorrow?"

"Possibly. We'll run more as we feel are necessary. We must be sure the heart isn't compromised. I'm hoping we've gotten this figured out soon enough, but we can't be sure until the blood work comes back clean."

"Yes, I understand."

Marcy didn't wake up or stir while her parents talked with the doctor. Colleen took her hand, but it felt like a cold fish, so she laid it gently back on the bed. She turned and looked up into Charlie's eyes he could see the tears glistening in hers, his own eyes felt scratchy. His young daughter had never looked so ill, it was such a foreign concept that it was hard for the Bernard's to grasp. Since Marcy didn't move, even after Colleen took her hand, they turned together to leave the room. The doctor followed them and pulled the door nearly closed behind him. After all, this was a men's surgery ward, Marcy was the only female patient on the ward.

After returning to the waiting area again, Charlie asked, "If she had no symptoms that anyone detected, how can you be sure she has Rheumatic Fever?"

The doctor smiled and nodded. "Yes, it makes you wonder, doesn't it? Her symptoms and the blood work results we have so far show a classic case. Rheumatic Fever is caused by a virus, you know how illusive a virus can be. I'm instructing my residents to keep a close watch on the blood work results. We'll be taking blood samples periodically until we're satisfied that's what we're seeing and they come clean."

The trio sat down in the lounge seats and Jason continued, "What we're really concerned about is heart involvement. At this point, we see no heart damage, but that doesn't mean there won't be some before she is totally recovered. The first twenty-four hours are always the most critical, I'm sure you know. Like I say, since she's been such a healthy young woman, that she'll be anxious to get out of bed, perhaps before she should be. Mrs. Bernard, I want to make sure you realize how important it will be when we do discharge her that she stay in bed for the week."

Charlie was nodding and Colleen said, "Yes, Doctor, I'll make sure she stays in bed. I know she'll want to be completely well."

Jason had his mouth open to say something else, but all three of them heard a page over the hospital intercom, "Dr. Wright, extension forty-eight seventy."

Jason made a face. "I must leave you folks. Feel free to page me with more questions."

"Thank you, Doctor," Charlie said, as the man rose quickly and disappeared onto the ward where they had been. Knowing his wife as he did, Charlie pulled her close inside his arms, laid his cheek down on her hair and stroked her back tenderly. Huddled into Charlie's strong arm, Colleen sat quietly studying her hands for several minutes.

Finally, she looked into her husband's face and saw his love. She was glad for his love, it had helped her weather many problems. She asked, "Where do we put Marcy when we take her home, Honey? He said she can't go upstairs. Would she be comfortable on the couch?"

Dumbfounded, Charlie shook his head and looked at Colleen, but took several minutes before he said, "Sweetheart, there isn't any choice! This is not a stop-gap temporary thing. We must put her in the music room, of course! You heard Dr. Wright say she cannot walk long distances or go upstairs. She certainly can't go to her room on second floor until she's well. You wouldn't hear her even if she had a bell. You know the couch isn't a choice, there's too much traffic through the living room and it wouldn't be comfortable for her to lie on for hours and days at a time. In the music room she'll have the much wider day bed and we can shut the doors so she can rest and have some privacy."

Colleen's head came up, as she leaned away from Charlie. Looking aghast at him, her eyes as big as saucers, as if he spoke sacrilege, Colleen shook her head and whispered, "But… but that's Sandy's room! Suppose she comes home? She can't go upstairs at all, you know."

Charlie shook his head, lifted his arm from around Colleen, shifted on the vinyl so he was facing her, then took both her hands and waited until she looked at him again. He swallowed, his mind was working in German, but he must speak English. Colleen took a long time before she looked up. There were tears on her eyelashes and she shivered. In a whisper, she said, "My baby is so sick! How did this happen? Did I cause it, could she have gotten it from me?"

Still concentrating on the need for the bed in the music room, Charlie said, "My dear, Sandy cannot come home while Marcy's sick! You know that Sandy is eight months pregnant in Georgia with her husband and under close watch by the doctors she's seeing in Vansville and Blairsville.

They would not let her travel for Christmas, so of course she can't come home now."

Charlie took a deep breath, this had been a litany for well over a year, almost two! Colleen seemed to have a closed mind to anything except that Sandy had to come home. He swallowed and said, "Please, Colleen, let's not go through this again! Sandy is not coming home, but Marcy must use that room so that she will be close to both the bathroom and the kitchen. Besides, how would she get hold of you if she's in bed in her room on second floor?" Taking another deep breath, Charlie said, "Colleen, I'm sure if the doctor suspected that either of us gave her the virus he'd have insisted that we be tested. He didn't mention it. My love, you always want to take the blame for every wrong that happens in our house. It isn't so!"

Silent tears slid down Colleen's face. Squeezing Charlie's hands until they nearly turned white, she whispered, "It's so awful! I was thinking I should go to be with Sandy during this last month and see if I can finally convince her to come home, but now Marcy is so sick. You think there is no way she can stay in her own room?"

Trying to swallow his frustration, because it seemed as if Colleen hadn't heard a word he or the doctor had said. It had been well over a year since Sandy left for Georgia, married Ramon and was now expecting their first grandchild. Charlie took a deep breath, how convoluted his wife's thinking had become in only a few hours! What was the problem? She certainly was too young to be senile! Besides this thinking only involved her daughters!

Finally, he said, "Colleen, listen to me! Look at me!" He waited again until she looked into his eyes. "Our older daughter will not be coming home, whether you go there or not! You might have helped her some in her home, which you did while we were there over Christmas. I know they were very grateful for your help. I know she would also have been glad for your help after she has the baby, there in her home. She is happy in her life in Vansville and has no intention of leaving."

Colleen gasped and tried to look away, but Charlie grasped her face with his thumb and finger, then continued, "At this point, Marcy needs the bed downstairs, in the music room." Charlie tried not to speak harshly to his wife, but there came a time when words had to be blunt and now was that time. "You've kept that room almost as a shrine to Sandy, even though there is nothing of hers in the room. Don't skirt around what needs to be done. Marcy will go in that room when we bring her home! You'll make up the bed, Ed and I'll bring down some of her things from her room so she will be comfortable."

In barely a whisper, Colleen said, "How can you say that?"

On a sigh, Charlie said, "Because it's true, Colleen! It's very true."

Silently, Colleen shook her head.

They had barely finished speaking, when a nurse came from the ward where Marcy's room was and said, "Mr. and Mrs. Bernard?" They looked at the nurse, so she continued, "Marcy is awake, but we'll give her an injection soon. Would you like to see her for a minute?"

"Yes, yes!" Colleen said and jumped up.

Charlie also stood and hurried after his wife. "We'll have just a minute with her?"

Colleen nearly ran to the nurse, Charlie close behind her. Compassionately, the nurse said, "Yes, but Marcy's a very sick girl, try to be pleasant when you speak with her. She may be napping or very groggy. In a few minutes the medicine nurse'll be in with another sedative injection, so be quick about what you say. But remember to be cheerful."

"Yes, Ma'am, thank you for calling us," Charlie said. "This development is so unlike Marcy it is hard for us to comprehend."

The nurse nodded. "I know, she's never been sick since she's been on our ward, but I knew you'd want to talk to her."

"Thank you so much for calling us, Miss." The Bernards went in the dark private room and moved close enough that Colleen could take Marcy's cool, almost clammy hand.

Colleen whispered, "Hi, Dear, the nurse said you're awake…."

Marcy had a struggle to open her eyes, but finally she looked at her mom. "Mom, Dad," she whispered, "I guess they called you?"

"Yes, my dear. We've been here a while and talked with your doctor. He's explained everything they know so far. Did you have any idea you were sick?" Charlie asked. "He couldn't believe you didn't have any symptoms when you were home last."

Marcy slowly shook her head, but left her hand in her mom's. "Daddy, I had no idea! I was caring for my first patient, doing his morning care and all at once I felt dizzy. The next thing I knew, a man was drawing blood and there were four or five men standing around waiting for him to leave. I had this IV and I felt like a wet noodle. Has the doctor told you anything?"

Not knowing what Marcy had been told, or what she should know, Charlie said, "He said you're very sick and must have many tests. He said his students are monitoring your blood work closely. When you're released we can take you home but you must stay in bed for a week. He was pretty strict about that."

Marcy raised her head off the pillow and tried to lift herself on her arms, but she couldn't make it happen. Exhausted, she fell back against the bed and her breath rushed out on a sigh. When she finally did speak, her words were barely more than a breath. "A week! Daddy! But I have two more weeks to this quarter. How can I stay in bed, at home for a week and still get through this quarter? Dad, surely the man is mistaken! I'll be up and out of here soon. I need to finish this quarter!" her voice became stronger as she spoke.

Shaking his head, Charlie reached for her other hand and said, "I think this quarter will be an incomplete, my dear."

"But Dad….!"

"I know," he said, compassionately. "I know how upset this makes you, but your body seems not to like what it's been doing and has rebelled."

"Oh, bother!" Marcy muttered.

Another nurse opened the door and walked in, holding a syringe and said, "Excuse me, folks, it's time for Marcy's next shot and you'll have to leave."

"Of course, we know she must rest to get better."

The nurse smiled at the couple and said, "Thank you."

"Yes, Ma'am."

Charlie looked down at his daughter and smiled, but even in the dim light, she could see the pain and sadness in his eyes, as he said, "My dear, we'll see you again. We'll be in the next time they call us, of course."

She shut her eyes, as the medicine went in her arm, she whispered, "Thanks, Daddy." She never heard the door close as the medicine nurse left the room.

After the initial blood work was finished and all the tests the doctor ordered were completed. Marcy was not released in two days as the doctor had told her parents initially. Even though she had been receiving sedatives and antibiotics ever since she was admitted and had slept almost all of three days, her resting had not been enough to keep the virus from attacking her heart. Her blood test for three mornings showed more damage to Marcy's heart and Marcy grew weaker and weaker. Colleen had been at her bedside most of every day and helped her eat the meal ordered. They hadn't helped strengthen her, either.

As soon as Dr. Wright discovered this he immediately prescribed more and stronger antibiotics, some of them given in her IV, which didn't come out for another two days. Finally, the third day the blood work showed that the damage had been stopped, but Marcy was very weak. It made her very unhappy that Dr. Wright only let her sit up with the help of the bed behind her. She was not allowed to even go to the bathroom. That was definitely against her religion! Marcy was never one to call attention to herself, but these days while she was in the hospital many people disrupted her sleep, doing procedures and blood work.

Colleen came early in the day, every day and stayed close to Marcy's bedside. Much to Marcy's displeasure, Colleen fussed over her and shed silent tears nearly the entire time she was in the room. Charlie came each afternoon when his shift at the post office was over, then stayed into the evening, of course, he was a steadfast rock, both for Colleen and Marcy. Ed came each day for a few minutes, but he was only a few weeks into his new semester of classes. This was his final semester and he needed to get the highest grades he could for the position he hoped to get after graduation.

Of course, Marcy slept a lot. The sedatives weren't as strong as they'd been at first, but they still made her sleep a lot, since she never took medicines. During the evening when Marcy slept, Colleen and Charlie emptied her room at the nurses' residence. The doctor had told them she might never come back to nurses' training, it was probably too strenuous and her heart had sustained a lot of damage from the virus. This he told them outside Marcy's room, she was already discouraged without knowing everything. Charlie was also discouraged, even though he tried for a strong front in Marcy's room, but it was hard, because Marcy's condition was not good, but Colleen was despondent, even in front of Marcy.

Finally, six days after Marcy had collapsed, still very weak; Dr. Wright determined that if Colleen would keep Marcy in bed, even for meals, that he would release her. Marcy was dozing when the doctor came in her room and said to her parents, "Colleen and Charlie, I'll write a release for Marcy, but I'm writing several prescriptions that the pharmacy downstairs will fill for you to take home. Also, I think it wise, unless she's in a room that has an attached bath, that you rent a commode for beside her bed. I want her on strict bedrest for at least a week. Marcy is still sick and very weak. Her heart has been damaged and must get as much rest as possible. Otherwise, she could be an invalid for the rest of her life. I know Marcy well enough and I'm sure you do, too, that she will not want that for her life."

"We'll do our best, Doctor," Charlie said.

Dr. Wright nodded. "Good, I'm glad to hear it. I'll go write those orders now. She should be ready in about half an hour.

Charlie nodded. "Thank you Doctor, we'll wait in the lounge here on the floor."

"That's fine."

Marcy woke while Jason spoke with her parents and watched them leave. When he turned to her, she scowled and said, "Dr. Wright! You can't be serious! not even the bathroom?"

Scowling at the young woman, Jason said, "Marcy, how far is the bathroom you'll have to use from where you'll be in bed?"

Marcy sighed, she wasn't sure yet where she'd be, but she said, "Probably several rooms away, Doctor. Only my parents' room has an attached bathroom."

His eyes nearly slits, the doctor looked hard at the young woman and said, "Listen, young lady, I need to be very blunt with you. You're suffering the effects of Rheumatic Fever, as I've told you. I know you've studied about the illness. You have been very, very sick and your heart is damaged. I know you want to get well, as well as possible. If that is true, and I'm sure it is, you must be in bed and sleeping most of the time for this first week or you'll be in the bed lots longer, perhaps for the rest of your life, believe me."

Marcy sighed, "Yes, Doctor, I hear you."

"And Marcy, several rooms away is absolutely too far for you to try for the bathroom, understood?" Marcy nodded, silent tears welled in her eyes, but as she swiped at them, more continued to form and she wiped her nose. "I want you back in a week to see me, but someone must bring you. After I see you I'll decide if you're well enough to be up around the house.

At that time I'll take several blood samples to see how you're progressing. Do you understand?"

"That's the pits!" Marcy grumbled.

"Yes, I'm sure that's how you feel, but it's real life, Marcy." The doctor sighed, he wasn't really an ogre, "Marcy, I know this is hard, but there for a few days your life did hang in the balances, I'm sure you know that."

Marcy let out a long sigh, "Yes, I think I know that, too."

Jason smiled and patted Marcy's hand. "Good, I'm glad you understand. You do know that I'm not a mean old troll."

Giving him her typical Marcy smile, she said, "Really?"

Shaking his head, glad to see just a little spunk in the very ill young woman, Jason said, "Thanks a lot, girl." The Chief of Staff gave Marcy a smile. He really liked this young lady. It upset him a lot to think that her nursing career had been cut so short that she'd never be able to truly become a full-fledged nurse. Also, she'd never been shy about her plans to be a missionary nurse. Those plans were out, too, but sometimes life handed out thorns with its roses. Marcy had gotten the bigger bundle of thorns. "Marcy, I'll see you in a week in my office downstairs – that's after total bedrest!"

In the car on the way home from downtown to their north Philadelphia home, Marcy fought to stay awake. She couldn't believe that the head nurse had insisted they only pull a coat over her flannel pajamas to send her home. She had clothes she'd wanted to wear, but it didn't happen. They were in a paper bag on the floor beside her. Her parents were quiet in the front seat, as she lay on the back seat. She could never remember feeling so weak and exhausted in her life before. She still couldn't believe she had gotten so sick so quickly. In fact, she couldn't remember a time in her life when she'd had more than the sniffles or a slight cough. Where in the world had she been exposed to the virus that gave her Rheumatic Fever?

She shook her head. Of course she worked in a hospital, there were always germs and viruses around, but they always took precautions, washing their hands between each patient and wearing gloves, changing them between patients. As far as she knew, none of her patients had Rheumatic Fever, how could she be exposed to it if no one had it?

She was about to drift off, when Charlie said, "Sweetheart, Mama's made up the bed in the music room. Ed and I've brought down some of your things so you'll be comfortable. Dr. Wright ordered a commode and we have it in the trunk. I guess you'll be tired of those walls real soon. It's good there are two windows for a slight change of scenery and plenty of light. It'll be hard I'm sure, as much as you like to be active."

Marcy didn't voice her astonishment, but she was very surprised that she'd be in Sandy's former room. It had stood empty for well over a year. At this time there was very little in the room and nothing of Sandy's. Soon after Sandy had left for Georgia, she'd asked to change to that room and her mom wouldn't hear of it. It was like her mom was keeping the empty room as a shrine to her elder daughter.

However, she said, "Daddy, a commode? I can't even go to the bathroom?" She shook her head. "Man, those things are for old people in nursing homes!"

Charlie smiled and looked at her in the rearview mirror, as he said, "That's what he said, girl. Mama will wait on you hand and foot. Doctor said, she must even help you when you get up to use that commode."

"Daddy! How horrid!" After all, she was in her twenties and hated being dependant on anyone, especially her mom and especially to go to the *bathroom*. She covered her face with her hands. "That is so horrid!"

Charlie chuckled, and said, "I know so much help is against your religion, but he was pretty adamant that you rest or the damage to your heart will be permanent, you don't want that."

Marcy sighed, "I know, I heard him. Dr. Wright is such a stickler. I had him as an instructor in one class. It was hard."

"Maybe so, but you know what they say, 'It's for your own good.'"

Marcy sighed again, "Daddy did you have to say that? You said that so much when I was little. It was almost like a broken record."

"It got you through, didn't it?" He chuckled.

"Yessss, Daddy," she grumbled.

"I'm so sorry, Honey," Colleen added.

It was a beautiful day, the sun shining all morning with only a few clouds in the sky, but of course it was very cold in Philadelphia. As Marcy looked out the window above her feet, she could see the bare-limbed trees in the huge Schuylkill River Park. This was Sandy's favorite place in Philadelphia and Marcy loved it, too, an oasis in the middle of the huge city. As children, their daddy had often brought them here.

That was before Sandy had her motorized chair, but their dad would lift Sandy into the car, fold up her chair and put it in the trunk while the rest of the family scrambled in. Ed and their dad took turns pushing Sandy's chair along the trails. It was a time in their lives that they loved to remember. Now they rarely did things together. Of course, Sandy was in Georgia, but Ed was in grad school and she'd been in nursing school.

Marcy sighed. "Daddy, thanks for driving through the park, I can see all the trees."

"I'm glad it makes you happy, Marcy," Charlie said. "I thought it might. Would you like to stop for a while and open the door so you can see more?"

"Would you? I'd love it. I know I can't do anything but look, but it's so pretty through here and it reminds me of the fun we used to have when we were all kids."

"Sure, we'll stop. It's a bit cold, but the sun's out and the wind isn't strong, so we can at least spend a few minutes here and then we'll go home."

"That's great, thanks."

Colleen opened her mouth, but Charlie shook his head. He was almost sure what pessimistic words would come out. He drove to the part of the park that was a family favorite. The road followed a big bend in the river that had a sandy beach where Ed and Marcy had played as children, swimming and making sand castles. There was a bench close by where Charlie and Colleen had watched. Many times, Sandy had brought her paints and painted pictures that she gave as gifts. It was a rare time that Sandy didn't have her paints. Marcy swallowed a sigh, now they were all grown, Sandy had moved away, Ed rarely was home, he'd rather spend any free time with Margaret and she'd left for nursing school.

Colleen interrupted her thoughts when she said, "Charlie, you won't let her get cold, will you? You know, what the doctor said." Marcy stifled a sigh, her mom was such a worry wart.

Patiently, Charlie said, "My dear, a few minutes with the car running and the heater blowing won't hurt, I'm sure."

Colleen sighed, "Yes, Dear."

When he stopped and put the car in park, he left it running then he opened the back door so Marcy could see the frozen surface of the river.

As soon as he opened the door, he went to the trunk and brought back a blanket. Even with her warm winter coat, a scarf and a warm hat and mittens, Charlie was taking no chances that Marcy would get a chill. He laid it over her, right up to her chin and Marcy smiled at her dad's care for her. Even so, he left the car motor running and the heater on to help keep the chill from the car, while Marcy enjoyed the scene before her.

Only ten minutes later, Marcy said, "Daddy, I think I've been here long enough, let's go home. I know it's cold, I'm warm, but you guys don't need to get cold just so I can look at the trees and a frozen river." *Besides, I feel like I'm about to fall asleep.*

Charlie stepped out and closed Marcy's door, then got back in and drove on through the park. "Sweetheart, it's okay. If it helps and gives you peace Mama and I can stand a little cold."

"Thanks, Daddy, it's been great."

Charlie smiled and said, "You're welcome, my dear." It wasn't that far home, but before they arrived, Marcy fell asleep.

Because she was so quiet, Colleen looked back, amazed that so soon she heard Marcy's slow breathing. "Charlie, she's asleep!" Colleen whispered. "I guess she's really worn out!"

"Yes, I see that, my dear," Charlie whispered back. "However, I think one of those pills they gave her before we left the ward was a sedative."

When they arrived at home, Ed met them at the back door. He'd been home for a little while from his classes. He never said a word, just walked down the incline, opened the back door of the car and reached in for Marcy. When he saw she was awake, he grinned and winked at her, then easily lifted her out and cradled her against his chest. He turned, never letting her down, and started up the incline.

Marcy scowled up at him and said, "Ed, surely I can walk up the incline! I'm not a baby, for crying out loud!"

Ed shrugged and patted her arm under his hand. "Not what I heard. As far as you're to walk is from your bed, two steps to some potty chair." He grinned at his little sister, enjoying her discomfort immensely.

"Ed! You're awful! I won't use a potty chair!"

Chuckling, Ed answered, "That's what I heard."

With long strides, Ed soon had his sister deposited on the high daybed in the old music room. Marcy whispered, "Was it you or Dad who finally got Mom to let me have this room? I couldn't believe it when Daddy said I'd be in here! Surely Mom put up a fight! Remember after Sandy left I asked to move down here?"

Ed shook his head. "Believe me, Sis, it was Dad. I guess he gave it to her straight and left her no choice."

"It's about time! Not that I wanted to be in here with this reason."

"I know, but you'll get better faster in here. Besides, you're too puny to walk upstairs." Ed's face split with a grin and he winked at her. The young man loved to tease his little sister, she always took the bait.

"Edwin! You can be such a trial!"

He chuckled again. "Not me. I'm your best brother."

"Yeah, right. You're my only brother. Thank goodness!" she huffed.

His eyes twinkling, he said, "Be glad."

Marcy sighed, "Oh, I am! Believe me, I am!"

He patted her cheek and said, "Now be a good girl and rest. And be sure to eat all your spinach when Mom puts it on your plate."

"Hsssss!" Ed heard, as he left the room and pulled the door behind him. Once he closed the door, Marcy closed her eyes. Everything wore her out, the trip home from the hospital was exhausting. Where had all her stamina gone? She guessed it had fled that morning when she ended up under Mr. Hain's bed. Used to, she'd do an eight hour shift on the ward then go to class. For two weeks straight, not too long ago, she worked two weeks of night shift, come off, eat breakfast and spend three hours in classes, then get about five hours sleep. She hadn't liked the routine, but that's what twenty-four hour care was. She fell asleep.

Colleen had moments before removed Marcy's supper tray, but Marcy was already asleep when the phone rang. Charlie was the closest, so he answered. A deep voice said, "Charlie, Ramon. Wanted to report that Stan's admitted Sandy this afternoon into Blairsville Hospital for the duration. He and Doc Weber feel she's best off here so she can be monitored."

Charlie had to drag in a breath and swallow, before he could say, "Ramon, what do I say? Actually, I'm amazed that Sandy's lasted out of the hospital this long. What has them concerned? Is she bleeding?"

"No, not bleeding, no cramps, everything about her pregnancy seems fine, the baby's growing normally, but the lower part of her, obviously where the baby is, since it's paralyzed, is compressed. Unless she lies down there's no room for the baby. Doc Weber feels the baby is pushing against Sandy's diaphragm. At any rate, she's short of breath most of the time and has a hard time filling her lungs. The baby's been pressing against her bladder, too and that's very hard for her, so they've inserted a catheter. It has relieved her."

Charlie sighed, "Ramon, Sandy's pregnancy is amazing, we'll call it a miracle. We never thought Sandy could get pregnant." What he didn't say spoke volumes to Ramon. "It is a joy to us and we want only what's best for her." He chuckled. "I'm sure you know this will be her mother's first grandchild, well, need I say more?"

Ramon chuckled. "I don't think so, Charlie."

Charlie sighed, "The other thing that seems unbelievable, since we have such normally healthy children, you caught us home tonight because Colleen and I brought Marcy home from being hospitalized for six days only this afternoon. Her doctor gave us very strict instructions to keep her on bedrest for at least a week or her heart will be permanently damaged. Somehow, no one knows how, she contracted Rheumatic Fever and it's affected her heart quite a bit. She may not be returning to nursing school any time soon."

"Wow!" Ramon exclaimed, his voice catching. "What! Unbelievable! Colleen is covered up, isn't she? Not returning.... Wow!" Ramon looked at his wife, who was obviously listening to his side of the conversation.

Charlie chuckled. "Perhaps that's the understatement of the year? Maybe since Sandy is hospitalized, you'd best not tell her how sick her sister is. Then again, Marcy could use Sandy's prayers, as we all could. Ramon, use your discretion. We're a very discouraged household tonight, as you can imagine."

"I understand, Dad. You pray for us and we'll pray for you. We all have the same God and He will keep us in His strong and mighty hand."

"Son, I needed that, thanks. Yes, we'll pray for you, too." After a pause, Charlie asked, "How are you running your business?"

Ramon was quiet for a few seconds, changing gear from that bombshell about Marcy. "Thankfully, it's not time yet for the season to start again. Sandy's been pushing herself to get everything caught up and she's done wonders, even as bad as she's felt. Actually, it's a relief for me to have her in the hospital, I've watched her struggle for days now, but she's in the hospital and the computer is back home and so are her paints and piano, thank goodness! We've notified all her piano students that lessons will stop for the time being, too.

"It looks like another busy season. We have bookings well into the summer. We hope to hire another guide, but so far, it hasn't happened. Duncan's married and with the baby, I don't want to be on long hikes. Neal's the only one who's single." Ramon chuckled. "I never knew how much a woman can change a man's life! Still, I wouldn't trade Sandy for anything!"

Charlie smiled this young man had grown so much since Sandy had met him. "Son, remember to always keep it that way! God will honor you as you do. I know without asking that you've been a tremendous help to Sandy since the season was over. Actually, it sounds like you're really busy and will be even more when the hiking season starts! Will they wait for Sandy to go into labor or what?"

"By all the calculations, they're still not sure of the due date, but Doc Weber thinks it's somewhere close to the end of March, so he's planning to do a Caesarean on the twentieth. That's the scoop right now. At any rate, if she goes into labor before that, he'll take the baby. He feels it would be too hard for them both to have her deliver normally, especially since she has no feeling below her waist. Neither of our doctors has experience with a paraplegic, so they don't know what to expect. I'm glad he's decided to take the baby, that's been worrying both Sandy and me for some time now." Ramon sighed, "Believe me; I'm so glad for all the wonderful people in Vansville that say they'll help us when the baby comes."

"I'm glad for them, too. I know Colleen wanted us to come down for a while around the time of the baby's birth, but that doesn't look like it'll happen, at least for a while."

Ramon chuckled. "I know Marcy, Colleen'll probably have to sit on her."

Chuckling, Charlie said, "Yes, I'd say that's about the size of it. Except that she fell asleep almost as the words left her mouth, she was disgusted with a week of bedrest!"

"You know, when Marcy's better, she could come down, we have plenty of room."

"Thanks, Ramon, I'll pass that on, but you know how her mama is."

Ramon chuckled. "Yes, Dad, I know all too well."

"Mmm, first hand experience." He couldn't say too much, Colleen was there with him in the kitchen and certainly was listening.

Charlie hung up, then went to Marcy's room. Ed had gone to his room to study, Colleen stood at the kitchen sink washing dishes and shedding tears into the cooling dishwater. Charlie knew that was her escape when she was stressed and he rarely bothered her as she slowly took care of the supper dishes. Besides, he felt the need to see his youngest child alone. He hadn't been able to for a long time, not even when she was in bed at the hospital. He walked in the room in the middle of the house and knew his daughter wasn't sleeping. She lay on her back, her eyes closed, but her head was turned to the side and tears were sliding down onto her pillow. With skin so pale, he couldn't help but see how sick she was.

Charlie closed the door to the living room and pulled up a chair beside the bed. In a whisper, he said, "What is it, Sweetheart? What is it that's making you cry? You're home now and Dr. Wright says you're on the road to recovery."

Marcy hiccupped and swiped her wrist across her eyes, opened them, then whispered, "Daddy, why did this happen? Why did it happen now? I really don't understand what's going on! I still have a year to finish my degree. Dr. Wright was pretty sure I won't be going back for a very long time, if at all! It's the pits! You know what this means?"

Taking her hand in his and wiping the tear that escaped onto her cheek, Charlie said, "Honey, I have no idea why this happened or why now, but we mustn't blame God. Sickness and disease came into the world because of sin. If we must lay blame, it should be at the devil's feet for tempting Eve and for her to give in to his tempting and Adam for not protecting her. Perhaps I don't know the answer to your last question. What do you mean?"

Marcy opened her eyes and tried to smile. Charlie squeezed her hand and curled his other hand around it. "Daddy, I heard Dr. Wright and the chief resident talking over my chart the other day. Somehow they missed catching the virus right away and it injured my heart. Even though I rest, some of it'll be permanent, so they said. Daddy, that means I can't be a missionary overseas like I wanted to be… like I thought the Lord wanted me to be!"

Charlie took one hand from hers and stroked her cheek. Tenderly, he smiled and said, "My dear child, leave it all in God's hands. He can do all things. If He wants you to be a missionary overseas, He'll make you completely well, if He doesn't, He'll have something even better for you. Let's get you better now and follow Dr. Wright's orders. He seemed to think you'd make a very good recovery if you stay on bedrest for at least this week. You only came home today, you know. Remember our verse, 'And we know that in all things God works for the good of those who love him.' (Romans 8: 28) This is part of 'in all things' my dear."

Marcy sighed, "I know, Daddy, but it's hard."

"Yes, it is, I know."

Charlie and Marcy were quiet for a few minutes, surprising Charlie, Marcy didn't like being quiet for long. However, he'd noticed with her illness, several things she used to do, she no longer did. She closed her eyes, but finally, after several minutes, she sighed again and asked, "Who was on the phone?"

"It was Ramon…."

Fresh tears slid down Marcy's cheeks and her eyes came open. Charlie easily saw the pain in her eyes; it wasn't her own physical pain, but pain for her sister. Marcy was truly a compassionate young woman. Charlie hurt because of that. Marcy surely deserved to be a nurse because of her compassion for people. "They put Sandy in the hospital, didn't they? Her body's cramping the baby, isn't it? I was afraid that would happen, I'm surprised, though, that she could stay out this long."

FOUR

Charlie nodded, reluctant to share such news with his very sick daughter, but knowing that being a nursing student that she would think of that problem immediately. "Yes, that's right. He said she's there until they take the baby by Caesarean. They need her on bedrest so that the baby can stretch out and they've put a catheter in her bladder."

More tears slid down Marcy's face and she shook her head. "Nobody can go be with them, either! Daddy, this is all so horrible!"

Charlie still stroked her face, pushing a curl behind her ear, then pulled his hand back and wiped a tear away with his thumb. He kissed the hand he still held and said, "Honey, remember, 'in all things God works **for the good** of those who love him.' Ramon reminded me that God is with us and with them. He is mighty, He created us for His enjoyment. He loves us unconditionally and means only good for us. Remember, He holds us in His hand, all of us. He has plans for you, perhaps not what you thought, but they are good plans."

"Yes, Daddy, I'll try to remember."

Charlie could see Marcy wilting in on herself before his eyes. He continued to stroke her face and whispered, "Sleep, my child, get your rest. God is with us, His love surrounds us each moment. Mama and I love you with all our hearts. I'll see you tomorrow, Sweetheart."

"Yes, Daddy," Marcy's eyes closed.

Moments later, Charlie knew his daughter slept. Carefully, he laid her hand on the bed and slipped from the room, turning out the light before he closed the door. His heart heavy, Charlie went to his favorite chair in the living room. It was dark outside, but the window reflected the quiet room. He pondered Marcy's questions. God had reasons for everything, sometimes they didn't fit in with what they, as finite humans wanted. Since she was little, Marcy was sure God had called her to be a foreign missionary. Why had God cut her down so she couldn't fulfill that calling? Surely there were people in the world whom Marcy could reach only because she was Nurse Marcy! Charlie shook his head. God surely worked in mysterious ways. Who was he to question that? He reached for his source of strength – his Bible.

Ramon replaced the receiver in the cradle. Sandy's eyes were open and she stared at the ceiling until then, then her eyes moved to his face. He didn't expect her to be asleep; she was too active a person to sleep just because she was in a bed. She had argued hard with Stan and Bruce Weber not to be hospitalized, but they had prevailed. They knew, as did Ramon, that she'd never stay in bed if they let her stay home. He was glad, she had been doing far too much, even though he'd taken on so much around the house and the business since the hiking season closed. He shook his head, not only was the hiking service current, she'd finished two commissions and just this morning, Heidi had come for a lesson. She was an unbelievable woman!

He sat looking at his lovely wife then laid his hand on the mound that was their child. He was rewarded by a gentle kick. Sandy couldn't feel his hand, but she had seen the movement and placed her hand over his. This wonderful, joyful woman was his wife, his soulmate, the person in all the world who knew him best.

"Honey, why is Mom covered up?"

Ramon sighed, so much for discretion as Charlie asked, he must tell her. He'd been sure Sandy had heard most of his conversation, that one statement he'd made clued her in. "Darling, Marcy is very sick; your folks brought her home today from six days in the hospital. She collapsed on the ward, so they hospitalized her immediately. She has had Rheumatic Fever and must be on bedrest or there'll be permanent heart damage."

Sandy swallowed, turning pained eyes to look into her husband's. "Wow! You have said a mouthful, Honey! If there is heart damage she won't be able to fulfill her life-long goal of being a foreign missionary! I'm afraid that'll devastate her more than the illness."

"I know, Sweetheart. I told your dad we'd pray for her and he assured me that they'd pray for us. Want to do that now?"

"Yes."

He turned his hand, still resting on her belly and grasped her hand, twining his fingers with hers. He watched as she closed her eyes. His love for her knew no boundary. What she was going through for them to have this baby was beyond believing. Neither of them had thought she could have a baby, or they might have tried to prevent it. However, she was ecstatic and would go through anything to have this baby. Because of that, he would do anything for her so she could carry this child to term. In fact, he wished he could carry the child for her.

He closed his eyes as she whispered, "My matchless Father, we didn't know until just now that my sister is gravely ill, but You've known all along and You've been with her, we know. Touch her body, I pray, my Father, make her well. If it is Your will that she be completely healed so she can do this missionary work she's always wanted to do, then make it happen, but if not, then give her grace to work with her body for healing and fulfill Your plan. Give her comfort right now and restful sleep. Bless Mom and Daddy; help Mom as she cares for Marcy. Thank You for Your love for us. I pray in Your Son's matchless Name, amen."

"Yes, Lord, thank You, amen," Ramon added. A second later, Ramon added, "And Lord, bless my darling, give her body rest, amen."

They stayed that way, holding hands on top of their baby for several minutes. Ramon was content to silently hold his wife's hand and as they stayed, he felt the baby kick their hands several times, but Sandy never acknowledged it, probably she couldn't feel it at all. Finally, Sandy sighed, "Honey, I hate to be here and it'll be such a long time, maybe as long as six weeks, but I know it's best for the baby."

He pulled his hand from hers, then put his arms around her and hugged her tightly to his chest. Before he spoke, he gave her a long, lingering kiss, then he said, "Yes, my love, I know it is and for you, too. You've been struggling for several weeks now to do so much and I'm glad you can finally leave it and rest. Our little one can stretch out now and I can tell already that you're more comfortable. I think tonight'll be truly a restful sleep for you." She heard the smile in his voice, as he continued, "The only thing, this isn't a queen sized bed so I can't join you."

After another long kiss, she said, "That I will miss the most, Honey!"

After another deep breath, like she hadn't been able to take in several weeks, she said, "Honey, it's been a busy day, you should go home. You know there may be messages."

Ramon sighed and hugged her again, "Darling, who cares about the messages! They'll be there when I get to them. Besides, I'm pretty sure Duncan's planning on coming over while Nancy works at the clinic tomorrow. Between the two of us we'll get all the messages taken care of. Both of us can do data entry in the program, we'll have the scheduling done in no time."

Sandy sighed, "I know, I hate to leave you with so much to do, that's all."

"Darling!" Ramon said, exasperated, "You have the business current! With just me at home, there can't be much to do. The business is shut down for the winter, you know that's so!"

She sighed, "I know, but things change daily."

"Yes, and since you're here, you can't take care of it. So, now it's your turn to rest and be treated like the queen that you are."

"Honey…" she chided.

"Yes, I mean that!"

Sometime after the end of visiting hours Ramon stood, moved her legs once more, into a position she often slept in, then cradled her close and kissed his wife a long, lingering kiss. "I'll be here tomorrow, Love," he said, straightening, letting all the love he felt for her show in his eyes. "Close your eyes and let sleep take you to a restful place. Our baby will thank you for it. You know I love you."

"Yes, Honey, sleep well. I love you."

Reluctantly, Ramon moved to the other side of the bed. Giving his wife a sad smile, he pulled the door open, then stood there and watched her. Sandy watched him. Finally, he blew her a kiss and said, "Rest, my love. I'll see you in the morning."

"I will, Honey." Reluctantly, Ramon pulled the door behind him and walked down the hallway and out to the elevator.

Ramon had made her comfortable before he left and she had fallen asleep soon after he left, but over an hour later, Sandy lay in the bed, not able to turn herself and realized how much Ramon had been doing for her since she'd become pregnant. He must have been sleeping with one eye open ever since the hiking season had closed, because she realized each time she became uncomfortable whether she was awake or asleep, he'd been awake to turn her. Tears came to her eyes and she murmured, "Thank You, my Father, for my wonderful husband. Bless him tonight; give him a restful sleep, since I won't be there to trouble it. Amen."

Sandy kept her eyes closed, listening to the soft sounds that came occasionally through her closed door, but couldn't get comfortable. She didn't usually sleep on her back, but no way that she turned herself above her waist seemed to relieve her pain and she couldn't move herself from her waist down. Ramon had been turning her and holding her against him night after night, giving her support and comfort she hadn't realized.

Ten minutes later Sandy pushed the button to call someone. A voice spoke from a box above her head, "Yes, Sandy?"

Sandy hurt badly by this time and she couldn't mask the sound of tears in her voice, as she said, "I hate to bother you folks, I'm sure you're very busy with others on the ward, but I need some help turning, please."

"Of course, I'll be right there!" the voice said, urgently. Seconds later the door opened and the night aid ran in. As she turned on the light over Sandy's bed, Brenda exclaimed, "Sandy! Please, don't wait so long that you hurt! Call us right away and we'll come turn you. That's why we're here! It's part of the reason you're here so you're comfortable all the time."

Immediately, Brenda put her hands under Sandy's legs and moved her lower body, positioning her in a totally different position. When the pain had left, Sandy sighed and said, "Thanks, Brenda, so much, I'm fine now."

The compassionate girl patted Sandy's arm and said, "Good, I'm glad. You rest now, but if you start hurting again, you be sure to call."

"Yes, I will. Thanks."

The aide turned off the light and left the room. Sandy breathed a sigh and let her body relax. She fell asleep almost instantly. When Sandy woke up again it was morning, and the nurses were bustling around. Lying there, still with her eyes closed, she breathed deeply; something she hadn't been able to do for a long time and realized how rested she felt. She smiled, she didn't want to admit it, but Stan and Bruce had done the wise thing by insisting she spend the rest of her pregnancy in the hospital. She chuckled; maybe she'd thank them when this was over. Maybe not. Why thank two men for doing their job?

It was still February, but finally, the sun came out and the sidewalks started drying off. The trees lost the glistening ice and snow finally melted from the ground. Everyone took a deep breath of the warmer air. Vansville was thawing out after three weeks of winter. It certainly wasn't spring, but the precipitation stopped and the sun came out.

When Natt took over running the store, while Brad was still hospitalized, he'd brought Joyce's coffee maker to the store, since she wasn't a coffee drinker. At first he planned to use it mainly for himself, what student didn't try to stay awake to study that one last page for the exam tomorrow? Because of that, he'd worked hard at perfecting his coffee. He was rather proud of all the compliments he'd received from his dorm friends.

His first pot was still brewing when someone walked in, smelled the rich aroma, and asked if Natt had coffee available for his customers. Being an enterprising young man, Natt quickly told the man that coffee was available as soon as the machine finished brewing. While that happened, Natt hurried to the shelf where he kept disposable cups and the customer browsed the store for the item he needed. In the little village of Vansville, it didn't take long for word to get around that Natt made excellent coffee and it was available whenever the store was open. That first man thought it was a good idea to leave a donation.

On the second sunny day in a row during the third week of February, Brad sat in his favorite chair behind the counter, he'd punched in the numbers and given the man the total, then put the money away and made change, but it had exhausted him. He watched as the customer held out a hand to Natt, then walked out with a steaming cup of coffee. Natt came back to the cash register and plunked the quarters the man had given him for the coffee down on the top of the register. There was no sign and Natt had never asked for donations, but they always appeared every time a cup left the building.

After the door closed, then nodding after the man, Brad grinned at his grandson and said, "Son, was a great idea you had, bringin' your gramma's coffee maker over. Them customers think it's great, havin' a cuppa! Achally, you should buy a bigger one, we run out too quick. Its only ten o'clock and you're about run out already. Besides, we keep Alex in business, too."

Putting his grandad's mug down beside the coffee maker and draining the carafe into it, Natt said, "Grandad; that is a good idea. I had an idea, myself, last night after I ate supper. Let me tell you and you see what you think of it."

Natt brought the mug of black coffee to his grandad, as Brad said, "Sure, Son, you've had some good ones so far. Ah, what is it?"

"Well…" Natt didn't want to yell, but he needed to make more coffee. His grandad drank it like a fish, as well as a possible customer. He turned his back, taking the carafe back to the sink for water to start the process to make more coffee. Buying a bigger coffee maker was a good idea, he'd put an order for one with the supplier next week. He'd better warn Alex to order more coffee, too. His idea had gone over much better than he'd imagined.

Pouring the water into the coffee maker, he was quiet until he'd counted out the scoops of fresh coffee grounds, then he said, "Grandad, since people like my coffee so much and most everybody who comes in wants a cup, I was thinking maybe we could make that corner up there by the two windows into a gathering place. You know, put four or five chairs there for people to sit on to chat and look out the window, while they drink coffee. What do you think?"

Not saying a word, Brad scowled, but rose up in his chair to look at the corner Natt was talking about. After several minutes of looking at the shelving and the area in general, Brad said, "But we'd be encouragin' people to waste time! Don't you think so? If there's comfortable chairs, they'll use 'em, won't they?"

Natt grinned at his grandad and asked, "Grandad, don't you think people waste time all the time? What's a couple of minutes here or there? Besides, some couple may come in together and only one of them wants to shop. What's to keep the other from sitting up there with a cup of coffee to wait?"

Brad sat and scratched his chin. "Yeah," he said slowly, nodding, "I guess people in this place waste lotsa time, achally. So you think people'd come in and sit and jaw?" Nodding, Brad answered his own question, "Yeah, I can think of a couple of 'em critters who'd set all day. Kinda like them old fashioned pictures ya see."

Natt chuckled. "Yeah, Grandad, and drink coffee. I think the chairs'd be full most all the time, 'cept at meal times."

"Yeah, you're probly right, Son. You find the chairs and I'll he'p ya clear out the place."

Since Natt had been thinking about doing this for several days, he punched the button and the machine started wheezing. Immediately, the rich smell of brewing coffee filled the store. He went back to the front of the store and started in moving the things from the corner. There were several shelving units he wanted to move, he had a vision of what his 'coffee drinkers nook' would look like. He didn't know where he'd get the chairs. He didn't think upholstered living room chairs would be suitable, besides, only two chairs like that would take up the space he had in mind. He didn't know anyone who would give up their dining room chairs for his coffee drinkers nook, but he'd find some somewhere. Buying a set of chairs sounded too expensive for his budget, but he'd figure something out. He could order a bigger coffee maker, but five or six cushioned chairs were another matter.

He was pushing a large set of shelves when Brad finally left his place by the cash register and wandered over to help. Brad gave his grandson a grin, as he pushed on the opposite corner of the shelving. It was a rather feeble attempt at helping, but Natt wouldn't complain. Actually, he was concerned that Brad sat in the same chair all day and dozed. He was in his seventies and he'd had a stroke, but wasn't there something that said if you kept moving you were healthier?

"You know what I think?" the old man said, "I don't think you jest thought on this last night! You ben thinkin' on it a while, haven't ya?"

Natt grinned back at his grandad, as he wiggled his corner to match up with the other shelves he wanted to put this one beside. "Yeah, I have, Grandad, but I wanted to run it by you. After all, this is your store."

The old man slapped the side of the shelving, as if it needed one last push and said, "Supposin' I give it to ya?"

Natt's hand dropped immediately from the unit. He straightened up, looked wide-eyed at his grandad and gulped. "Grandad! I'm hoping you'll get all recovered so you can take it back and I can go back to the university in the fall." That was his greatest desire. He still wasn't giving up on his dream if he could help it.

Even though the spot for the nook wasn't empty, Brad caught his grandson's arm and led him back to the counter, the move not nearly completed. He nodded to the counter, then hobbled back and collapsed into his chair, then took a long swallow of tepid coffee. He wouldn't waste a drop of it even if it was cold. Since Joyce didn't drink coffee, he didn't get much at home, at least not brewed coffee, she'd make him a cup of instant stuff in the microwave when he asked. Natt leaned against the counter, folding his arms across his chest and waited for Brad to speak.

After another long gulp, Brad put the mug down on the counter and said, seriously, "Son, I really don't think I'm gonna get much better than this, now nor by summer nor fall. I'm an old man. Next birthday I'll be seventy-eight. It's time a young fella like you started pumpin' some young blood into a place like this. Right now I can't think of a better person to do it, neither."

Natt didn't grin, still keeping his arms crossed, he looked back seriously at his grandad and said, "You know, I was taking courses toward being a journalist, Grandad. I have two and a half years under my belt."

Brad sighed, "I know that, Son, and I was proud as peanuts of ya for doin' that. I know your dad had a place all set for ya, there at the paper, too and I know you was wantin' to travel the globe. I'm sorry you couldn't keep on that way, but I tell you what, you done a bang up job here since you took over. I ben grateful for what you done around here while I was sick and still do. This business of addin' coffee and a place for them loafers in town is down right brilliant. I'm just sorry I didn't think of it years ago. I tell you what, if you don't want the place, I'm thinkin' of sellin' it anyway and gettin' out from under it anyhow." He sighed, "I started workin' here when I was in knickers, mind you."

The weight of what the old man said, gave Natt the shivers. Finally, he said, "Grandad, can you give me a week? I'd like to think about it a while."

Brad brought the mug to his lips and drained it, before he said, "Sure! Mind, I'll keep on with ya while I'm able, but it'd be yours."

Nodding, Natt headed toward the corner again, intent on finishing the move and said, "Give me a week, Grandad, I'll give it some serious thought."

"Fair 'nough, Son."

Natt went back to moving two other things from the corner, but Brad was obviously tired out, he sat by the cash register and watched. After he moved the shelving, Natt found the broom and swept the years of accumulated dust from where the units had been. There were still stripes of dirt stuck on the floor, so he found a mop, wet it and started scrubbing the dirt lines off. Finally, the floor gleamed like the rest of the walk space. It looked like a big empty space, but he knew, once he put whatever would hold the coffee maker and the chairs he wanted to put in the space, it wouldn't be very big at all. People's knees wouldn't touch, but it would be cozy for conversations. While he worked, Natt glanced outside, the sun had slipped behind another cloud.

Natt took the broom and mop and headed for the back of the store. On the way, he said, "So, Grandad, you said I should find the chairs. Who do I ask? Who would have five or six dining room type chairs they don't use, but that would still be good? All I know are a few of the customers that come in and Isabel. I've never asked where any of them live, for goodness sake! That's not something I think I should do."

Brad chuckled. "You ben in our garage lately?"

"No, Grandad, but you and Gramma always park outside. It must be full of something."

"It shore is! It shore 'nough is! That's 'cause there ain't no room for a car!" Brad huffed, "What's a garage for? Ain't it fer puttin' cars in? You go in the garage through the kitchen when we close up and you'll find you some good chairs. Achally, you take a bit for lunch taday and go get them chairs. Your aunt talked your gramma into a new dining room set here a while back and made me put all the old stuff out there. Wasn't nothin' wrong with the old stuff, but you know women! Nuthin' would do!"

Natt shrugged, walking back to the front of the store after putting away his cleaning supplies. "Not too well, Grandad, but you've lived with one for a long time. I never had too much success trying to talk any woman out of anything."

Brad made a face, before he said, "You could say that. I'll talk 'er outta that stuff at lunch, you jest watch, see if I cain't."

"Mmm," he said, under his breath. Knowing his gramma, he'd had to live with her for several days by himself, Natt said, skeptically, "Sure, Grandad, I'm sure you will."

Brad grinned at his grandson, thumped his empty mug down on the counter and said, "Now, don't make it sound like that! I'll get 'em chairs, just you wait! This here's the best idea you had since I got this store."

"Okay, Grandad," he said, with a grin.

Brad lived on the street behind the store in a ranch style house with a two car garage. They never left the store unattended over the lunch hour, Brad would take lunch and when he returned, Natt took his usually doing some grocery shopping while he grabbed a sub at Alex's grocery store. It was where he learned more of the small town gossip. Besides, he learned some valuable lessons on being a store owner from the other store owner in town. Alex was younger than Brad and hadn't had a stroke, a 'go get 'em' kind of guy. He had learned some valuable lessons from Alex since he came to Vansville

Not long after Natt had the area cleaned, Brad left for lunch and Natt was alone. He had a lot to think about and was glad that he had no customers while his granddad was gone. It wasn't a big city store where there were several employees he was it, as far as being the responsible party in this place. Did he want the responsibility of a good sized store, a Laundromat and gas pumps? He shuddered, just thinking about it. This was all so far from his life's dream, but then, 'best laid plans....'

When Brad came back from lunch all smiles, he shooed the young man out the back door, giving him his truck keys before he sat down behind the cash register to wait for that first customer after lunch and said, "You go on over to the house, Son. Gramma's had her snit and I backed my truck up to the garage door. All you gotta do is open the door and start loadin' them chairs and the table in and bring it back."

"The table, Grandad?" He looked at the not too large space. "I don't see how we could fit a dining room table and six chairs in that spot."

Brad waved at the area. "It's a fold down job, or somethin'. It'll do real fine for the coffee pot and that other stuff folks think they need in coffee. Them chairs'll fit just fine."

"Okay, Grandad, I'll get them," he agreed, skeptically.

However, when Natt arrived at the house, Joyce was hardly over her snit. The young man walked up the driveway and saw the old truck in front of the garage doors, so he went to the door and tugged on the handle.

It didn't move, so he walked to the back door beside the garage door that led into the kitchen.

Joyce was waiting.

Her fists on her hips, Joyce scowled at her grandson. "Tell me, what did that old man promise you, young man?" she groused.

Natt shrugged, it was easy to see that Joyce didn't think much of Brad's idea of raiding her stored furniture. Trying to be the world's best diplomat, any journalist knew that's how to get what you wanted; Natt smiled and said, "Gramma, he said you had a spare dining room table and chairs in the garage we could take to the store for a coffee drinker's nook. If that's not so, I'll get some somewhere else. It's no big deal, really."

Joyce sighed, "First you take my coffee maker, while I'm gone and now you're gonna clean out my garage!"

Chuckling, Natt went to her, put his arm around her shoulders and said, "Gramma, look at it this way. You don't like coffee anyway, so taking the pot to the store for Grandad wasn't a sacrifice. Besides, we've got a big urn ordered, so you'll get your pot back soon. Your dining room's full now, you couldn't put the table and chairs from the garage back in there anyway."

Joyce harrumphed, "But I like that set a lot! I was thinking of bringing it back in here and putting this stuff in the garage."

Unlike many journalists, Natt had learned that sugar, rather than vinegar helps the medicine go down much easier, so he walked through the kitchen into the dining room and looked at the ultra-modern chairs gathered around the glass-topped table. It was a large table and no leaves could be added or taken away, but it filled the dining room, with not much room to spare. From experience, he knew the chairs weren't all that comfortable, either. "Gramma, I guess I could make the switch for you after work. I'd really only need the chairs at the store."

Joyce sighed and shook her head. "No, we can't do that; Maryann would have my head if I took this set out and put that other set back in here. She says I'm too old fashioned and set in my ways, as it is. Besides, it's easier to load those things from the garage to take over there. Besides, your grandad said you needed a small table."

Natt grinned at his gramma. "Yeah, just think; you could park your car in the garage."

Pointing her finger at her grandson, a gleam coming into her eyes, she said, "Now that would be a treat! I would have kissed you a week ago for thinking of that. I sure would have loved parking in that garage in all that bad weather, don't think I wouldn't."

Walking up to his gramma and tapping his cheek, Natt said, "You still can, Gramma. Here's the spot you usually peck on my face."

Joyce clicked her tongue, but didn't lean over to kiss her grandson. "Oh, go on! You'll miss your lunch if you don't get that stuff moved!"

"Okay, Gramma, it's as good as done."

"You got the place all ready for those chairs and things?"

Grinning, Natt said, "Yup, I did it even with all the hundreds of customers I had this morning and you know Grandad even helped."

"Nathaniel! I know for a fact you had no hundred customers this morning! Where in the world did you get your sense of humor? It sure wasn't from your dad or grandad."

Natt chuckled. "You don't think so?"

"No, I know so!"

Natt walked through the kitchen to the door into the garage. He didn't remember the set they were talking about. He'd been too young to care about furniture when his grandparents had the new set delivered and they didn't visit much except during Christmas. What he saw was a huge sideboard, a china cabinet, a small sideboard, six chairs with upholstered seats and a table that pulled apart to accept one or more leaves. Even without the leaves, the table was large. Silently, he took in the entire set. What he had cleared at the store would never hold so much.

Joyce followed him and closed the door. Natt looked over the set and said, "Gramma, there's no table here to stick in that nook I made! I can't have more'n a cardtable in that spot."

"Natt, your grandad always called that thing right there a table. I know that's what he's talking about. Go ahead, load those chairs and that little sideboard. You can store extra coffee and your creamer and sugar in the bottom, it'll work just fine."

Walking over to the garage door, Natt turned the handle to raise the big door and said over his shoulder, "Okay, Gramma, it's as good as done! You get on back in the house, it's not very warm out here and you only have a sweater on."

Nodding, Joyce said, "I'll do just that. See you again."

"Sure enough, Gramma!" he called after her, glad again that he didn't have to load all seven pieces while his gramma stood watching and yapping. Grandad was the one who had the stroke, but Gramma sure did talk about her ailments a lot! He took a closer look at the small sideboard, it would be just right and the tiny cupboard would be perfect.

Joyce turned and hurried back into her warm kitchen and had the door closed even before the garage door had made its way all the way open. He was surprised how light the little sideboard was; he lifted it with ease and loaded it on the truck. Six chairs later he slammed the tailgate, pulled the garage door down, climbed behind the wheel and turned the key. The old truck growled a little, but didn't start. Natt looked down at his feet and unhappily discovered three pedals. The truck had a standard transmission and he'd never driven one before, but he knew enough to push in the clutch before he turned the key for it to start.

"Great! Just great! Alex, save me a ham and cheese," he grumbled.

When Natt returned to the store with his truckload of furniture, Roger was at a gas pump pumping gas into his Jeep. Natt ground the gears on the old truck and backed it with several spurts and gasps up to the front door, where it died. Natt immediately opened the door and got out. Roger grinned at the young man, as he slammed the door behind him. "So it's a long walk to work at lunch time?" Roger asked.

Disgruntled, Natt shook his head and started toward the back and said, "If you've never driven a stick before it might as well be across the world! Granddad didn't even tell me it was a stick when he gave me his keys."

Roger chuckled. "I hear that! So why'd you drive?"

Natt looked at the chairs grouped in the back of the truck and said, "I'm putting in a coffee drinker's nook up here in the front of the store. As we moved shelves out of the way, Grandad said to use some furniture from his garage that he and Gramma don't use anymore. I went to get it over my lunch break, I had it all loaded before I learned the truck was a stick. It took so long and I stalled so many times I don't have time even to get a sandwich from Alex." To emphasize his plight, Natt's stomach took the opportunity to growl right then. Heat crept up Natt's neck, he knew the customer heard the noise unfortunately, the growl wasn't a quiet one.

Being always hungry had been his lot in life ever since he'd hit puberty. "I could have walked them over one at a time faster!" Natt reached for the handle on the tailgate.

Roger really laughed. He set the nozzle on automatic and leaned back against the door of his Jeep. His eyes twinkling, Roger said, "And a growing boy like you will be dead on his feet by the time the store closes at five."

Natt grinned and said, "You got that right! Especially since I gotta move all this stuff into the store and unfortunately, we don't sell that first sniff of food." He shook his head and put down the tailgate, then lifted out a chair. Brad had always told him to be friendly with the towns people, so Natt said, "I know I've seen you before, why don't I know you?"

Roger sighed, "The reason for that, young fella, is that you don't come to church with your grandparents. I'm Roger Clemens, the pastor of the church across the street."

"Oh, yeah, you came to the house when Grandad got sick after Gramma called you on New Year's Day."

Roger heard the gas nozzle click off, so he turned toward it and said, "That's true, but you should check us out this Sunday. What I say hasn't killed anybody yet, you might even enjoy it. We even got a pretty good praise team, does the music."

Natt set the chair on the pavement, turning back to Roger, he mumbled, "I haven't done church since I left home and lived in the dorm. Sunday's about the only day I get to sleep in a bit. After all, gotta be here by eight."

Roger finished pumping his gas, hung the nozzle on the pump and fitted his gas cap back in place, then walked to the back of Natt's truck and lifted off a chair. Natt picked up the chair he'd taken from the truck and started walking toward the door into the store, so Roger fell in beside him with the chair he'd lifted off and said, "You know, I walked in your shoes for a while, too. Leaving home and being on your own does something to a guy. I was a long ways from where I was supposed to be for over six years. It's hard when the profs scoff at what you've been raised to believe. I know, been there, done that."

"Yeah, that's true. But the preacher at my folks' church didn't do much either. Tell me, what's the point of sittin' there for an hour to listen to somebody do what I can do in my dorm? Man, by Sunday morning I'm ready to sack in!"

Roger shifted the chair to one arm and pulled open the door to the store, then followed Natt inside. "Oh, man! You've hit the nail on the head! That's what I did here at this church for five years! I read stuff anybody could read who could do public speaking. When people called me I'd go and pat them on the back."

Inside the door, Natt set the chair down in the empty area, so Roger followed him. Natt sat down on the chair, so Roger set his chair down, but Natt said, "So you don't now?"

Roger turned the chair he'd brought in then straddled it, placing his arms on top of the back. He shook his head and after a long pause, he said, "No, thank God, I got rescued! Over a year ago God grabbed me and turned me around. I can't imagine how I lived with myself back then. You know, I was sick and tired of my life here in this little place, I was lonely and grumpy, and felt sorry for myself. Of course, I couldn't leave, people of the church asked me to come, but I sure wished I could!"

"Yeah? How so?" The man seemed happy enough now. What had changed? God grabbed him? What did that mean?

"You know, it was really something, believe me. Almost as soon as God turned me around I met a wonderful lady and as soon as I started preaching God's Word instead of reading stuff, people started filling the church. Your grandad shut his store on Sunday and started coming to church and believe it or not, I got a raise!"

Natt sat forward and dropped his hands between his knees. "Wow! There was even a woman your age here in this Podunk?"

Roger grinned, remembering. He shook his head and said, "No, she came to visit over the long Thanksgiving weekend from Michigan, but in two weeks God made it possible for her to move here. He sold her house and fired her from her job. There was no reason for her to stay there, so before New Year's last year she was here to stay and we were married soon after that."

Musing out loud, Natt said, "Huh. Grandad shut down on Sunday and came to church."

Nodding, Natt looked at Roger and said, "Yeah, maybe I'll check you out come Sunday, Preacher." Natt looked at the young man. He wore jeans and a polo shirt. He had a slight beard that hardly showed, since he was blond. He didn't look like any minister he'd ever known.

"That'd be great, Natt!"

Roger stood and pulled out his billfold. He grinned at Natt and said, "I'm Roger to all my friends and I haven't met a soul here in Vansville who I don't think of as a friend." He turned toward the counter and saw Brad behind it in his chair with his eyes closed. "Hey, Brad, you taking money for gas today?"

Brad's eyes popped open and he pulled himself to his feet. "Young man, if I don't take your money who will?"

Roger handed over a few bills and said, "Good question, Brad. How come you haven't brought this fine young man to church with you yet?"

Brad punched in the amount for Roger's gas on the machine and saw that he'd given him the correct amount, so he parceled it out in the drawer then closed it and sighed, "Roger, you know, on any given morning I have a hard time gettin' myself outta the house to come here to work, never mind gettin' a young squirt like that out on a Sunday to go to church. He don't even live at my house."

"You got a point. I'll have to see what'll get him off of dead center. Maybe I need to come in the store more often."

Brad grinned, as he handed Roger his receipt and said, "He's a good kid, Roger, I guarantee he'll come one of these days."

"Good, we'll see you Sunday! Take care, both of you." Roger saluted Brad, then turned to leave the store and said to Natt, "See you soon, Natt. Glad to know you."

"Yeah, take 'er easy." He saluted Roger as he made his way out the door, but soon Natt followed him out, he had to get the rest of the chairs while the store was empty. Those chairs and the sideboard didn't bring themselves inside; that was sure.

When he opened the door a cold gust of wind blew in and when he stepped on the black-top he realized the sun was behind a cloud and other clouds were quickly covering the sky. He shivered and hurried to the truck to grab off a chair, took it to the door, but decided to empty the truck before he opened the door to the store again. It was still warmer than those three weeks, but maybe they were in for more winter weather. The foothills of north Georgia were lots colder than Atlanta, it seemed. Natt shivered, as he grabbed the small sideboard from the truck bed. He hoped those clouds didn't send any more precipitation on them. Business had suffered during those winter weeks, all except for the bags of ice-melt they'd sent out by the dozens. Coffee heated people up, that was a definite calling card. The aroma didn't hurt, either.

Before the afternoon was too old, Natt had the little space fixed the way he'd imagined. He found an extension cord on a shelf and put the little sideboard against the back of the shelving, then brought the coffee pot, the cups and all the accessories and arranged them on top. He put the chairs around the other two sides and was surprised when they all fit in the space. His grandad must have sized up the space better than he'd thought.

Brad came over when he was finished and looked around. He nodded. "This is right good, son. I like your idea."

"Thanks, Grandad." Natt nodded. "Since I like coffee so much it made good sense."

Brad looked out the window and grunted. "You know, it looks like it could rain."

"Yeah, when I was out bringing in these things it was downright cold."

Brad shrugged. "Well, it ain't August."

Natt chuckled. "No, that's sure, Grandad." Waving his hand around the new area he'd created, he said, "Thanks for this stuff, Grandad."

"Hey, it were a right good ider."

Marcy made it through her strict bedrest until Sunday. She called for her mom whenever she needed to use the commode, her mom helped her wash up and clean her teeth and she sat up in bed with help to eat her nutritious meals. She'd been taking her medication regularly everything seemed to be going well. Even though all the help grated on her, she was determined to give her heart as much chance to get as well as it could. She took long naps in the afternoon and her mom and dad made sure she had a quiet evening and a restful night's sleep.

However, Sunday, about eight thirty, Charlie, Colleen and Ed all left for Sunday school, then church, making her promise she would stay in bed. They would be gone for about three hours. Only moments after the house was empty and quiet, she fell asleep, but she'd had a glass of milk and another glass of orange juice for breakfast and before the three hours were up, she woke up needing to use the commode badly. She raised her head and looked at the beast sitting only inches from her bed and sighed.

Scowling at the thing, she muttered, "Surely I can make it to that thing! If I sit up and put my feet on the floor, if I swivel around I'll be sitting on it." *Right! Piece of cake!*

She pushed the covers from over her and pulled her feet closer to her chest, then pushing up, using her elbow, she put her feet over the edge of her bed, as she'd been doing all week, only her mom had been there to help her sit up. By the time she was in a sitting position, her heart was hammering and her breath was coming in gasps. Being in training to be a nurse for more than two and a half years, she knew enough to sit still until her heart settled down and her breathing evened out. It only took a few seconds for that to happen.

Meanwhile, her full bladder was clambering to be emptied.

When everything settled down, she leaned over and put the cover up, eased back for a minute, then carefully scooted to the edge of the bed. "Now comes the hard part," she murmured and sat for another minute. "Heart, don't give me any fits, I gotta use this thing and it can't wait for another hour or so until the folks get home."

She eased forward until her feet rested on the floor, then pushed herself up and swiveled toward the commode. However, they had never carpeted the floors, since Sandy's wheelchair didn't do well in the fabric, so there was a small rug beside the bed, which the commode sat on. When Marcy put her feet down, it was enough outward movement on the small rug that it moved and instead of finding herself on the commode, she landed quite heavily on the floor in front of it. Silent tears slid down Marcy's cheeks, tears of frustration, anger and a bit of hurt.

She still had to use the commode!

FIVE

Spending only a minute on the floor, her heart pounding and her breath coming in gasps, Marcy reached for the commode seat and the high bed to pull herself up, she made it to the seat and sat. While she relieved herself, she also realized that her breath came in gasps, but her heart not only thumped hard but it hurt. Those tears continued to fall; she knew she wasn't getting better very fast. Tomorrow was her appointment with Dr. Wright. Sniffing, she wondered what the doctor would say. Would he tell them that she must spend another week on bedrest? Oh, what a horrid thought! At this very time in her life she wanted desperately to be independent, but instead, she was totally dependent on someone to wait on her!

She sat on the commode quite a while until her breathing was normal; her heart stopped thumping so hard and the pain eased. When things seemed better, she leaned over and put her hands on the bed, then bending over, put weight on her feet. Quickly she leaned forward and fell onto the bed, then drew her feet up. Exhausted, she lay on the sheet and gladly laid her head on the pillow. After another few breaths, she pulled the blankets over her and soon fell back to sleep in the quiet house. That little escapade had showed her just how well she was and how quickly she was getting better. Not. So. Much!

Forty-five minutes later, Charlie let Colleen and Ed out at the back door then parked the car in the garage. Ed bounded up the incline, then looked down at the tiny patch of garden he'd planted. Colleen waited for Charlie, then the three who lived in the house along with Marcy came in the back door. Marcy wasn't calling, so Colleen hurried to her room to change clothes. Ed and Charlie didn't hurry quite as fast, but they also went to their rooms to change into comfortable clothes for the afternoon. After Sunday dinner was a quiet afternoon for naps and who wanted to keep on Sunday clothes to take a nap?

When Colleen left her bedroom, she passed the open door of the music room. She noticed that the commode was farther from the bed, the rug wasn't under the bed at all and the cover for the commode was up. Marcy was asleep on the bed. Colleen scowled and turned back, as Charlie came from the bedroom. "Honey," she whispered, "look in there. Doesn't it look like Marcy tried to get up?"

Charlie put his arm around Colleen's shoulders, looked in the room and saw the same scene as Colleen. Nodding, he said, "Yes, it does look like that, but she promised not to get out of bed until someone was here to help."

Colleen shook her head then turned with a grin to Charlie. "I know, but when you gotta go, you gotta go!"

As if she knew they were talking about her, Marcy stirred and looked out the door. She saw two sets of eyes looking at her and pulled the covers over her head then mumbled from under them, "I tried to use the commode."

Charlie looked at his wife and said, "Sweetheart, go ahead and get our lunch, I'll talk to this mound of blankets for a few minutes."

Colleen gave the mound of covers another look and nodded. She said, "Okay, I'll have things ready shortly," then went on to the kitchen. The aroma made his stomach growl appreciatively, but he knew Colleen had other things to fix for their meal. Right now, it looked like his daughter needed him. He loved this child, she was so unique he felt blessed.

Charlie watched his wife make her way to the kitchen and disappear from the doorway. As the refrigerator door opened he went in the music room and pulled up a chair close to the bed, but didn't move the covers. He didn't move the commode or the rug, just sat on the chair and watched the mound under the covers. With a smile in his voice, he said, "What was that you mumbled from under that tent, my dear? I didn't quite catch it."

She lifted the covers and peered at her dad. "Daddy, when you gotta go, you gotta go!"

Charlie nodded, then took the edge of the covers and moved them from Marcy's face and said, "Yes, I understand that, so why is the commode and the rug so far away?"

Marcy tugged the covers so they fell back down over her head, then from underneath, she muttered, "The rug slipped when I put my feet down and I sat on the floor."

Charlie chuckled, turning to look specifically down at the rug. "Are you sure there's no little wet spot on the rug, too?"

That sent the covers off her face, as Marcy's hand pushed them away. She rose up on her elbow and glared at her dad. Fiercely, she said, "No, Daddy! There is not! I made it to the commode for that."

Charlie really laughed and said, "Ahhh, I'm glad to hear that. Mama has enough to do without having to wash a good sized rug. What with making those good smelling meals.... So you couldn't wait for us to get home?"

Marcy sighed dramatically and said, "Daddy, you know that Mom makes me eat and drink everything she puts on my tray! I had a huge glass of milk and another glass almost as big of orange juice for breakfast. With all the food she insists on putting on that tray, my stomach is stuffed. The liquid wanted out! It would not wait for you guys to come home."

Charlie nodded and smiled. "I understand, dear girl. Did you make it okay? Did it hurt to get up?"

Tears glistened in Marcy's eyes, but she fiercely dashed them away, she made a face and said, "Daddy, I'm not getting better very fast! Just to sit up by myself made my heart thump and when I tried to get up from the floor, my heart hurt. I sat there on the commode a long time then I barely made it back into bed." Marcy sniffed, but two tears welled up onto her eyelashes.

Charlie bent over and put his arms around his daughter. Tenderly he kissed her cheek. "Sweetheart, maybe it's a little setback, but you are getting better, you must remember that. Let's pray right now, shall we?"

"Yes, Daddy, please will you?" she said and closed her eyes, as she snuggled into her dad's strong arms. "I know your prayers reach heaven."

Charlie swallowed, the tears scratched his own eyes as he closed them, she didn't seem to be getting better very quickly, at least not that he could see. Maybe he was asking too much, but he'd sincerely hoped she'd be doing very much better by now. He cleared his throat, then after a minute, he said, "My heavenly Father, touch my child, I pray. You are the Great Physician, You know how best to ease Marcy's hurting and to heal her heart and her body. Put Your hand upon her now, we pray. Make her strong and well again. Thank You, in Your Son's Name, amen."

"And God, please be with my sister there in Blairsville Hospital," Marcy whispered. "I know it's so hard for her to be there, she loves to do so many things and she can't there. We pray everything is all right with her and the baby. Please don't let there be any complications, we all know that baby will be a special blessing to them, amen."

Marcy was glad for her dad's arms around her, she felt safe and protected encased in them. Nothing could possibly go wrong when she was surrounded by them. She didn't squirm out, but let her dad hold her for several minutes after they prayed. After several moments of quietness, Charlie said, "By the way, when Ramon called the other night he invited you down to spend some time with them after you're well enough."

"Really?" A smile spread across Marcy's face. "I'd like that! It would be awesome to spend time with Sandy!" The smile disappeared and she said, "But I'd have to be completely well, Daddy. Really well. Sandy couldn't take care of me and I wouldn't let her. She'll have enough to do with the baby."

"Yes, she'll have a lot to do when the baby comes, but let's get you better now. We're taking you to see Dr. Wright tomorrow, you know. You know I have time added up and I'm taking the day off."

Marcy sighed and hugged her dad's neck, "I know, Daddy. That'll be a chore. I'm really not looking forward to that long trip downtown. It does take a long time." *Not to mention the little episode with the commode earlier.*

"I know you aren't, but we'll go in the car, my dear."

"Good, I'll be glad for that." However, Marcy was amazed. Her dad never took off work. He hardly ever took a vacation and of course, he was never sick.

In the morning, Colleen helped Marcy dress. Disgusted, Marcy said, "Mom, this is so nasty! I hate it that you must help me with every little thing! For crying out loud, I'm past twenty years old!"

The lady, some salt in her brown hair, patted her arm and said, "You'll be better soon."

Marcy let out a long sigh, "I know, that's what y'all say, but it's not happening! It sure does get boring to be in that bed all the time!"

Looking in the tiny mirror her mother brought to the side of the bed and styling her hair a little, Marcy said, "What I'd like to know is how I got sick in the first place! We've studied about Rheumatic Fever already in school and I didn't have any of the symptoms, nothing! Nobody I was caring for had it that I know of. It makes no sense."

"I know, but God meant it for good."

Marcy sighed, "I know, Mom, I think I've heard that all my life."

Colleen smiled. "Yes, you probably have, let it sink in, Dear."

"I know, Mom. You've said it so many times I know the verse by heart; '…We know that in all things God works for the good of those who love him, who have been called according to his purpose.' (Romans 8:28) I'm trying to remember."

Colleen smiled. "I'm glad you remember, Dear."

To herself, Marcy grumbled, "Mmm, how could I forget?"

By nine o'clock, Charlie, Colleen and Marcy were making the long drive to General Hospital and an appointment with Dr. Wright. By the time they reached the hospital, Marcy wanted to curl up and pass out. She'd taken a short nap, but it hadn't helped. She hadn't done anything, yet she felt exhausted. Charlie found a wheelchair, so he pushed her from the entrance to the office in the ER. When they arrived they found that the doctor had been called to an emergency, so they had to wait in his hospital office for him to come to them. Marcy was glad there was a couch in the room. Charlie helped her to it and she rested, but wouldn't let herself go to sleep, even though her body told her it was the thing to do. However, the doctor had left word that Marcy needed some blood work done and the tech came to the doctor's office to do that before the doctor arrived.

Finally, he came rushing in, his stethoscope bumping his shoulders and slumped into the chair behind his desk and pulled in a deep breath. "Finally! Ah, Charlie and Colleen, you both came! So, Marcy, how are you?"

"I could be better, Dr. Wright," she groused.

"She is improving, Doctor," Charlie said.

Nodding, Jason said, "Yes, her color's good. So have you gotten up by yourself yet?"

Marcy made a face. "Yesterday, while they were gone to church I tried to use the commode myself, but I ended up on the floor. I got myself up, though," she added quickly.

"Why was that?"

"The rug slipped."

"Any ill effects?"

Holding out her arms, Marcy said, "I'm still in one piece. No bruises, cuts or scrapes."

"Marcy," Jason admonished, putting his hands together, then resting his chin on them and looked at her very sternly, as if he was reprimanding one of his students, before he continued, "I think you know I mean your heart."

Like a little kid, Marcy whined, "Do I have to say?"

"Uh huh, I think so."

Marcy sighed and made a face before she said, "When I sat up on the bed I had to rest a minute so my heart wouldn't beat so hard and my breathing became normal. When I pulled myself up from the floor I had to sit lots longer on the commode because my heart was thumping and hurt just a little."

"Just a little?"

Marcy made another face and glared at the man. "Dr. Wright, you are no help, none at all! Okay, so it hurt, my breathing was labored and I fell on the bed and hardly covered up before I was asleep. Are you satisfied?"

Jason turned his chair, stretched his legs, crossed his ankles, folded his arms across his chest and smiled at Marcy. "Not really satisfied, of course, it's not the news I wanted to hear, but I'm glad you told the truth. I know what you were hoping, but with that statement I'll tell you what you didn't want to hear. Another week of bedrest and a trip down here next Monday."

On the tail end of a huff, Marcy said, "You know, Dad makes me lie down on the back seat when I'm in the car!"

"Does he? So are the springs poking up through the seat?"

Charlie was smiling, but of course, Colleen was not. "Of course not, Doctor! Mom and Dad don't have any little kids, so the car stays in pretty good shape."

Jason chuckled. "I'm glad to hear that."

There was a tap on the closed door and Jason said, "Yes?"

A young man in a white jacket opened the door a little and said, "Doctor, here are the results you wanted from the blood draw."

Jason held out his hand toward the young man and said, "Oh, good! Bring that over, would you?" The young man walked the papers in, so Jason took them and said, "Thanks, Oliver. I'm glad you put a rush on those tests, since Marcy's still here. This'll tell us what needs to be done to the girl," Jason said, with a smile.

"Done to me?" Marcy grumbled.

The young man smiled and as he closed the door, he said, "Welcome, Doctor."

However Jason read the results, taking several minutes. "Uh huh, done to you."

Jason nodded and said, "I'm glad I have you on those antibiotics still. Charlie, I'm calling the pharmacy right now and order up some more. She can't be out of them for a while."

Marcy sighed, "Doctor, you have me on so-o-o many pills now!"

"You want to get well?" Marcy nodded. "You take more pills." Jason reached for the phone on his desk.

Charlie scowled, but waited for Jason to finish talking on the phone, before he said, "Did those results show she's not getting better?"

Looking at the papers again, Jason shook his head. "There's some improvement, Charlie, but not near what I'd hoped for. With what she told me happened when she tried to get up yesterday, I think I'd rather err on the side of caution than hold out great hopes. She's doing okay but not anything spectacular. The virus seems to be arrested, but her heart doesn't seem to be bouncing back as quickly as I'd hoped. If we give it another week on bedrest I think perhaps we'll have it licked."

Marcy sighed, "Surely I can go back into training after next quarter, can't I? I mean, that's into the summer!"

Jason took his hand from the phone, pulled his feet back, rolled his chair up to the desk and leaned his elbows on the desk, as he looked Marcy in the eye. Very seriously, without a trace of a smile, Jason said, "Marcy, I know you want to go back. I know how you've performed in your training and believe me, not many other nursing students would surpass you. You're a dedicated young lady, but as things look now, nursing school is out."

The look on Marcy's face was as if she'd been slapped. Jason made a face. "Unfortunately, your heart has been damaged. It seems to be healing, but it's very slow and it may not heal completely, there may be scars on it permanently, which will leave it in a weakened condition. As you know, nursing school is very strenuous. Any time you can't get eight hours or more of sleep, you'll compromise yourself. Just going to college, sitting in regular classes and doing homework will tax you. I'm sorry, but that's what Rheumatic Fever does."

Marcy shook her head, she could feel the tears scratching her eyes, but she refused to let them fall. Finally whispered, "That's the pits!"

Jason sat straighter, then put his hand over the receiver and lifted it. As he dialed, he said, "That's true, but as resourceful as you are, I'm sure you'll have a long and productive life. Let's see you again next Monday. Two weeks may do wonders for you."

"I'd be glad for that!" She shook her head as Charlie reached for the wheelchair. "You have never had to deal with my brother. Doctor, he re-e-eal-l-ly picks on me! He even calls that commode a potty chair!"

Jason sat back and laughed. "I'd say he's a swell guy! A potty chair, huh. I'll be…"

"Mmm, yeah, real swell," she grumbled.

Winking at her, he said, as Charlie turned the chair, "Next time, try to sit on that chair the first time instead of making a trip to the floor."

Charlie grinned, but Marcy grumbled, "Thanks, Doctor, you must know that wasn't part of the deal at all."

By the time Charlie pushed Marcy's wheelchair from Dr. Wright's office back to the car in the parking garage, she was happy to lie down on the back seat. She immediately curled onto her side as Charlie closed the door. Charlie wasn't back on the street off the hospital campus before Marcy was asleep. Colleen glanced back at the sleeping girl then looked at Charlie with tears in her eyes. "She's exhausted! She's asleep already!" Colleen whispered.

"I know, the closer we got to the car the more she leaned over. We'll go straight home and get her to bed. Mama, it's the first she's been out of bed in a week, you know."

"I know, but I thought she'd be much better than this."

"It'll come, my dear, God's in control. He'll do His work in His time." A few stop lights from home, Charlie asked, "Have you heard anything from Georgia? A letter or phone call? Sandy usually writes or calls each week, doesn't she?"

"Not since Ramon called that night. I wish we'd hear from him."

Charlie sighed, "No news is good news, I guess."

"I hope so," Colleen whispered.

"Mama," Charlie sighed, "you are the world's most pessimistic person!"

Colleen shook her head. "Oh, no! I tell it like I see it." Charlie held his judgment on that. His assessment; Colleen was a faithful wife, a devoted mother, but definitely a pessimist.

Ed wasn't home when they arrived, so Charlie lifted Marcy from the back seat to take her inside. She woke up when the cold air hit her face and she looked up into her dad's face. "Daddy," she gasped. "Surely I can walk inside! You shouldn't have to carry me! I know I weigh more than Sandy does."

He kissed her cheek and walked up the incline. "My dear, how much walking did you do once we got to the hospital this morning?"

"None," she grumbled, reluctantly.

Colleen opened the back door and Charlie walked in. As he walked through the kitchen, he asked, "And how long did it take you to fall asleep when you got back in the car?"

"Oh, stop! I get the picture, but still…."

Charlie deposited Marcy on the bed and pulled up the covers. "Mama will be in shortly to help you change out of your clothes."

Marcy sighed, "I know, thanks, Daddy."

After her dad left the room and before her mom came in, Marcy closed her eyes. The words the doctor had told her were frustrating and discouraging and two tears leaked out between her closed eyelids. "*God, why?*" she murmured. She wasn't used to the tight clothes she had on, so she waited for her mom to come help her get back into her pajamas. However, as soon as she was comfortable, she fell asleep before Colleen had supper ready. Her trip to the doctor had totally exhausted her.

It was March fourteenth the first hikes of the new season for DeLord's Hiking Services were leaving at eight o'clock. Ramon stood stirring the scrambled eggs in his huge frying pan as the coffee ran through the coffeemaker. Duncan and Nancy were coming, along with Neal for breakfast. Only moments later Ramon heard car doors slam on his parking lot and knew his friends were about to break the silence of his home.

Duncan threw open Ramon's front door, then followed his wife in and said, "So, I smelled the coffee. I know it's not as good as Sandy's, but it'll do."

"Humph! Thanks a lot, friend!"

Duncan came to his friend and slapped his back. "You, friend, have a lot on your plate. Are you getting any rest?"

Ramon gave the eggs one last stir and said, "Need you ask?"

Duncan nodded. "Just as I thought."

"I miss her so much!" Ramon whispered.

Neal followed before the door closed. "It's good to be back!" he exclaimed. "Been looking forward to this day for weeks. So we each have a three day hike, right?"

Ramon set the eggs on the table, while Nancy filled the mugs with coffee. "Yes, that's it, man," Ramon said. "You'll be back on Saturday."

"And you will be at the hospital."

Nodding vigorously, Ramon exclaimed, "You got that right!"

"So Sandy has another week?"

"Maybe, maybe she'll go this week, Nancy. Bruce never has said for sure when he thinks her due date is. If she hasn't started into labor he'll take him on the twentieth."

The three men filled their mugs again after finishing off the toast, bacon and eggs and headed for the office while Nancy cleaned up the kitchen and started the dishwasher. They booted up the computer and found the maps for the two hikes and as the printer finished printing, car doors slammed on the parking lot. As they did, Nancy rushed into the office and straight for her husband. She grinned up at him and put her arms around his waist.

Duncan bent over and put a kiss on her lips, then he sighed, "Seems the hoards are upon us, let's go!"

"Here you are, man. Here's your print-outs. You got a new area open?"

"Yup, you'll get to take some groups there soon."

"All right! That'll be a treat!"

Duncan lingered over another kiss then said, "Hold that thought, Love."

"I'll try, Honey. Be safe."

"Believe me, I'll work on that!"

Neal headed out the door with Duncan at his heals to meet their respective hikers. Ramon held the door and said, "Each of you have a good hike. Be safe, but be sure to take your phones. I'll see you when you get back on Saturday."

"Yeah, wish Sandy our best," Neal said. "Miss her cheery face in the office, you know? Hope she's doing alright."

Duncan said, "Yes, be sure to tell her we've been praying for her."

"Thanks, guys, I will. See you!"

Ramon closed the office door and heard the dishwasher door close. He hurried to the kitchen archway and sighed. Looking at the clean kitchen, he said, "Nancy, thanks for doing that! You know I can do the clean up, but I really appreciate you doing it for me. That means I can leave right away for the hospital."

"Hey, it's no problem, you fed us, I can at least clean up after us. I know Duncan told you we've been praying for Sandy, but tell her 'hi' for me, will you?" She rushed to the living room window to watch Duncan's group head away from the parking lot. "You know, working can take so much precious time out of a day. I've wished over the time she's been in the hospital that I'd had more time to go see her."

Ramon chuckled. "Thanks, Nancy, I'll tell Sandy hi for you."

As the men and their hikers left the parking lot, Nancy walked out the front door to her car and Ramon raised the garage door and literally jumped into his truck. He roared out of the garage as Nancy reached her car. They waved, and Ramon hit the remote to close the garage door then squealed around the corner onto the highway headed for Blairsville Hospital. It was a good thing there wasn't any traffic coming, he barely looked. He wanted to be with Sandy every minute he could be.

Nancy watched as he vanished and said, "Father, bless Sandy. It'll soon be time for her baby to be born. May everything be fine, I pray the baby will be perfect for them." She slid into her car and left, she needed to be at the clinic in only a few minutes. Being a newlywed, she missed Duncan already. She had to smile, he'd given her such a hard time the first time they'd met, but it hadn't been long....

In record time Ramon wheeled his truck into the near-empty visitor parking lot at the hospital. Mornings were good it was easy to find a parking spot. He stepped from his truck and slammed the door then his feet started running toward the entrance. For five weeks he'd been a daily visitor and today was no exception. His body hardly kept up with his feet.

Long ago he'd abandoned the elevators, they were too slow. He made for the exit stairs, taking them two at a time to the second floor maternity ward. His pulse a little elevated, he burst through the door and headed for the room where his beloved Sandy lay in her bed. He smiled, knowing that she'd be awake and watching for him. It had been a daily occurrence.

He pushed the door to the private room open and a voice that wasn't quite what Sandy usually spoke in, said, "Honey! Oh, Honey! Please, I feel awful!"

He rushed to her side, took her hand and said, "Darling, what is it?" As he asked, he pushed the button on the call box.

"I don't know, but something's not right!" she wailed.

Quickly, Ramon put his arms around her and murmured, "Love, it'll be okay, they know down at the desk. Someone'll be here real soon. Try and relax."

"Oh, Honey," she whimpered, tears in her eyes.

Someone at the desk had opened the line to answer Ramon's call, but instead they heard Sandy's anguished words. Those words galvanized the staff into action. The charge nurse picked up the phone and quickly jabbed some numbers into it. Another nurse grabbed a stretcher sitting right around the corner precisely for this moment and the third nurse, whose patient Sandy was, took off at a run for her room. Linda pushed the door open wide, as Ramon gathered his wife tenderly to his chest. He kissed her and lifted her off the bed. Linda rushed over and disconnected the catheter bag from the bed, then held it, so that by the time Andrea arrived with the stretcher, they were waiting to place Sandy on it. A voice came out of the box over the bed and said, "Doctor Weber's on his way take her to delivery room one right away."

Andrea and Linda looked up at Ramon, who gave them a weak smile. "I guess we're out of here," he said, around the lump in his throat.

"Seems so, Ramon. Sandy, I think your waiting's over."

Tears were sliding down Sandy's cheeks, no words came from her mouth she could only nod, as they whisked her from her room. The minute they began to move, a wet spot appeared on the sheet covering Sandy. She didn't see it, but she groaned in pain.

Moments later, they had reversed the process and Sandy lay on the delivery room table. She groaned again, but she was in Ramon's arms and he absorbed most of the sound. Amazed, he looked at Sandy's protruding abdomen he could see her contraction through the nightie she had on. He realized she was in labor, but she couldn't feel the contraction itself, only the results that went through the rest of her body. His love and admiration for her hit a new high, as he realized again what she was going through for them to have this baby. Tears choked the back of his throat, but he wouldn't let them fall for Sandy's sake.

A few minutes later a nurse hoisted a frame over her lower body, then covered it with drapes. Another nurse came hurrying into the room in a surgical gown, gloves and mask in place. She carried a tray covered in clear plastic. Another nurse grabbed a rolling table and pushed it over Sandy's legs. As soon as it was in place the scrub nurse put the tray on it and as she took off the plastic wrap another man came in the room.

He looked at Ramon still holding his wife's shoulders. Ramon and Sandy weren't looking at anyone else, only had eyes for each other. In fact, Ramon bent over his wife several times and took her tears into his mouth, as he kissed her. "Excuse me, Ramon," the doctor cleared his throat. "I need you to lay her down. It's time to start the IV and put her to sleep. Both Bruce and Stan are scrubbing now. This show'll be on the road in a few minutes."

Tenderly, Ramon kissed Sandy once more then laid her shoulders gently on the cold table. "I love you, Sweetheart. I'll be close by when you wake up. Don't you worry one second, you're in excellent hands and God is with us."

Sandy didn't speak, but her eyes told him to stay. He tried to smile, but this was a brand new experience for both of them. He kissed her again, moved back and took her hand. "I'm here, Love," he whispered. "You know we've talked about what'll happen, you'll do fine, I know." He couldn't help it he leaned over and planted another kiss on her lips. He had no idea what this was doing to his wife, but he wished he could do it for her.

The anesthesiologist moved to the other side and quickly pushed a needle into Sandy's hand, then taped over the spot. Soon he opened a valve in the tubing and liquid dripped steadily from a bag hanging over the table. A few minutes later, he pushed a needle into the tubing and pumped the syringe full of liquid so it went into Sandy's vein. Seconds later, Ramon watched her body relax and her eyes close. Only then he let out the breath he hadn't realized he'd been holding. Yes, they wanted this baby, but he wanted his wife to be safe and well much more.

The anesthesiologist smiled at the anxious father and said, "Ramon, come around to this other side. I'll pull up a chair for you so you can be close and hold Sandy's hand without bothering the IV. Bruce will be operating from that side and you mustn't touch his sterile outfit. The nurse'll be on this side, but you'll be okay."

"Yes, Doctor," Ramon sighed. "We'll never try this again. It's been so hard on Sandy."

The older man chuckled and sat back down on his chair to monitor everything. He looked up at the drip from the IV bottle, but wanting to reassure the anxious husband, he smiled and said, "You know, lots of folks swear they'll never have another when they're here in this room, but you know, I usually see them again in about two years."

Shaking his head, not taking his eyes from his wife, he said, "Maybe that happens when everything's normal, but we're anything but normal."

"I know, but this should all go just fine, Ramon. Have faith."

The doctor smiled, trying his best to be reassuring to the anxious young man, but also understanding exactly why Ramon was so apprehensive. He knew dealing with a pregnant paraplegic was a new experience for all three doctors. When he'd learned about this patient he'd been amazed that she had done as well as she had.

Ramon sat in the chair Dr. Flanagan brought for him. *'Have faith...'* Yes, he needed to let God have complete control, he could do nothing.

Bruce Weber and Stan Miles walked in, both in surgical gowns, gloves and masks. Muffled a bit in his mask, Bruce said, "So she's decided to speed things up and go into labor."

"I believe so, Doc! It sure was a shock when I came in this morning. You know, I think she could feel the results of the contractions, but not the contractions themselves."

Nodding, Bruce said, "I'm sure that's so. Believe me; I am ever so glad we decided not to let her have this baby vaginally."

"Yeah, I'm with you on that!" Stan concurred. They both watched in amazement as another contraction tightened Sandy's abdomen.

Soon Sandy's sleeping body was draped and the area scrubbed. Ramon looked away as the doctor made the incision. Only a few minutes later he gently lifted out a perfect baby boy. The little guy felt the air in the room touch his body, he pulled in his first breath, scrunched up his face and let out a lusty wail and Ramon let out a loud sigh of his own. His baby, the product of his love for his wife, lay in the doctor's hands. He stood up and looked for the ten toes and ten fingers. He saw the tiny nose and the dark hair. This was his son! Much to his relief, even though he knew in his head that his wife's paralysis would not affect his baby, he made sure all his extremities moved normally.

Stan took the baby from Bruce and looked at Ramon standing beside him. His eyes crinkled as he said to Ramon. "So, Daddy, here's your son! Has he got a name?"

"Sandy and I've decided on Jonathan David," he said above another squawk from the baby. "We both love those names and since we're not expecting to have any more ourselves, we decided to give him both of the names we love."

"They're really good names, Ramon."

"Thanks," he said, simply.

The circulating nurse had a warm blanket she'd draped over her hands. Stan laid the baby on them then she took him to get him presentable for the world. Soon, Bruce had finished stitching up Sandy's abdomen and Stan covered it with the dressing. Dr. Flanagan turned off the IV and both doctors pulled off their gloves and pulled down their masks. Bruce and Stan both grinned at Ramon, but he didn't notice, he was looking down at his peacefully sleeping wife. This beautiful woman, inside as well as out, had given him a possession they would both prize. She was the joy of his life; he cherished her, beyond words. He ran a finger down her soft cheek.

Before he looked up, he bent and kissed her, then whispered, "It's all over, Love. You have given me everything I've ever wanted. We have our son, thank you. And thank You, God, for being with my Sandy all the way to this point." Finally, he looked up at the two men who stood silently watching the young man. He whispered, "Thank you for all you've done."

With tears rolling down his cheeks, Bruce Weber said, "You're welcome, Ramon." This couple had been an inspiration to him from when he first met them.

Even though Sandy had been given a general anesthesia, the doctors had determined she could do recovery in her private room. They knew Ramon wanted to be with her all the time and that was the only way he could. When everything was disconnected from Sandy's body except the catheter, Ramon carefully lifted Sandy from the delivery table to the stretcher. Ramon took the head and another man took the foot. Moments later they came through the door onto the ward then entered Sandy's room, Sandy's nurse followed them. The bed was freshly made, so tenderly Ramon lifted Sandy and the other man pulled the empty stretcher from beside the bed.

He hooked the catheter bag over the proper place on the bed so Ramon wouldn't have to leave Sandy. As he left the room, Ramon placed Sandy on the bed, then crawled up beside her, found the control and raised the head of the bed several inches. Ramon's heart was so full; he looked down tenderly at his wife and kissed her. They had their son, he was a beautiful baby. He would be cherished.

Still asleep, Sandy let out a long sigh and moved her upper body closer to her husband. Tears glistened in Ramon's eyes and he placed his cheek on his wife's hair. "My darling," he whispered, "we have our son and this ordeal is over for you."

Several minutes later, Ramon sighed, "I guess I need to call your folks."

"Hello, Bernard's," Colleen said.

"Hi, Colleen, your grandson was born this morning. He weighed eight pounds and was twenty inches long. He squawked like a fog horn!"

"Oh, my, oh, my! Thank you, Ramon, I must spread the word!"

Ramon chuckled. "You do that, Grandma!"

Flowers were blooming around Isabel's cabins. It was spring, as least the calendar said it was only days away. Of course, spring was also the time for rain and after only a few days of nice weather, Natt opened his eyes to a dark, rainy day. The heater in the cabin hadn't been running for several days, but it came on as Natt brushed his teeth and Natt decided a warm shirt was necessary. He quickly fixed his coffee for breakfast then pulled out an egg, a sausage patty and two pieces of bread. He planned to make an egg sandwich. There wasn't a fast food place in town, but he could pretend and make his own.

He wondered, now that the town sported a real live clinic that was open six days a week, would a fast food chain decide that the 'booming metropolis' of Vansville was a place for its business. He sighed; he guessed he'd be here for several years he'd probably be one of the first to know. Life sure could put a wild spin on a guy's plans.

He looked at his clock, knowing he must hurry. His grandad took his 'constitutional' each morning, walking around the end of the block to come in the front door of the store instead of the back. He always arrived at the store by eight like clockwork, but he only opened the hardware store. Since his stroke, he hadn't remembered to open the Laundromat and turn on the lights or flip the switch for the gas pumps. People who worked in Blairsville often needed to fill their gas tanks this early. It seemed their gas was cheaper than any in Blairsville. This surprised Natt, he always thought gas was cheaper in a large town, but he was glad for the business. The gas station kept the whole complex open and in the black, he wouldn't complain.

His little cabin was small, but large enough for him. He sat at the table, staring out the window at the mountains, then glanced at the clock and washed down his breakfast with the last mouthful of coffee, then headed for the door. He didn't realize how solid and sturdy the cabin was until he walked outside. The evergreens out behind Duncan's house and the tree between his cabin and number one were bending dangerously in the wind, but he hadn't noticed until he opened the door. It couldn't be a hurricane, it was much too early for that, but the wind was fierce. Quickly, he stepped off his porch to the ground and ran down his walk to the parking lot.

As he turned from the parking lot to the sidewalk on Main Street, he looked up and saw his grandad moving much more slowly toward the store.

Even so, he was sure the old man would reach the store before he did. As he continued to move toward the store, he watched his grandad and to his horror, a large dead limb from a tree in the church yard snapped and the wind carried it across the street, knocking the old man to the ground.

No one could have heard him, but he yelled anyway, "Grandad!" and started running full out, his heart beating wildly. What if this triggered another stroke? Of course, there was nothing he could have done to prevent this, but he felt badly. To stop himself, he buckled his knees and fell to them as he reached his grandad's side.

The old man groaned and whispered, his eyes still closed, "What happened?" The rain spattered his face, so he closed his lips tightly.

Glad to hear his voice and that it sounded normal, Natt said, "A huge limb blew across the street and knocked you down. Are you hurt, Grandad?"

Moving his arms, legs and head, he groaned again and said, in a little stronger voice, "No, I don't think so. Help me up, we're gettin' wet."

"Sure, Grandad." Natt pushed himself from the sidewalk, the knees of his jeans wet from the pavement. He could also feel the grit on his palms as he pushed up from the wet sidewalk. Brad opened his eyes, but Natt reached for his hand and eased him up, letting him rest momentarily until he was standing.

Taking Brad's one arm and placing it around his own neck, Natt held him around his waist, so that he took most of his weight Natt helped Brad get his balance. Still supporting him, he moved slowly to the store, unlocked the main door and helped Brad to the first chair in the coffee drinker's nook. He heard the old man sigh as he relaxed in the chair. He didn't say much to Brad, because he knew what his grandad would say, however, he went to the phone by the register, turned his back to his grandad and called his gramma.

Speaking quietly, facing the back of the store, so Brad couldn't hear him, he said, "Gramma, a big limb hit Grandad out front here and knocked him down. I don't think he lost consciousness or is really hurt, but would you come take him down to the clinic? I'd hate for him to be hurt some way and we not know it."

"Of course, Natt! I'll be there!" After a second, she asked, "Does he know you called?"

"Ah, no, but I'll tell him before you get here."

Knowing her husband quite well, she exclaimed, "Yes, you'd better!"

Natt dropped the phone back in the cradle and hurried back to Brad, who sat with his eyes closed and his head leaning back on the window frame, his hands folded serenely in his lap. Natt took the chair along side his grandad and said, "Grandad, Gramma's coming to take you to the clinic. She thinks you need to be checked out."

Brad's eyes popped open, his head jerked forward, he groaned again, leaned his head back and demanded, "Why? What for? I'm okay, I'll just sit here a while." Scowling at the young man, he said, "Did you call that blame woman?"

Shaking his head, Natt said, "Grandad, we want to be sure you're okay. You know it hasn't been that long since your stroke, so we need to be sure."

Brad's head drifted back against the window frame again. "You critters'll be the death of me yet! Ain't nothin' wrong with me!"

Natt was glad to see his usual feistiness and said earnestly, "I'm glad, Grandad, Gramma's here now, she'll take you to make sure of it."

Bringing his hands to his hips, Brad glowered at his grandson and said, "Boy, if I could, I'd wallop your hide!"

Natt chuckled. "Grandad, I'm too quick for you to even catch me."

"I know it! But I'd sure like to try!" he groused.

SIX

Joyce appeared in the doorway and said, "What happened?"

"Nothin' Joyce, go on home!" Brad grumbled.

"Brad Thomas, not what I heard! Natt'll help you to my car and I'm taking you to the clinic. No argument!"

As the three headed out the door, Joyce pointed and said, "Goodness! It's that huge limb still on the sidewalk?"

Natt nodded and eased Brad off the nook chair and out the door to the car parked very close by. "That's the one, Gramma. It hit him square in the head."

Touching his head gently, but dragging a groan from Brad, she said, "Yes, I can see a knot coming up. Bradford, don't you tell me you aren't hurt! Why, this knot's as big as a half dollar! It's sore, I can tell. I touched it and you groaned. Don't you tell me it's nothing! We'll have Dr. Stan check it out."

"Just go on! Get this confounded checkout over," Brad grumbled, stepped carefully into the car and waved at his wife, then flopped back against the car seat. As she hurried to the driver's side, Brad looked up at his grandson, shook his finger and muttered, "Just wait, fella, I'll think a somthin' to get you back."

Natt winked at his grandad. Completely ignoring the last part of what Brad said, Natt grinned and said, "She's after it, Grandad."

Natt had barely shut the car door behind Brad when someone pulled in to a gas pump. He waved to the man and said, "Hold on a minute, I haven't got the pumps turned on. Grandad got hurt by that limb out there and needs to go to the clinic to be checked out."

"Hey, that's too bad!"

Natt raced inside and soon the pumps lighted up and began to hum, so the man raised his hand in acknowledgement and took hold of the nozzle with his other hand. Natt came back outside with his fistful of keys and went to the Laundromat. Rain pinged against the window, as he unlocked the door. From the Laundromat, he called back. "It's a dismal day, isn't it!"

"Sure is! It could be worse, though. Actually, I'm on my way to the hospital to bring home my wife and baby, that'll make it a great day!" Ramon said. He couldn't help the smile that was spreading across his face from ear to ear.

Natt couldn't remember seeing the light blue van before, so he said, "They been there long? Have they been sick?"

Shaking his head, Ramon said, "My wife's been on bedrest for over a month until our baby was born. I get to bring them home today!" He gave the young man a huge grin. "I got the house all ready for them." Natt had no experience with babies or children. Did the man have other children? Had they made a mess? Who knew?

Ramon followed Natt inside, slapped down his credit card on the counter and waited for Natt to run it through his machine. But as Natt worked his machine, Ramon nearly danced in front of the counter. As Natt turned the paper for Ramon to sign, he said, "I'm happy for you. Best of luck. Was your baby a boy or girl?"

Like any new dad who's proud of his son, Ramon grinned and said, "Jonathan David is our son's name. We're so proud of him!" Ramon took his receipt and turned to leave. "We'll see you again, I'm sure, Natt. I hope Brad's okay."

"Yeah, so do I."

Natt followed Ramon and stood at the window to watch. It still sprinkled, so he didn't follow him outside. Natt scowled as Ramon stepped up into the van and pulled out. "I've seen that man before he always drives a green pickup truck. Why's he driving a blue van now?" He shrugged, "I guess you can't fasten down a baby carrier in a truck. At least not in a one seater like he's got." Natt shook his head as the van disappeared. He couldn't hear because the store was closed up, but he saw steam on the wet pavement from the tires. "I sure don't know much about babies. Little brother's the last one I've had to deal with, thank God!" Turning back into the store, Natt headed for the storage area. He had to get the coffee maker running and the bigger one took a lot longer that his gramma's.

Joyce drove onto the parking lot of the clinic as the first customer of the day. She stepped from the car and hurried around to the passenger door, solicitously opened the door and helped a grumbling Brad from the seat. When she reached to put her arm around his back, he glared at her and said, "Woman, just walk along, I told ya, I'm okay! It was just a bump from some dead log!"

"Bradford, I'm gonna hold onto you, you could fall on this slippery pavement!"

Still grumbling, he looked at the glass door and muttered, "Fine!"

Inside, Brad sat down quickly in a chair in the waiting area while Joyce went to the counter to sign him in. It was so early no one else was in the waiting area. Nancy appeared only minutes later and walked over to the grumbling Brad. "Brad, what's happened to you?"

"Nuthin, I ain't hurt."

Nancy grinned at the contrary man, reached out to help him to his feet and said, "Joyce tells me you were knocked down by a big limb that was blown off a tree in this wind. I can see a goosegg on your head we need to look at."

Brad touched the tender swelling on his head. He made a face, pulled his fingers away, then looked up at Nancy and said, "I tell you, if my grandad had somethin' like this he'da slapped a wet rag on it and gone on with his work! People these days are wimps and they make wimps outta everbody else!"

"Maybe so, and maybe that's all we'll do, but that may not be all that's hurt."

Feeling the room spin just a bit, as he tried to stand, Brad held the armrests and stood up slowly. Reluctantly, he muttered, "Yeah, mebe so."

Nancy grabbed his arm, nodded to Joyce to follow, and said, "Here we go, Brad, Dr. Stan's here today and he'll give you the once over."

"I was afraid you'd say that," the old man groused.

Stan came in to the exam room a few minutes later and said, "So, Mr. Thomas, what happened this morning?"

"The wind blew some big limb acrost the street. It hit me and I slipped on the sidewalk and fell down. No big deal."

"Anything knock you out?"

"'Course not! I had my wits about me the whole time!"

"So this knot on your head's all the damage?"

"I…"

"Doctor! I just noticed a blood stain on the sleeve over his elbow!" Joyce exclaimed. She jumped up and came up beside her husband. "And look, here's a place on the back of his head where there's some blood!"

"Aha, you're trying to cover something up, Brad?"

"No, I ain't! Nuthin hurts much, I tell you!"

Stan pushed a button on an intercom and said, "Nancy, need you in here for a blood cleanup on Mr. Thomas, please."

"Be right there, Dr. Stan." *Why can't the CNA do that?* Nancy sighed, they had no other patients, of course she could do it.

Stan reached to touch the lump on Brad's head and watched to see Brad's reaction. "So, Mr. Thomas, does this hurt?"

"Yeah, a bit. Not nuthin I cain't stand, though. You got other stuff ta do more important than dabbin' my head."

Stan took his hand from Brad's head, but picked up a small scope to check his pupils. "Okay, we'll get some help in here and get you fixed up in a minute."

Nancy came in snapping on a pair of latex gloves. She pulled a basin from a cupboard, filled it with warm water and squirted some disinfectant soap in it, then found some soft cloths. She started dabbing the place on Brad's head with a damp cloth. "Is this it, Dr. Stan?"

Stan nodded to Brad's elbow and said, "No, there's blood on the sleeve of his left elbow, we haven't seen what's there yet."

Seeing Nancy had gloves on, Joyce bustled around and helped Brad take off his jacket and roll up his sleeve. By this time, the blood had dried and his shirt sleeve was stuck to his elbow. "Ouch! Woman, be a little careful, would ya?"

Becoming agitated, Joyce sucked in her bottom lip and whispered, "I'm sorry, Brad, dear, I didn't know it was stuck."

Nancy took her cloth again and wet both the sleeve and the elbow. After a few times over his shirt it loosened and came away from Brad's elbow. Joyce took his shirt out of the way. When the blood was gone, both Nancy and Stan noticed how deep the gash was. Stan said, "Mr. Thomas, we'll need to numb this and put a few stitches in it. It's pretty deep and won't heal right if it's not stitched up."

Letting a long sigh slip from his mouth, Brad grumbled, "Well, be about it! I need to get back to the store. Natt's there by hisself, I need to run the cash box."

Watching what he was doing, Stan didn't look at Brad, as he said, "I was sort of expecting Mrs. Thomas to take you home to rest for the day."

He jerked as he looked around at Stan. Very unhappy, Brad scowled at the doctor and said, "And have that woman hound me to lie down all day long and feed me chicken soup? You have got to be crazy! I'll go sit at the store with my grandson and drink his coffee. I can rest better there, believe me!"

Stan was glad he hadn't stuck the needle from the syringe into Brad's arm when he jerked, but before he answered he pricked the skin around the deep laceration and pumped the anesthetic into the area. "Mr. Thomas, it won't hurt you to lie down and have chicken soup for lunch. After all, you were hit on the head by that big branch."

"You never been around my wife," he mumbled under his breath.

Winking at Joyce, Stan said, "No, Sir, I never was."

Again, Brad grumbled, "Be glad."

Joyce looked at her husband and huffed, but didn't comment. Stan, of course, wasn't married, but he had to hide his grin. Some old couples could be real characters.

Ramon parked the van under the big drive through in front of the hospital. He'd talked with Bruce Weber the evening before and had everything worked out for Sandy's release. He'd already brought clothes for both Sandy and Jon. He opened the big passenger door and lowered the lift level with the van floor. He pushed the wheelchair, with the baby carrier, onto the lift then lowered it to the ground. When he had everything off, he closed up the van to keep the warm air inside, but left it running, then went in the door to the information desk.

"Ma'am," he said to the pink lady, "I'm going up to maternity for my wife and our baby. I've left our van there. Please don't let anyone move it, since it's running."

The woman looked out the door and saw that the van was the only vehicle there, but she obviously didn't know Sandy or recognize Ramon, she scowled at Ramon. For some reason, the large wheelchair that Ramon was pushing didn't register with the woman. "Why not?"

"My wife is paralyzed from the waist down, this is her chair and that is our wheelchair accessible van. I don't want to load her and our newborn in the rain and I don't want to leave them out in the cold while I hunt up the van from wherever someone has moved it. It's the only vehicle out there, it shouldn't be a problem."

The woman didn't seem convinced, she said dubiously, "I'll do what I can, sir."

"Thanks." Ramon said on the way to the elevator.

Ramon had told the staff when he'd be coming for Sandy and the baby the day before so when Ramon came off the elevator onto the ward, Sandy's nurse went with him down the hall to her room. Sandy was dressed and sat up in the bed holding their baby in her arms. The little tyke was dressed, even to the tiny blue knitted hat on his head. When Ramon walked in the room, Sandy's smile was radiant and his answered it.

Taking several gigantic steps toward the bed, Ramon asked, "How are my two most loved people this morning?"

"Honey, we're great! We're all ready to go!"

"I'm glad!" He bent over immediately and kissed her. His heart was pounding he was so excited to take them home at last. The nurse took the baby carrier from the wheelchair and reached for the baby. Ramon locked the chair then turned to lift his wife from the bed. "Darling," he murmured, "I get to take you home after so long. That house has been so lonely!"

With her arms empty, she held them up and Ramon stepped into them. After a kiss, she smiled and said, "I am ready to get there, believe me! It's raining out, isn't it?"

Putting one arm under Sandy's knees, he said, "Yes, Sweetheart, but you know you won't get wet. We'll load here in the dry and unload in the garage. The only thing, it's blowing a gale, I hope it doesn't blow us off the road."

Sandy chuckled, knowing what a good driver her husband was. "Honey, don't be silly! You know you'll do fine."

Ramon shrugged. "We can only hope."

Ramon settled Sandy in the chair then fixed the controls so she could use it. He gathered all the remaining cards and one vase he wasn't able to take home yesterday and put the cards in Sandy's lap, while he carried the vase. He walked beside her, as the nurse picked up the baby carrier and led them from the room. At the nurses' desk all the staff was gathered to wish the little family well. All the nurses were smiling through their tears. Sandy had been such a brave and cheerful patient during her entire stay. They all loved her.

"Guys," she said, looking around. "I don't know where you'll put it, but I'm sending you a picture as soon as I can get my hands on my paints again, so be expecting it."

"Sandy," the head nurse said, "you're great! Take good care of that husband and little Jonathan, that's all we ask."

Smiling up at Ramon, Sandy said, "You don't need to worry about that! We'll take good care of each other and Jonathan."

When they reached the main floor, a hospital security man stood at the information desk, his hands on his hips. They heard him say to the pink lady. "Listen, Trudy, rules are rules! Why can't we move that van? It's been there for at least fifteen minutes running. You know it's against the rules for any vehicle to stay there that long and running, too. Hospital policy, it is!"

The woman shrugged, obviously immune to the man's tirade. "All I know is the man who drove it said to leave it there, he needed it warm for his wife and new baby."

"Humph, he'd better come real soon! That's all I can say!"

The woman nodded. "I'm sure he will."

The nurse carrying the baby carrier had her mouth open to speak to the two at the desk when the little group arrived. However, Sandy's smile came with her. Before anyone else spoke, Sandy said, "Thank you so much for not moving our van! Want to have a peek at our baby? Isn't he absolutely the most beautiful baby you ever saw?"

The man and woman both looked at the lady in the wheelchair. Astonished, the woman said, "You… um, you had that baby?"

"Yes, isn't he perfectly beautiful?"

"Yes, Ma'am!" the man said. "You have a good day!" He vanished as fast as he could.

"Thank you, we will!" Sandy said over her shoulder, but the man was already gone, the lady smiled broadly as she looked at Jonathan. Ramon stepped up to the automatic doors and they opened. Sandy's chair began to hum as she followed her husband outside. The young nurse aid followed them out with the sleeping baby.

After the doors closed behind the DeLord's, the pink lady looked at the security man, who really hadn't gone far and said, "So, there, Woody, what do you say now?"

The man sighed, "Baby's are nice, too bad they don't stay that way for long. But she's crippled! How's she gonna take care of that little rapscallion?"

"Hey, don't ask me, I got my own brood at home that was enough for me to handle. Besides, you need to get back to your busy schedule."

"Woman, are you bein' sarcastic?"

"Would I be sarcastic with you?"

"Humph! Just all the time!"

Giving Woody a broad smile, she said, "See, you didn't have to move that van!"

The nurse aid watched silently as Ramon opened the van with the keys in the outside locks and lowered the lift. When it was on the ground, Sandy drove her chair on, but Ramon reached back for the baby carrier from the girl. "Thanks, Alisha," he said.

"Oh, you're welcome! Sandy's been our best patient since she's been here. Jon, well, he's great, too. Take good care of each other!"

"Thanks," Sandy said, as she moved toward the front of the van and Ramon put the infant seat on the back seat and fastened it in.

Soon, Ramon left the hospital and drove home, pulled onto the full parking lot, hit the remote for the garage door and backed toward the door as it went up. Sandy looked at the cars and sighed. The people on the ward where she'd been had been wonderful to her, but there was no place like home. As Ramon put the stick in park, Sandy reached back and released the lock holding her chair in place. Ramon left his seat and went to the controls for the lift. As the door grumbled open, he took a step to the back seat and brought the baby's seat to Sandy's lap. Before doing anything else he bent over and kissed his wife.

He whispered, as he looked down at his sleeping infant. "Here you are, Mommy, we're home at last."

With her special smile, she looked up at Ramon and held up her arms. "You can't know how glad I am to be home, Honey."

Ramon's arms circled Sandy's shoulders and he bent to kiss her. After their kiss, he said, "Darling, I am *so* glad you're here! You can't know how lonely it's been."

"Honey, you've been wonderful, coming every day so faithfully."

Ramon shook his head, as he looked at his beautiful wife. "Darling, I couldn't stay away! You mean everything to me."

Inside, Sandy took a deep breath. She could smell the lemon cleaner that Nancy had used the last time she'd cleaned. "Oh, my! I'm home!"

"Yes, Love, we're all home."

Natt looked out the window of his cabin and saw the sun shining brightly. He hadn't set his alarm, but decided to let his body wake up when it wanted to, today was Memorial Day and the Thomas complex was closed all day, even the gas pumps wouldn't be lit today. Except for Sundays, today was the first day the whole complex would stay closed all day. Not for the first time Natt wondered how he would survive the summer, let alone a year as a store owner in a small town. Being cooped up inside any building was against his religion in the summer.

He looked out the window and for almost the first time since he'd moved into Isabel's cabin he saw the magnificent mountains behind the town which he now called home. He'd lived here since the first of January and today was the first he was even aware of the mountains. Of course, he knew they were there, Vansville was known for its hills and the hiking service. He wished he had more than today off, he'd like to go on a hike Vansville had become famous for, but he knew DeLord's didn't do hikes for just one day and that's all he had. Tomorrow the store would open again and he had to be there. He sighed, if Grandad hadn't had his stroke, he'd be done with his junior year and be a mighty senior. He'd be nearly done with classes.

His coffee maker was running when the phone rang. He grabbed up the receiver and almost answered as he did at the store, but caught himself in time to say, "Hello? This is Natt."

"Hi, Son, what's on for your day?"

"Not much, Dad, only to be away from the store," he sighed. "I'm fixing my breakfast and wishing I could take a hike, but the store's open again tomorrow."

His voice wavering, since the SUV was moving on the highway, Nathan said, "We've left Atlanta to come up for the day, maybe Dad could tell us where to go for a one day hike."

His excitement building, he danced a little and exclaimed, "Oh, super, Dad! I've been sitting here looking out my window at these mountains and realized I hadn't really looked at them until today. They are awesome! There's still some snow in some places and it's been really warm around here."

Feeling almost the same as his son, Nathan said, "I don't think we can take them in in a one day hike, Son, but I know there're trails not far from Vansville. They wouldn't have that hiking service otherwise. We've already left I'm calling on my cell, so we'll be there before the hour's up. Maybe you could ask Dad for some hints? They've lived there forever, surely, even if he's never gone hiking, he'll know where some are. Oh, it's great to have a day off!"

Natt almost acted like a teenager, dancing around his kitchen, as he said, "Sure, Dad, I'll call as soon as we hang up. See you in a bit. Thanks for calling; it'll be great to see you guys."

Natt didn't hang up, just disconnected then punched in another number, while he danced a little jig. He stuffed the last of his muffin in his mouth just a Joyce answered. Natt gave his mouthful a few chews and said, "Gramma, Dad called and asked me to call you to find out about some trails we could hike. Do you or Grandad know any? It's such a gorgeous day to be out! He thought maybe we could spend it outside!"

"Of course! Come on over, surely Nathan will come here anyway. We know some places I'm sure you'd love to hike to that aren't too far away."

"Great, Gramma! I'll be over as soon as I gobble down my last three bites of breakfast and wash out my coffee mug."

"Okay, we'll be looking for you!"

Natt changed into hiking clothes, including hiking boots instead of tennis shoes, opened the door to feel the temperature and left for his grandparents' house. He didn't use much gas now that he lived in Vansville, it was silly to start his car when he could walk the three blocks in almost the same time as it took to start the car, wait for traffic on the highway and drive the distance. Besides, he needed the exercise. You didn't get much just walking the aisles of a store. Three blocks wasn't a long walk, but it was enough to get his blood flowing.

He was about to turn the corner onto his grandad's street when he saw a familiar car coming. He waved, ran down the block and across the street to his grandparents' home. He was on the porch, about to push the doorbell when his dad pulled up onto the driveway. As Natt pushed the doorbell, four doors on the SUV opened and four people spilled out.

"Ha!" Joylyn exclaimed, "Thought you'd get in first, did you?"

Grinning at his sister, he said, "I'd hoped."

The door opened and Joyce exclaimed, "You're all here!"

"Hi, Mom!" Nathan called from the driveway. "We came to spend the day. Some of us want to go hiking, but some of the puny ones want to stay here. Is that all right?"

Pushing the screen door open so Natt could walk around her and grinning at her son, she said, "Whatever any of you want to do is just fine with us! Natt called and I've started making some sandwiches so the hikers'll have some lunch, while your dad's looking at the map for the trails. Who's going hiking?"

"Natt and I are, for sure. I'm still trying to convince the two ladies that they could use the exercise, but so far, it hasn't worked."

Natt looked at his little brother and asked, "How about squirt, is he going?"

Danny drew himself up to his full height and said, "I'm no squirt!"

Natt ruffled his hair and looked down at him, his eyes twinkling and said, "Well, you sure are! You aren't near as tall as me!"

"Listen, Bro, Dad measured me the other day, I've grown two inches since New Years, so there! Besides, I'm going on your hike. You, major pain in the… will not keep me from going on this hike!"

His older brother gave a long sigh, "So we gotta watch out for big holes, like rabbit holes and keep you from falling in one."

Danny made a face and said, "Just 'cause the last time we went on a walk I tripped in a hole doesn't mean I fall into rabbit holes!" Letting out another huff, Danny said, "You, big brother, are a pain in the neck!"

Giving his little brother a grin and a wink, Natt said, "Well, you never know, we might be searching for you in La-la-land like Alice in Wonderland, or something like that for boys. Surely somebody wrote about that, who was it? Was it Danny in La-la-land?"

"Humph! I don't fall in holes that end up in La-la-land! You're the one who's living in Podunk, USA, don't forget!"

"Boys, two seconds and you're at each other!" Nathan reprimanded.

"Ah, Dad, the kid needs a good tease!"

"No I don't!" Danny exclaimed.

They walked inside and Brad sat at the dining room table with a map spread out. Natt and his dad walked up to look over his shoulder and Brad said, "Hello, Son. Looks like if ya drive down the highway a mile or so there's a country road off to the left. Down that road a bit is a trail to a picnic area and a hikin' trail a mile or so long off from there. Would that be good?"

"Sounds like our cup of tea, Dad. Especially that picnic area," Nathan said, with a chuckle. "I've been cooped up at work too long!"

Nodding, Brad said, "My thoughts exactly!"

Surprised, Nathan said, "You'll come with us?"

Brad folded up the map on all the proper creases and said, "I'll take the drive and guard the food at the picnic area while you boys hike."

"That's great, Dad! Mom, have you got those sandwiches made yet? Natt, here's, about to jump out of his skin." He grinned, knowing the response his son would make, he said, "You know how Natt is, he's still a growing boy."

Before Natt could answer, Joyce clucked her tongue and said, "I'm wrapping cookies for dessert and Eleanor's making iced tea for the jug, so it'll be ready in the shake of a lamb's tail."

Natt and Danny looked at each other and laughed. "How long is that, Gramma?" Danny asked. "Is a lamb's tail very long?"

"Not at all, young man." She walked into the dining room from the kitchen with a big basket. "See, here's everything, we even fit the thermos of tea in the basket. There should be enough to feed even you growing boys."

Nathan took the basket from his mom, looked around the room at the rest of his family and asked, "So who's going? Is it just us men?"

"Dad," Joylyn said, in a pained voice, "you think I'll stay here with them? All Mom and Gramma wanna do is talk!"

Nathan smacked his forehead. "Of course, how could I forget you can't abide talking unless it's you that's the main speaker." Before Joylyn could come back with anything, Nathan continued, "Okay, let's go, we only have today, it's a gorgeous day and we don't want to waste it. It's good we brought the SUV so we'll have enough seats for five of us and the picnic basket." Danny was already headed for the door.

Joyce looked at Brad, as he started to get up. "Brad, you aren't going!"

Brad scowled at his wife. "I most certainly am!"

"But…but you've had a stroke, you were clobbered on the head by a log! What are you thinking? You should stay home!"

"None of that spilt any brains out! I didn't lose an arm or a leg! Give me a break! Why would I wanna stay home and listen to two females chatter all day?"

Joyce sighed, as she looked from her husband to her son. "Bradford, we weren't going to talk all day, we were planning on watching the parade down Main Street for part of the day. Did you forget about the parade?"

"What if I did? It don't make me no never mind. They don't need me to do their parade. I don't need to be here to guard the store, either. All the more reason to get out of town. See you ladies later!" Brad grinned and waved jauntily as he followed his son off the porch to the SUV. When he reached the walk he pulled in a deep breath of the fresh air. It felt really good to be outside for a change with no responsibilities.

Anxious for her husband, Joyce said, "Nathan, watch your dad, I don't want him hurt."

Brad huffed, but Nathan said, "Don't worry, Mom, he'll be safe with us. He said he's just watching the picnic basket for us."

"Well, yes, but…"

Brad moved quickly down the walk, away from his wife then climbed into the front passenger seat while Nathan opened the back and put the large picnic basket behind the back seat and the three from the younger generation climbed in the two big doors and found their places. Joyce continued to stand in the doorway, a concerned look on her face. Brad did not turn around to see that she was there. Soon, Nathan slid behind the wheel and looked from his dad to his children and grinned. It had been some time since he'd had a leisure day to spend just as he wanted. He'd even turned off his cell phone after talking with Natt. Today he intended to enjoy every minute he could. Normal, daily routine could get to be a rat race. He was excited to leave the rat race back in Atlanta, at least for the day.

"So, Dad, where is it we go?"

Grinning himself, Brad said, "Follow the highway out of town and I'll show you the turn-off. It's not real visible."

Nathan immediately followed Brad's directions and drove down the highway, then turned on the country road. The day was young when he pulled up beside a light blue van in a space only big enough for one and a half cars. "I know that van!" Natt exclaimed. "It belongs to a man getting his wife and baby from the hospital a while back."

Brad nodded. "That's Sandy's van; she did have a baby a while back. Was in the hospital for a long time before he was borned." As Nathan pulled in to the not very wide opening beside the van, Brad remembered something and added, "Oh, yeah, you can't park on this side, she needs the space to open her door."

"She has a brand new baby on a trail?" Nathan asked, incredulous, wondering why she'd need another whole parking space to put her baby on the back seat.

Brad shook his head, still looking at the van beside them. "Probably just down here at the picnic area, I reckon. She'll be paintin' pictures. She probably got behind while she was in the hospital, if I 'member right."

Looking at his dad as if he were speaking Greek, Nathan said, "Oh, I see." He hoped his dad didn't hear his skepticism.

The SUV was still running, but Nathan was looking in vain for another parking space when Brad said, "Oh, just pull around her van and park beside the road, nobody much comes down this way. It'll be okay."

"Whatever you say, Dad," Nathan said, dubiously.

"Yeah, it'll be okay."

Nathan backed up, then drove by Sandy's van and pulled back to the side of the dirt road. "Yep, this is fine," Brad said and nodded.

They parked. Brad slowly left the SUV while Nathan retrieved the picnic basket and the three younger ones piled out of the back seat. Brad walked up beside his son, but Danny reached for his hand. "Grandad, we go down this road? Does it lead to the mountains? I see a house down there a ways."

Brad looked down at the boy beside him. "No, young feller, when we pulled in that other place didn't you see the trail in front of us?"

"Yeah...."

"That's where we go."

Scowling, very perplexed, Danny asked, "So why did we move from there?"

"'Cause Sandy has to open her side door. Didn't you see how big that door is?"

Scowling, the little boy asked, "To get her baby out?"

"No, to get herself out."

"Grandad, you don't make sense!"

"Son, the lady lives in a wheelchair. There's a lift on that side of her van she's gotta put down to the ground to get out of the van."

"Oh." A profound statement, since the child had no clue what Brad was saying.

Joylyn and Natt both looked at each other and shrugged, wondering what their grandad was talking about. Natt had never seen a lady in town who was in a wheelchair. The one time he'd seen the van, a man, who was quite handsome and walking normally, had driven the van to the gas pumps and had filled up. What his grandad said made no sense. As they reached the van he looked inside and did a double-take. The space behind the wheel was empty there was no seat there at all.

The first thing out of Natt's mouth was, "She's here alone?"

Brad nodded. "Probably has her baby. Ramon's probably out on a trail somewheres. He heads up that hiking shindig."

"Huh, interesting." That was about as non-committal a response as possible.

As they reached the trail, Brad kept Danny's hand and Nathan fell behind him with the picnic basket, while Natt and Joylyn straggled behind. In only minutes, the questions the younger Thomas's had were erased from their minds as the beautiful scenes unfolded before them. All of them slowed down, happy to let the warm breeze and the lovely scene enfold them. Here was something they couldn't get in Atlanta, the air was clean and sweet, the sky a deep blue, with puffy white clouds scattered across it and the hills and mountains beyond were spectacular through vistas in the trees. Even Danny was quiet, so that the birds still chirped and sang their songs among the trees.

"Wow! Grandad, this is awesome! I'm sure glad we came here today," Natt said. "This is really good for the soul."

Nodding, Brad said, "I figgered you'd like it."

"Wow! How could we not?"

Danny's head was on a swivel. "Wow!" he whispered.

"I guess you moved here after I left home, I wish I'd seen this before, Dad!" Nathan exclaimed. "This is awesome!"

"Well, ya know, Son, you could come home more often. It ain't that fer from Atlanta on any given day."

"I know, Dad," Nathan sighed, "but sometimes life gets in the way."

Brad nodded. "That is a fact!"

Not far down the trail it widened out into a grassy place where three wooden picnic tables stood under a few trees. Brad had been right, beside one of the tables sat a wheelchair and on that table rested a baby carrier with a sleeping baby in it. In front of the lady in the wheelchair stood a large easel. The lady didn't even look up to see who had come she was too busy splashing paint on the canvas with her paintbrush.

"Hi, Brad," she called.

"Hi, yourself, Ms. Sandy. This your first outing?" Brad walked up beside her and patted her on the shoulder.

"My first by myself, Brad. Ramon's taken us out a few times to take pictures, but it looses something when I have to paint from a photo. Besides, the day's perfect for being out and Jon has been so good. I needed to get out of the house."

Nathan reached another table, so he put the basket down, but Danny rushed over to look at Sandy's painting. Momentarily, he exclaimed, "Wow! Dad come look at this! It looks just like what I can see over there." The boy pointed passed the painting Sandy was making.

Sandy chuckled. "That's what I was trying to do, make it look just like that. What's your name, fella? I haven't seen you before."

Proudly, Brad said, "I got my family here today! That's Danny. This is my son Nathan, my grand-daughter, Joylyn and my grandson who runs the store, Natt."

Sandy took her brush away from her painting and looked around at the others with a smile. "I'm glad to meet you folks. I'm Sandy DeLord and our son Jonathan."

"So you guys run the hiking service," Natt said.

"Yes, my husband's out with his first hike this weekend. He's been so good to stay home with me until last Friday."

"So ya took off," Brad said.

Nathan wasn't talking. He was tongue-tied. This lady should be a feature in his paper! She was phenomenal! No one he'd ever known in a wheelchair was like this lady. He looked at her painting, when he lifted his eyes the scene was exactly what he saw on the canvas. Several minutes later he said, "Ma'am, you drive that van out there on the road? That light blue van?"

"Yes. I have for a couple of years now." She smiled, as she put her brush back in a blotch of paint on her pallet. "It's a bit more complicated now with Jon, but I'm happy to do both. It's great to be back in God's out-of-doors." Giving them another smile, she said, "If you'll excuse me, I need to get some more paint on this canvas before the light changes so much I'll have two pictures instead of one, like the lady wants."

Brad chuckled. "If she's anythin' like Joyce that would never do."

Aiming the brush at the canvas, Sandy laughed. "Brad, that's it. Not that she'd come to see if it was right, but she'd figure it out. People who commission paintings are funny that way."

"That painting is awesome!" Nathan said softly to his dad.

Nathan collected his family and Brad sat down on the bench of the table they'd claimed with the picnic basket. Nodding, Brad said, "Yeah, she's great! She's brought life to our town. You folks head on down that trail. When you get back I'll have this spread ready for your lunch. You'll be hungry for it by then."

Nathan pulled in another deep breath and said, "We'll do that, Dad. Don't work yourself up, we'll take our time and enjoy the views."

"Yeah, I know you will. Have a good one."

After they left the picnic area, Nathan said to Natt, "Have you ever seen that lady before? I guess it's obvious she drives that van herself."

Natt shook his head. "No, Dad, I never saw her before. The last time I saw that van for sure was when her husband drove it to the gas pump and while he filled up, he told me he was going after his wife and new son from Blairsville. I had no idea she was handicapped. It took me a minute when I saw no seat behind the wheel!"

"Dad!" Danny exclaimed. "Did you see that picture she was doing looked like what we saw? Even now, what she had on that thing looks like the mountains! She's some painter!"

"I know, Son. I guess you don't know what she does with her paintings, do you, Natt? Does she sell them, give them away?"

Looking around at the beautiful, quiet scene around them, Natt said, "No, I don't know, Dad. Believe me, I never knew we had a resident artist in town. I guess Grandad would, he knows her pretty well, it seems."

"I guess I'll ask him when we get back. Maybe your mom would like something like that for her birthday. It'd be different from the jewelry I get her all the time."

Natt looked at Joylyn and nodded. How many years had his dad given his mom jewelry for her birthday? If he ever got a wife he'd make sure he'd give her something besides jewelry ten years straight. "Yeah, Dad, she might like that."

It was well over an hour later when the Thomas's walked into a clearing. They had taken their time, enjoying the peaceful out-of-doors and watched a few wild creatures scamper across their trail. In fact, they'd even noticed some of the newly blooming plants around them. The May apples and Jack-in-the-pulpits were showing themselves. Of course, the mountains in the distance were awesome. Once in a while a cloud blocked out the sun for a few minutes, casting shadows on the mountainsides as it moved.

Joylyn looked up and gasped. "Dad! Look! Wow! Look what's beyond that pipe rail! That is so awesome! I'm sure glad Grandad showed us how to come here."

"I agree with you there, Joylyn, it's sure great to be out-of-doors! Hey, and you know, that lady could probably get all the way down here to paint this!"

Natt didn't speak instead he took long strides and reached the rail first. Immediately, he put his arms on the top rail and rested one foot on the bottom. The other three hurried to the rail that seemed to end the trail. Danny squatted down, resting his arms on the bottom rail, since he couldn't see over the top rail. Joylyn and Nathan also put their arms on the top rail. They were all silent as they took in the awesome scene.

In front of them was a huge expanse of acres and acres of wilderness that stretched out before them. Below them, only a foot or so beyond the pipe rail the ground dropped off to a sheer rock formation, probably a thousand feet straight down. Far off, the valley turned hazy, but beyond the valley, were the majestic mountains they had seen from every angle since they'd left the city behind hours ago. Some of them were so far away that they looked purple, just as the song said.

In some places on those mountains they could see bald places where there had been landslides, taking the soil and leaving only the shear rock. Faintly, in other places they could see color. They stood in silence for many minutes, gazing out in all directions, awed by the vastness and splendor of the scene. All they could see in any direction in front of them were trees and nature. They couldn't see any roads or buildings, nothing man made to mar the beauty.

SEVEN

At the foot of the rock formation ran a stream. From where they stood it looked as clear as glass, they could even see some of the clouds reflected in it. In one place off to their left, just before the stream flowed into the trees, they saw white water and assumed it was a waterfall. They all stood silently looking out every way, taking in the beauty and the splendor before them. As they watched silently a hawk took off from a tall tree below and began circling and screeching in the vast valley. Behind them in the trees birds chirped and sang. The sun was nearly overhead and warmed them. Both Nathan and Natt decided that this was the perfect way to enjoy a day off.

Back at the tables, Brad sat and watched Sandy paint. "How you doin' girl?" he asked, after several minutes. "Hain't seen you much, not since you had that little squirt you got there."

Sandy glanced over at Brad and said, "Brad, I'm doing okay. It's taken me a while, with Jon getting us awake during the night, but I think we have it down to a science now. Actually, I think Jon's helping us out, he seems to sleep longer maybe he'll sleep through the night pretty soon. It's a bit harder when Ramon's gone, but we manage." She glanced up, holding her brush in her hand and smiled at the older man. "At least I have my shape back now. I can hold that baby on the outside so I can breathe better he's not squashing my breathing apparatus all the time. Believe me, that helps a lot!"

Brad chuckled. "I'm glad of that! Of course you're painting again, have you got your students back yet?"

"I've been working them back a little at a time. Of course, Raylyn, Heidi and Lenny came over that first week I was home to clean, so I gave Heidi her lesson that day, but I've been adding two students each week since then. I'm almost back up to my peak again. The one thing I haven't been able to get back to is doing enough paintings to send off to Philadelphia. Jon takes up enough time that I can't do any extra besides the commissions I have here. You know, it seems these people keep wanting my paintings."

Brad scowled at Sandy, even though she wasn't looking at him, as he said, "Young lady, what with all that and your man's hikin' stuff, you got enough on your plate! That Casbah fella ain't takin' you off to Atlanta again, is he?"

"No, Brad, he hasn't asked me for anything this year. That time last year was something I won't forget for a long time, but it'll last me a long time, too."

Brad hoisted himself from the bench and sighed, "I guess I'd better get this food spread around, them hungry critters'll be back soon wantin' some food and drink. I'm sure glad that Natt got his own place, he was about to eat the Missus and me out of groceries!"

As he arranged the tablecloth and place settings, Sandy asked, "How's your grandson working out for you at your store, Brad?"

Pulling the thermos from the basket, he grinned at Sandy and said, "Achally, it ain't mine no more, it's his place."

"Wow! I'm impressed, Brad! He bought you out?"

"Achally, I give it to him. I'm just his partner now. I get a salary and live mostly on my Social Security. He's done a lot for the store, lots more'n I ever thought of doin'. I told him there needed ta be some new blood piped into that place and he done it. He's purdy conscientious about it, really."

"I'm sure you're glad of that."

"Yeah, I am. Him and me, we're a good team."

"I'm glad to hear that, Brad."

The pair ran out of things to talk about soon, since Sandy kept painting and never looked at him. Brad wasn't offended, he knew how Sandy worked and appreciated her paintings. He set the picnic basket in the center of the table and slowly took out all the things Joyce had sent along. Sandy gave Jonathan's infant seat a slight push and lightly touched his body, but he continued to sleep, so she went back to her painting. When Brad had finished setting the table, he sat back down, his back to Sandy and looked out at the awesome scene before him, his eyes closed and he dozed. He was content.

Finally, the four younger Thomas's appeared, coming into the clearing from the trail. Their talking woke Brad and he grinned at his family. Sandy had finished one painting and had turned her easel a different way and was now painting a totally different scene. When the four appeared in the clearing they heard an eagle screeching overhead and Sandy wasn't talking, but busily painting on her new picture.

Danny ran to look at Sandy's new painting then he ran back to his dad. "Come look at what she's doin' now, Dad!" he exclaimed. "She's doin' another whole painting! Come see it!"

Danny grabbed his dad's hand and pulled him to behind Sandy's chair. They both looked at the new painting and saw what she was busily working on. The eagle in the sky was taking shape on Sandy's canvas as they watched. "Wow!" Danny whispered. "It looks like it'll fly right off that picture!"

"It sure does, Son. Let's let her paint and go eat Grandad's lunch. I sure can eat after that hike we took, can't you?"

"Yeah, Dad, I'm ready to eat a horse!"

After saying grace, Brad said, "Ain't she somethin' else?"

"She is, Dad! She finished that other one already?"

"Sure did! She told me that first one's a commission, but this one ain't. She's hoping to hang it in her gallery in Philadelphia."

"She wouldn't sell it to me?"

"Sure, she ain't no different from somebody else tryin' to make a livin'. She'll sell it to ya, probly for a good price, too. You wantin' it for Eleanor's birthday?"

Nodding, Nathan said, "She'll have it done today?"

"Sure! You'd have to promise you'll let it dry real good. She's pretty fussy about that, but I know she'd sell it to you."

Nathan glanced over at Sandy and said, "If I could have it today, I'd sure promise!"

Nodding, Brad raised his voice, "Ms. Sandy, you game for a customer out here in the boonies? I gocha one."

"Brad, what did you do, talk your son into buying my painting or twist his arm?"

"Not on your life, young lady! He done it hisself. He brung his family up fer the day from Atlanta and wanted to take a hike. He got a birthday to remember, though."

"Send him over I'll have it done in about a half hour."

"Believe me, Ma'am, I'll be over real soon," Nathan said, around a mouthful. "You're painting is awesome!"

Sandy continued to splash paint on her canvas. The bird still soared in the sky. "Thanks, Mr. Thomas. Believe me; I try to do all my work to bring glory to my heavenly Father. He's the One who deserves the praise."

"Yes, Ma'am."

Marcy was fit to be tied, the Memorial Day parade was about to begin on the Avenue two blocks away. The weather was spectacular, she could see the sparkling sun, but here she sat with her pillows, a book she didn't want to read in her lap. She'd always been either a spectator or a participant in the Memorial Day parade and today she would miss it. For many years, Charlie wore his postal uniform and always walked in the parade. Although he hadn't been born in America, he was a patriotic, naturalized American. When the three of them had been young, Charlie'd push Sandy's chair and brought his younger children dressed as something special. Colleen watched from the side of the street with the other spectators. As they grew older, Ed and Marcy had ridden decorated bikes with the other children. In recent years, Marcy had been on the sidelines with Colleen, but this year, she couldn't go at all. Dr. Wright had said she couldn't leave the house until he saw her later this week and of course, Memorial Day was on Monday. Charlie and Colleen left for the starting point and Ed came to Marcy's door.

He leaned his tall frame against the door, folded his arms across his chest and grinned. He watched her, knowing she was fuming. "So, lazybones, you're staying home in bed, I see."

Scowling fiercely at him, she waved her paperback book at him and said, "Edwin! If you come in here I'll clobber you! You know I wouldn't be here if I had my way! I feel okay, I feel like I could walk up to the corner." Motioning him closer, Marcy said, "Come on, I dare you to come closer! You're despicable, you know that!"

Making himself shake all over, but grinning broadly, Ed wiped his forehead, as if wiping sweat and said, "I'm shaking in my boots, I'm so scared! With what, you'd hit me with that flimsy paperback you have?" Without entering the room, he turned and said over his shoulder, "So I'm out of here. Gotta go watch that really super parade. It'll be spectacular I know! I'll see you after the parade, wimp. Rest up real good, just like the doctor said. One of these days you'll be all better, maybe."

"Oh!" Marcy growled to the empty doorway. "I absolutely hate being stuck in this bed! If Dr. Wright doesn't let me out, I think I'll……" It was only thin air she spoke to she heard the front door click shut as her words died away. She collapsed back against the pillows and opened the book. However, only minutes later she slammed it closed.

Tears slid down her cheeks. She threw her head back and looked up at the ceiling. "God in heaven, when will I be back to normal again?" she whispered, but no one answered. Of course, she didn't expect an answer. Now that she was alone, she couldn't stop the tears. She felt like she'd cried a bucket full since February.

Her hopes and plans had gone up in smoke back in February. Her heart didn't hurt and she got up to the commode herself. Still, she knew she wasn't up to par, maybe she never would be. What she hated the most, her mom wouldn't let her get dressed her clothes were upstairs. If she'd had clothes here, she'd probably talked her dad into letting her go to the Avenue.

Thursday was Marcy's date with Dr. Wright. Charlie didn't take the morning off, so Colleen went with Marcy to General Hospital for her appointment. Of course, Marcy couldn't drive yet, Dr. Wright hadn't released her and Colleen wouldn't think of driving downtown, so she drove to the Avenue to the trolley stop and waited for the next one. They would take the trolley to the Elevated that would take them downtown and had a stop in front of General.

All week long Marcy was hoping for a statement of release, but she wouldn't say anything, not to her family. She knew she wasn't as strong as she'd been before her bout with Rheumatic Fever, but she was much stronger than she'd been when she first became ill. Now she could do everything for herself, even climb the stairs slowly to her old room without her heart hurting or her breath coming in gasps. Both Charlie and Colleen were happy with her recovery, still she knew she'd never go back to nurse's training. That hurt the most.

She cried when she was alone, it was a crushing disappointment, but she didn't want her family to know how much. She'd been so sure that the foreign mission field had been in her future, she felt at loose ends now. What could she do with her life if she couldn't finish nursing school and have to stay stateside because of her heart condition? She'd been praying, but so far nothing had come to her. She read her Bible every day, but even that seemed like only words, no inspiration seemed to come from the pages.

After the long ride on the trolley and Elevated and surviving all that noise, they walked into the emergency area, moved across the big receiving room to the offices beyond where Jason Wright's hospital office was. They had to take seats in the hallway because his office door was closed, but at least there was no one else waiting to see him. He was either seeing another patient or he was off somewhere in the hospital, working some case with his residents. He was a very busy man.

Moments later, the door opened and a lady walked out with Jason behind her. He said, "See you in two weeks, Melinda."

"Yes, Doctor, I'll be here."

As the woman walked away, he turned and smiled down at Marcy. Motioning to both Colleen and Marcy, he stepped back and held the door open. Then he said, "Ah, my favorite patient, Marcy, come in and let's have a chat."

After they were seated, Jason sat in his desk chair and folded his hands. Grinning at Marcy, he said, "So, Charlie didn't come? You didn't have to lie down on the back seat today?"

Marcy grinned at the doctor and said, "Nope, Mom and I came on the Elevated by ourselves. Since you wouldn't let me drive yet and Mom didn't want to drive downtown, that was our way of getting here."

Nodding, Jason grinned and said, "And I don't want you to drive yet, anyway, Marcy."

"Doctor!" Marcy said, exasperated. "Why not?"

"Because you've been really, really sick. You aren't back to full power yet and I don't want any added stress put on your heart," he said, succinctly.

With a big sigh, Marcy asked, "So how much longer? When will you release me? I absolutely hate sitting around when the weather's super. Besides, how can driving be stressful?"

Since he was Chief of Staff, his hospital office sported a window. He looked out at the beautiful day and said, "You can be outside. If you don't live on a hill, I'd suggest you start walking, say around a city block every day that's nice. Not in the rain, of course, but walking will be good exercise. It'll build up your stamina and your muscles."

"Suppose I walk to the market, it's two blocks, but up a little grade."

"If all you do is get an ice cream, it's fine, but no carrying bags of groceries home."

Even more exasperated, Marcy exclaimed, "Doctor! For crying out loud! What good is it to walk to the market if you can't bring home the groceries? I've felt like an invalid so long, I want to start being useful."

Jason winked at the pretty girl. "Your day'll come, Marcy. I want to see you completely well. If we can get that heart of yours up to snuff, I'll feel like I've done my job." He looked sternly at her. Making sure she looked at him, he said, "Unless you cooperate, that won't happen. It won't be so noticeable now while you're young, but I guarantee it'll come crashing down on you when you're older."

Sighing, Marcy said, "Thanks, Doctor, I really needed to hear that." She took her eyes from the man and looked away at all the books she could see on his shelves. There was definitely that scratchiness behind her eyes, they were trying to cloud over, but she blinked furiously, she would not cry in the doctor's office, especially with her mom in the room.

Watching her closely, therefore seeing her reaction, Jason cleared his throat and said, "You start walking and if you don't have any pain or shortness of breath, you can walk a little farther each week. But don't you push it!"

"So you won't tell me when I can drive or when you'll release me?"

"Nope, I'll see you in a month and we'll see. I'll give you this form for the receptionist when you come in then for a blood draw. We should have the results back before you leave, that'll tell us how things are going." The man scribbled on a small prescription pad and handed her the top sheet. "There, that should do for the bloodwork. Keep up the good work, girl!"

Marcy let out a big sigh, "Yes, Doctor. I'd like to whip whoever gave me that virus! Did anybody else have it or get it when I came down with it?"

Leaning back, so that the chair squealed, Jason put his fingers together in a steeple, shook his head and said, "Not that I've been aware of, Marcy. You know, of course, there are viruses in the air all the time. It just so happened that you were susceptible to that particular one and it zapped you. We may never know where it came from."

Sarcastically, she muttered, "Great! Just great! Anything else?"

"No, go home and start walking and be back in a month."

"All right, Dr. Wright. After my walk I can sit outside, right?"

"Yes, that's perfectly acceptable."

"Great!"

"Thank you, Doctor," Colleen said, from the doorway.

Jason smiled. "Not a problem, Mrs. Bernard, it's Marcy you need to keep corralled."

She smiled at the doctor. "You know that is very, very hard."

"Mmm, I had that feeling."

That evening at dinner, Charlie said, "So, what did Dr. Wright say, my dear?"

"Daddy, he said to go home and start walking and be back in a month. I still can't drive and he won't release me yet."

"So did you walk today?"

"While Mom drove home, I walked from the trolley stop, then I walked down to the corner and back. I wasn't out of breath and nothing hurt."

"I'm glad to hear that!" He grinned. "How about walking with me on my postal route?" Marcy didn't say anything, but she grinned.

Colleen gasped, but shaking her head, Marcy said, "I'd do it, Dad, but he said start walking around the block, then each week go a little farther. I doubt he had a five mile walking postal delivery route in mind when he told me to walk."

"Sis, I'll walk with you," came from the young man slouched in his chair at the table.

Incredulous, Marcy held up her hand, pointing at her brother, then back at herself. "You'll walk with me? You who must take his wheels to go two blocks to the market for a six pack of cola? I don't believe I heard you say that!"

Ed smacked his flat abdomen and sighed, "It seems as though I'm getting a bit of flab from sitting in the stacks all day. I'm in need of working it off. You wouldn't deny a request from your big brother to walk with you, would you?"

Marcy grinned at her very in-shape brother, her eyes twinkling, and said, "By all means, Bro, wouldn't want you to get any unwanted flab, it would really hurt your image, I'm sure." The grin covering her face, she added, "Was that why Marg broke up with you, because of your flab, Brother dear?"

Ed made a face at his sister. "Be kind, sister dear, you who have been laying around for weeks. It makes a body wonder sometimes."

"Humph! I'd be out of here if I could be, believe me."

Chuckling, Ed said, "Sure you would!"

A month went by, Marcy walked. She coerced Colleen into walking with her, when she couldn't, she talked Ed into walking. Each week she did as the doctor said and went half a block further. In fact, she fudged a little by the time the month was up she was walking around two long city blocks with no shortness of breath or pounding heartbeats. Usually she walked early in the morning or near dusk, since the days were getting longer and also hotter. She found that the heat was harder on her than the distance. When she walked in the evening, Charlie often joined her. She liked that a lot. They had a lot of father - daughter talks that way.

A few days before Marcy's appointment, Colleen found out her sisters had something planned that they wanted her to go. Not remembering that was the day for Marcy's appointment, she accepted. When she hung up the phone and told them, Marcy was ecstatic she could finally get to do something on her own. Clapping her hands, she said, "Mom! That's great! Super! You've been stuck here with me for so long, you should go with them. That'll be perfect!"

Scowling at her daughter, Colleen nearly came out of her chair, as she said, "I most surely will not! You have your appointment with Dr. Wright that day and I forgot all about it. Your dad can't go with you and Ed, well, he's busy with school. I most surely will go with you. I'll call the sisters back and tell them!"

"No, no! I'll go see him, you go with your sisters," she countered, quickly, even putting her hand over the phone. "Mom, I'll be just fine! Really."

"But..."

"But nothing, Mom. It's only two blocks to the Avenue, then I ride the trolley to the Elevated. The train stops right in front of the main entrance to General."

"Suppose you get a weak spell and you're alone?" Colleen, ever the pessimist, countered.

Marcy sighed, "Mom I haven't had one in weeks. I've been walking around two full blocks all this week and the El stops right in front of General. Isn't that so, Dad?"

"I can take you, Sis. It's only a few blocks out of the way."

Marcy glared around the kitchen table. "No! I'm going by myself! I will be fine! I've been cooped up at this place so long!"

Still not convinced and overly worried about Marcy, Colleen said, "Really, I forgot about your appointment. I'll call and tell the girls I can't go."

Marcy swallowed, willing the tears of frustration away. It had been weeks she'd been cooped up and waited on. She blinked to make the tears go back and said, "Mom, listen to me! I'm twenty-two nearly twenty-three, I know what I can do, I've been walking this whole month and haven't had a weak spell or any palpitations since I saw the doctor. Please let me do this! I really, really need to do this by myself!" Silently, Marcy looked at her dad, her eyes pleading.

Charlie came to Marcy's defense, knowing how Colleen was she'd fight this tooth and nail. He covered Colleen's hand and said, "Colleen, Sweetheart, it's okay. You know you've nursed her right along. It was your purpose to get her to be independent. We talked about it last night that she's so much better."

Colleen sighed, "Yes, I guess that's so."

Marcy sighed, "Thanks, Daddy."

Charlie reached over and squeezed Marcy's hand. "You're welcome, my dear. I'm sure you'll do just fine."

"Yeah, Sis, you need to get off your duff."

Marcy sighed, "Oh, Brother."

Thursday came. Charlie left to be at work by seven, Ed left for class at the university at eight. Colleen's sisters came and blew the horn. Marcy jumped up, found Colleen's purse, took her keys from the hook by the back door and dropped them in the purse and handed it to her mom. "Here you go, Mom! Have a great day with Aunties. I'll see you when we both get back! I know you'll have a great time with them. Tell them I said, 'hi'."

Scowling at her daughter, Colleen said, "This just isn't right! You're my daughter I should be going with you to the doctor."

"It sure is, Mom!" Marcy took Colleen's arm and ushered her down the incline. Marcy's next oldest aunt was stepping from the car, so Marcy added, "Hi, Aunt Collette, here's Mom, she's ready to go with you guys." Marcy kissed Colleen's cheek and said, "Have a great day, Mom, do all the shopping you can and don't think about me."

"I most certainly will think about you!" Colleen muttered, as Collette took her arm.

Her face could hardly contain her grin, as she waved. "Bye, Mom, have fun!"

"Bye, Dear, do be careful!"

"Oh, I will, Mom!" She waved at the ladies in the car. Marcy watched her aunt's car leave their driveway then she hurried inside and grabbed her own purse and keys.

She heaved a sigh, but felt like doing a dance. She'd gotten sick in early February, now it was almost July. It was the first time she'd been alone since she'd collapsed at the hospital nearly six months ago. She looked at herself in the mirror in the bathroom and grinned. She'd gotten a tan, she'd spent so much time outside in a month and best of all she didn't have those horrid black half circles under her eyes.

She left, locking the door behind her and walked at her usual pace to the Avenue to catch the public transportation to the El. The El came every twenty minutes, so there was no rush to get the one in the station when she left the trolley on the street. She found a seat on the El, it wasn't rush hour, so it wasn't hard. She'd brought her book, since it was such a long ride to the hospital downtown and she'd done it so many times in over two years. Finally, it was her stop and she left the noise behind. Quickly, she went down the stairs to the street, she didn't want to be late for what she hoped was her last appointment with Dr. Wright.

In the ER, she handed the receptionist her paper for the blood work, then followed her instructions to the lab. There were two ahead of her. After that, she returned to the ER to wait for Dr. Wright, since his door was closed. As always, the ER was organized chaos, with nurses running between exam rooms. Tears stung Marcy's eyes, but she scrubbed them away fiercely. She longed to be here, to do what those women were doing. She shook her head, according to Dr. Wright, it would never happen. She still had a year and a quarter of class and practical work to be able to take state boards. The doctor had informed her several times she couldn't do it. She wondered what to do with her life. She knew it wasn't right to question God, since He was all-knowing, but sometimes, it didn't seem like He knew what He was doing. She stopped that train of thought before it went any further. God was sovereign He knew the end from the beginning.

The door to the doctor's office opened and three young men walked out. Marcy looked up and saw Jason sitting at his desk. He looked out the door and motioned to her, smiling as she stood. Jason looked around her, as she closed the door and scowled. "No one came with you?"

"Nope. Dad had to work and Mom's sisters wanted her to go with them shopping. I finally convinced her she should go with them, that I could do this myself. I even ushered her out the door when they came for her."

"So you came here by yourself. You didn't drive, did you?"

"No, Dr. Wright. I wanted to do everything just as you told me. Maybe you'll find I'm much better than you think. I had that blood work done, too."

"Good, they should have it here very soon."

"Yes, I was hoping so. There were only a couple of people ahead of me. Depending on what it says will you release me today?"

"If all looks fine, yes. I see you have a nice tan. I guess that means you've been out walking each day."

"I sure have! I have my brother back in shape, since I got him to walk with me most of the evenings after supper. I've been spending lots of time outside, too. It's much better than being cooped up inside for hours on end."

Remembering her first statement, Jason said, "You have your brother in shape?"

"Yes, he's been stuck in the stacks this summer trying to get his dissertation finished for his masters. He can teach in the junior college once he gets his degree." She grinned. "He told me he had to get rid of his flab from being in the stacks so much, his girlfriend didn't like him looking so paunchy."

"Hmm, sounds like a real dud."

"Well, sometimes he does act like one."

Grinning, Jason asked, "Isn't he the one who called that commode a…"

Fiercely, Marcy scowled at the man and said, "Don't you say it! Dr. Wright, you'll be no friend of mine if you do!"

"I won't touch that with a ten foot pole! Why do you want to be discharged so badly?"

"The day I came home from the hospital my brother-in-law called to tell us about my sister, but he also invited me down to Georgia to visit with him and my sister when I was better. They have a new baby who's now several months old. Sandy still needs lots of help, but I knew I couldn't do much until I'm well."

Jason scowled. "If the baby's several months old why does she still need help? Usually by the time a baby is several months old mother and baby have their routine down pat."

"Doctor, it was a miracle she was able to carry a baby to term."

"Really?"

Marcy nodded. "She was paralyzed at birth from her waist down and has always been in a wheelchair. She spent the last six weeks of her pregnancy in the hospital on bedrest, because sitting in that chair cramped the baby so much he pushed against her diaphragm and her bladder and in her condition that was really hard for her. She has so many things she loves to do that the doctors had to put her in the hospital to keep her from doing them and making herself any worse off. However, now with the baby, she's trying to do all she ever did as well as take care of the baby and that's almost impossible. Her husband is a hiking guide and has to take hikes every week, so she's alone with the baby a lot."

"What will she do when the baby walks?"

Marcy shrugged. "Your guess is as good as mine!"

"Wow!"

There was a tap on the door, but before Jason could answer, it opened and a head and arm came in. "Doctor, here's the blood work results you wanted."

"Thanks a lot and for putting a rush on it."

"Not a problem, Doctor." The young man walked in, handed Jason the forms, then left and closed the door again.

Marcy folded her hands and sat quietly for several minutes, while Jason looked over the results. She couldn't tell anything by the look on his face. Marcy felt like chewing her nails, she could wish all the results were normal, perhaps if she had snapped her fingers before the tech had drawn the blood or maybe she needed a fairy-god-mother to wave her magic wand to make it all normal.... No, God was in control, if He wanted the results to be normal, she didn't need to do anything, He'd take care of it.

Jason looked up from the slips of paper and smiled. "I guess you're on your way to Georgia, young lady. When'll you be back?"

Marcy sighed, "Are you saying I must come back?"

Laying the papers on top of others in a file folder, he said, "Marcy, any doctor wants to follow his patients from start to finish. I will release you today, but I really would like to see you in six months." He grinned at her and it took ten years off his age. "Some of us like to brag about the cases that make a good recovery."

Marcy grinned back at the man. "Are you saying I've recovered?"

Shaking his head, Jason said, "Young lady, I'm not saying that! If I do, you'll be on the next boat to China or enrolling back in nursing school for the next quarter. Actually, you've come a long way from that first time I saw you. I don't think you'll ever be as strong as you were last Christmas and you'll need to protect yourself from things like the flu, but you are well on your way to good health and I'm pleased with your progress. Still, there is residual heart involvement, sad to say. Yes, I'll let you drive. I suppose you're planning to drive to Georgia?"

"Sure! I'm positive I'll need my car."

Looking at her seriously, Jason leaned onto the desk and looked Marcy in the eye, as he said, "Marcy, if you drive that far, please take it in two days. I want you to drive no more that a couple hundred miles at a time, with good rest stops before you get in to drive again. If you try to push yourself too much you could end up with a relapse and I know you don't want that."

With another loud sigh, Marcy said, "All right, Doctor, I'll do as you say. Thank you for all you've done. In case I stay longer than six months, should I try to see another doctor? Maybe Sandy knows one down there."

Jason sighed and looked at the reports again. "If you must stay, or if you need to see a doctor for anything, they can ask for your records and we'll fax them anywhere. Try really hard not to get yourself into any trouble and everything'll be fine."

"You know me I try to stay out of trouble!"

"Mmm, that's questionable." Jason stood up and reached for Marcy's hand. "Take care of yourself, Marcy. Like I say, I'd like to see you in six months, but don't come back just to see me if you're still gone. In that case, have a good life." Jason grinned and came around his desk, then opened the door for Marcy.

As she walked out, Marcy smiled and said, "Thanks, Dr. Wright, thanks for everything."

She looked up at the doctor as she walked by. "I'm still in a quandary as to what to do with my life now, but surely it'll come to me. Thanks again."

Standing in the doorway, he smiled and said, "You're welcome, Marcy, see you around."

"Yes, but I can't say it'll be around the water cooler."

Jason laughed. "Nope, that's true."

Marcy was ecstatic as she left the hospital. She nearly skipped down the street. Since she had lived in the nurse's residence for over two years, she knew the area quite well, so before she climbed the stairs to the El station, she went shopping for some clothes. It seemed when she hunted in her closet for something to wear today, she didn't have much of a choice, the ones in her closet didn't fit her quite as well as they once had. She was grinning as she walked into the huge department store and bought several outfits before she went home that afternoon. They made quite a stack around her on the El seat.

As she walked in the house, her mom was bustling around her kitchen, but she looked at Marcy and saw her bags with the store logos and exclaimed, "Where have you been!"

"Hi, Mom, I see you beat me home. I've been shopping."

"You should be home resting!"

Working hard not to let her mom's pessimism get to her, she said, "No, Mom, Dr. Wright released me today. He said I can drive."

Charlie walked in while Marcy was talking, so he said, "He's released you! I'm sure you're really glad of that."

Marcy grinned and said, "Absolutely! I think I'll call Sandy and tell her I'm coming."

"WHAT!" Colleen exclaimed. "You're what?"

Marcy set her bags on her chair at the table. Looking at her mom, her elation dropped. "Mom, don't you remember that Ramon invited me down way back when I got out of the hospital? Dr. Wright and I discussed it this morning and since he released me, I think I'll go as soon as I let them know."

Colleen took two long steps and grabbed Marcy's arms above her elbows. Shaking her, she said, fiercely, "Marcy, no! You're doing no such thing! You must build up your strength. You need to be here! You just said, he wants to see you in six months!"

Marcy put her hands on her mom's arms and pushed herself from her grasp. Fiercely, she said, "Mom, my strength is fine, Doctor said it was. My blood work was very good. He said I'd come a long way and told me I can drive, all I have to do when I drive that far is take breaks. Like I said the other day, I'm almost twenty-three and I *will* be leaving for Georgia very soon. I'll do like Sandy did and stay off the interstates."

Since Colleen wasn't holding Marcy, she began wringing her hands. She looked at Charlie. "Please, Charlie, make her stay here! Tell her she needs to build up her strength!"

Charlie shook his head. Seeing tears form in Colleen's eyes, he came to her and put his arms around her. After a kiss, he said, "I can't, Colleen. Like she says, she's an adult. The doctor's released her. You had to let her go when she went to nursing school, now you must let her go because she's well again."

Tears streaming down her cheeks, Colleen broke from Charlie's hold and ran from the room. She never stopped until she reached her own bedroom. The door slammed behind her, but both Marcy and Charlie heard her wail, "No-o-o, please no!"

Looking at the empty hallway, Marcy shook her head and said, "Dad, will she always be this way? It really bothers me when she's like this!"

Charlie shook his head, also looking down the hallway and sighed, "I don't know, my dear, I don't know. I know for sure you must get on with your life and not let her smother you."

"Thanks, Dad," she said, simply. "You know how hard it's been to get to do anything, especially since I've been feeling so much better."

"Yes, my dear, I know."

Sandy had finished another painting and put it in the place for it to dry. Clouds had moved in since noon. Sandy now held Jon who had been jarred awake by the clap of thunder. He was still sniffling in her lap. She had fed him and he was content, but the lightning and thunder startled him each time they snapped and boomed outside. Sandy was also unhappy, all three of the guides were gone on hikes each of them had more than five in their group. Of course, everyone was instructed to bring raingear in case of rain. Still it was less than ideal to have to be wet as they hiked and muddy trails were not fun either.

Maybe with the rain this early in the afternoon, it would clear off for their overnight. She could only hope. Pitching a tent in the rain was horrible, but they'd have to eat their supper, too. Granola for supper didn't seem like such good fare, how could they find any dry wood to start a fire? A hot cup of coffee would taste wonderful, but without dry wood, it wouldn't happen. Sandy knew that, remembering how wet she'd gotten when she first came as Ramon's receptionist. She wouldn't forget that time in her life for a while.

She looked down at the baby on her lap, tears of joy came to her eyes she loved Jon so very much. He was such a good baby, even only a few months old he had his own personality. He was a miracle, she'd never thought she could give her husband such a gift, but he was such a perfect, beautiful baby, she was blessed. Also, she was thankful for a warm, dry home. Ramon was a wonderful husband, an excellent provider. She thanked God for him every day, without fail. God had truly blessed her.

The lightning and thunder grumbled off finally, but the rain still fell when she had to turn on the lights to fix her supper. A few days ago they had passed the longest day of the year, but the clouds were so heavy and dark it seemed like late evening at supper time. It was on nights like this that Sandy wished Ramon did something else beside lead hikes in the hills of north Georgia, but she would never discourage him. He loved the wilderness he hiked in.

Jon was in his infant carrier. He was awake and looking around the kitchen. Sandy wheeled herself to the chair where she'd put his carrier and smiled while she ran her hand over his tiny body. She loved this baby so much he was a miracle, a true gift from God. His legs wiggled under the blanket and her heart turned over. She always knew her paralysis could not be inherited, but to see Jon's legs moving made her extremely happy.

She had the ingredients for her evening sandwich on the counter when the phone rang. She looked at the display and saw it was their private line, not the hiking service line, so she reached for the phone and said, "Hello, DeLords."

"Hi, Sis! How are you? How's Jon, how's everybody?" came the cheery voice that Sandy hadn't heard in a long time.

Happily, Sandy exclaimed, "Marcy! You sound great! We're all fine. Ramon's out on a hike, but it's rained today and it's still misting. They'll have to camp in a wet place tonight, probably pitch wet tents and eat granola for supper."

Marcy waited for her sister to finish, but she seemed like she had a one track mind when she asked, "Can I come down?"

Sandy's face lit up. She grinned at Jon, as she exclaimed, "You're all better! You don't have to see the doctor any more?"

"Sis, I'm great! I saw the doctor today and he released me. He said I can drive and I can come down if I take it easy."

"Super! Sure, come on! I can't wait to see you!" Then Sandy asked, "Mom's not trying to keep you there?"

"Oh, sure, of course. When I said I was coming down, she threw a fit and tried to get Dad to keep me here, but he wouldn't, so she ran to their room. It's Thursday, Dr. Wright said to take the trip in two days. Suppose I leave in the morning and get there Saturday afternoon. Would that work for you guys? Believe me; I am so anxious to get out of this house! The four walls of the music room hold no appeal anymore."

"It would be fantastic! Ramon will be home tomorrow. It'll be great!" Sandy sighed, "Sis, I'm sorry to hear about Mom. I never thought when we were growing up that she'd be quite so possessive of you and Ed. It's really sad."

"I know, but while I was sick I had a feeling she'd do the same with me that she did with you. She followed doctor's orders to the letter. You know she always did. My last appointment with Dr. Wright, she and I almost came to blows. I mean, REALLY! The Aunties wanted her to go shopping with them that day and I practically had to walk her out to their car to get to go to the appointment by myself. After that, I went shopping for a couple of hours. Then when I came home…. Well, I'm sure you can picture the scene!"

Sandy shook her head. Thank goodness for their dad, he kept his children sane. "Marcy, I can tell you I know exactly how you feel. You know that is precisely why I'm here and not there. Life goes on much better without a smothering mother."

"Absolutely! Okay, I'll let you go and go pack. It won't take me too long at least I don't have paints and a piano to bring."

Sandy chuckled. "Great! We'll see you Saturday, I'm excited! Jon'll be anxious to see his Auntie. Be sure and drive carefully."

"I will, I promise."

Marcy hung up the extension Charlie had installed in the music room only days after Marcy was discharged from the hospital. She sat on the daybed, that was back to being a couch, since she now was sleeping in her bedroom upstairs. She looked up to see a female storm cloud standing silently in the hall doorway. Colleen had obviously heard her making plans over the phone. She was intent on keeping her daughter at home perhaps she thought she could physically hold her daughter herself, since no one else was doing it.

EIGHT

"Marcy, you are *not* leaving in the morning!" Colleen said, angrily. "The doctor wants to see you in six months. How can you do that if you're not here?"

Nodding, Marcy slid off the bed, carefully, she would never forget the first time she'd left this daybed on her own and landed on the floor. It had hurt nothing but her pride, but still... Firmly, but as kindly as possible, Marcy said, "Yes, Mom, I'm leaving for Georgia in the morning. Sandy and I made all the arrangements. I'll get there Saturday afternoon sometime. I'll take it slow, just like Dr. Wright said I should."

Colleen started wringing her hands and shaking her head. The hand wringing was her usual way of coping with anxiety when it was more than she could bear. "You can't! Marcy, listen to me! You aren't all better! Dr. Wright wants to see you in six months, you told us! How can you if you're gone? And... and driving all that way...! I get tired when we go down."

Walking toward her mom, since she needed to go out that door to reach the steps to the second floor, she said, "Mom, I can do that. I am all better. Dr. Wright released me today. A doctor doesn't release a patient from his care unless he feels they are well. He said I can drive to Georgia, only I must take it in two days. That's like Sandy did. It's a good ways and there's lots to see. Every time we've gone, we've been in a hurry and haven't stopped to do any sightseeing. Dr. Wright said he wanted to see me in six months **if I was here**, if I'm not, he said to have a good life. I can see another doctor somewhere else if I need to."

Silently, Colleen shook her head. Her hands twisted around each other.

She stopped in front of her mom, who hadn't moved, and said, "Mom, I'm going to my room now to pack. I plan to leave when Daddy leaves for work, so I need to get upstairs now. Will you *please* move so I can?"

Tears came to Colleen's eyes and started sliding down her cheeks. "No-o-o!" she whispered and stayed where she was. "No-o-o, Marcy!"

Marcy turned from the doorway and went to the other door from the music room, but when she turned the corner to the hallway, her mother stood there. It was much too serious to laugh, but Marcy felt a bubble of laughter come into her throat. She hadn't played cat and mouse since she was a toddler and that was with Ed. However, the hall was wider than the doorway, so Colleen couldn't block the entire opening. Marcy turned sideways and moved around her.

From a few safe steps away, Marcy said, "Mom, I'm sorry you feel you have to be an obstacle, but it won't keep me from going to Georgia. You were happy enough for me to leave for General to go to nursing school a few years ago. Just pretend I'm going back there." Marcy felt a sigh, but swallowed it and said, "And another thing, you were always pleased that I'd planned to be a foreign missionary. Mom, missionaries leave for overseas and don't come back for years, remember? I'm only going to Georgia!"

Marcy kept walking and was at the bottom of the stairs when Colleen said, "It's not the same, you've been really sick." It wasn't hard to hear the tears that clogged Colleen's throat as she spoke those words.

Trying not to sigh in exasperation, Marcy said, "I know, but I'm well now. Be sure you remember that as I drive away."

"I can't," Colleen whispered.

Nodding, Marcy said, "You must, Mom." Marcy started up the stairs, intent on getting out of the way in case Colleen came after her.

Colleen rushed back and stood at the bottom to watch Marcy all the way to the top. Marcy never looked back, but walked into her room. She shook her head. Why couldn't her mom let her go? She'd done the same to Sandy, only she'd done it to Sandy all her life. Marcy realized now even more why Sandy had wanted so desperately to leave and go so far away.

Their mom had always been like that with Sandy. She remembered as a little kid her mom had carried her sister, even when Sandy had been six years old! Even though Sandy had been so small from her waist down, by the time she was six, she weighed much more than a normal woman should carry. Remembering what she'd just done, escaped from her mom, she realized how Sandy's handicap had prevented her from doing that. Sandy couldn't walk away.

However, never before she'd gotten sick had her mom been like this with her. Did she think she could keep her daughter from all germs if she kept her close at home? Marcy didn't have an answer, so she pulled her two suitcases from her closet, threw them on her bed and started filling them. She remembered doing this each time when she came home on her days off from nursing school and smothered a sigh.

They'd finished supper there was no reason to go back downstairs before she went to bed. She'd wanted to talk with her dad, but she knew her mom would try to interfere. She'd pack everything she could claim then set her clock radio for when her dad got up in the morning. That would be plenty of time to box her appliances and take everything to her car. She'd eat breakfast with the others and leave when her dad left for work. Her mom would just have to accept her decision it would make it easier on her when she was gone.

Upstairs, with the door closed, Marcy continued packing, so she didn't hear Colleen tearfully confront Charlie in the kitchen. "Why are you letting Marcy go? Charlie, she's been so sick! The doctor wants to see her in six months. If she's in Georgia she can't go to see him." The dishwater gurgled down the drain and Colleen wiped her hands on her little towel then turned from the sink to face the kitchen table, where Charlie still sat with his Bible open before him. While Colleen did the supper dishes was his time to read and study his Bible. It was his favorite time of day and he was with his two favorite people, the Lord and his wife.

Ed had been sitting in his chair at the table reading the newspaper, but he quickly closed it and stood up, giving his dad a sympathetic look, then silently headed for the stairs. Charlie sighed, left his chair at the table, then took Colleen's hand and led her to the couch in the living room. He sat down, pulling her down beside him. He placed one hand on the top of the couch behind her, sitting sideways on the couch so he could look directly at her then placed his other hand on her leg. He sat very close so he could look at her as he spoke. Colleen tried to look away, her hands wringing themselves together in her lap, but Charlie waited in silence for several minutes until she looked back at him.

Finally she looked up and opened her mouth to speak. "Charlie..." she began.

When he had her undivided attention, he put his finger over her mouth to stop her words, then curled his finger under her chin so she couldn't look away and said, tenderly, "Mama, our children are grown, all adults. Our first born left home a couple of years ago and is making her life in Georgia with her husband and son. We can probably go see them this Christmas. Our son has finished his Master's degree and will teach at a junior college in the fall. He has asked a young lady to share his life. You've been happy for them and are waiting for the wedding. You were happy when our youngest went into nursing and planned to be a foreign missionary, but she's had to change those plans to something else. Why is it so hard for you to let go?"

"But Marcy's been so sick!" Colleen whispered, not answering Charlie's question. She continued to look at her husband, the tears glistening in her eyes. "She's had that terrible virus, it could come back! Doctor said you never get rid of a virus it's always in your body! I remember him saying that."

"I know that, but she is well now. Dr. Wright released her. He said she can drive to Georgia and you know Ramon invited her."

Colleen shook her head. The eyes she turned to her husband glistened with tears and abject misery. "But why? Why can't she stay here?"

Feeling helpless, knowing his words wouldn't cheer his wife, Charlie said, "Mama, no one said she'll stay in Georgia as Sandy did. She may come home, she's going to visit. Why is that so bad? She's not a child you can't take care of her all her life. She wouldn't let you perhaps she's the most independent of our three children."

Shaking her head slowly, Colleen stood up, didn't answer Charlie's last question, but walked down the hall. Charlie let her go and heard the door to their room close behind the dejected woman. Charlie shook his head, too. He also stood up and went to his favorite chair by the window and sank into it. There was nothing to see outside.

Only moments later he bowed his head and on a sigh, said, "My Father in heaven, please cheer my wife. I have no idea how to comfort her, how to make her happy with her life again. It seems she isn't happy unless she has someone to care for, please fill her cup, Lord. Give her life meaning besides what she's done for her children over the years. I pray for her, Father, in Your Son's Name and for Your glory, amen." It was still in the house, but Charlie felt the ache in his heart. It felt like a living thing.

Charlie didn't need an alarm to rise as five o'clock he had done it for years. But Marcy hadn't been up at that hour since one of her courses in nursing school. Since she'd been sick she'd been sleeping until her dad and brother left the house. Sometimes, her brother got on her nerves, so she stayed out of his way. Her alarm turned on the radio. It was barely light outside and for a minute she lay under the sheet pondering why her radio was on. She turned toward the radio, which also meant she faced the window. Her mind was still foggy as she stared out at the gray of dawn there weren't any streaks of color even.

"Oh!" it finally dawned on her, as she saw the numerals. She scrambled from her bed and raced to the bathroom. "I'm leaving for Georgia today!" Her heart started to pound, only in an excitedly good way. This was definitely a good day, she'd be on her own again, no mother to fight with and she'd see her beloved older sister and see her new nephew that would be a treat!

She took a quick shower, grabbed all the things she kept in the bathroom and ran back to her bedroom. She heard the shower come on as she dressed in what she had saved out, then finished packing. She had a box, which she soon had full of her appliances. She had no reason to stay in Vansville, but if she did, she wanted everything she owned with her. This was her life, she had no obligations in Philadelphia or Vansville so she could do as she pleased or if the Lord opened up something, she'd be ready to do it. She sure hoped He'd be about it she was tired of not knowing what she was to do with her life. After all, she'd known *forever* she was supposed to be a foreign missionary! But God had zapped that faster than the trip under the patient's bed.

She opened her door at the same time as Ed. She wondered how a man could shower, shave and dress so fast. "So you're leaving me to the wolves, right?" he said, as he came to her.

Setting the box she'd brought last on top of the two suitcases just inside her door, she grinned at her brother. *Yeah, leave him to the wolves! Wouldn't that be great!* After a minute, she answered, "If you're saying that Mom's a wolf, then, yes, I'm leaving you to the wolf. I'm out of here when Daddy leaves. Mom is **not** going to stop me!"

Putting his arm around his little sister, he grinned. "Good. You know, of course, that Marg and I are engaged now, so you'll have to come back for our wedding sometime. She'll probably want you to keep the name register." He knew that would get a rise out of her. He loved to tease his little sister – she took the hook every time.

"Oh, you are such a pain! The register! I know for a fact she wants me as a bridesmaid, but I'll be back, I will, I promise." She grinned at the handsome young man, but knowing what kind of wedding Margaret wanted, she asked, "And when will that be? Have you guys set a date yet? I mean, after all, us mortals need to plan our schedules."

Ed sighed, "Sis, it's anybody's guess, especially me, why should the groom know what the bride wants? As I understand, I'm along for the ride. I find out on a need-to-know basis."

Marcy chuckled. "I guess that's how it goes when the bride wants a big, fancy church wedding at the fashionable Episcopal church on the Avenue."

Reaching for the box and pointing to the larger suitcase, he said, "Great! I'll carry the box and a suitcase down. Can you manage that little one or should I come back for it, little Sis?"

"Listen, Bro, I'm quite capable of pulling my suitcase down the stairs. The wheels don't make noise or scratches on the carpet."

"I hope that's true, because Mom may try to stop you, like she did when the movers came for Sis's piano." Ed shook his head, remembering what he'd had to do to get the piano gone. "You missed quite a show on that one."

Marcy shook her head. "I cannot understand her at all! It's like she's trying to tie those apron strings again, only tighter."

"I know. She sure has done that to you. Hurry, come on, I hear her in their bedroom, I think you want to have your stuff in your car before she comes out," Ed whispered, as he hurried down the stairs in front of Marcy with his arms full.

"You're right, I'm right behind you." She grabbed the handle of her pull-behind suitcase and rushed for the stairs. Soon the suitcase was bouncing down each step behind her.

Ed reached the bottom and made the turn with Marcy on his heels. Colleen pulled her door open and rushed out of her room, leaving the door open behind her. Ed with his arms full moved on, down the hall and Marcy tried to follow, but Colleen rushed up behind her, grabbed the handle on top of the suitcase and held on, whirling Marcy around.

Marcy glanced down at her suitcase, then back at her mom. "Mom, what are you doing?"

Fiercely, Colleen exclaimed, "You. May. Not. Go!"

Marcy continued to look at her mom, but she slowly pushed the pull-handle into the suitcase, hoping her mom wouldn't notice. What she intended to do then, she wasn't sure. She kept her hand around the handle of her suitcase, but at the same time looked Colleen square in the eyes and said, "Yes, Mom, I will go. I'll eat breakfast with you all then leave when Daddy does. Have you fixed breakfast? Daddy needs to eat before he leaves for work, you know."

Colleen's determined look turned to perplexity. "No, I need to get to the kitchen to fix breakfast. Let me by."

Giving her mom a strained smile, Marcy moved her hand to beckon her mom by and said, "Of course, Mom, by all means. I'll let you by if you'll let go of my suitcase."

"But you're not going!" The words came out almost as a wail.

Hearing the tick of one of her dad's many clocks, Marcy said, "I guess we stand here and you don't get Daddy's breakfast, is that it?"

Tears welled up in Colleen's eyes. "Please, Marcy, don't go," she murmured.

"Why, Mom?"

"I... I... you need me to care for you!"

"No, Mom, I'm well now. There's nothing you need to do for me, I can take care of myself. Dr. Wright released me yesterday and said I can drive to Georgia. I do not need you to care for me any more. Please let go of my suitcase."

Colleen did wail, "Marcy, please!"

Finally, Marcy felt the suitcase come back into her possession. She pulled in a sigh of relief, glad she hadn't had to call in her dad for reinforcements. She pulled the suitcase to her and turned so Colleen could move by her. Of course, there had been room for her to pass all along. When her mom was three steps passed her, she pulled up the handle again and walked behind her mom, through the kitchen and on into the utility room, while Colleen stopped at the refrigerator to pull out things for breakfast. Neither of them said anything once Colleen was in front of her. Still it wasn't hard to hear Colleen sniffling as she rummaged in the refrigerator.

Ed was coming back inside and met her at the back door. He shook his head and whispered, "I can't believe what she's doing!"

Marcy also whispered, "With Sandy gone and now me, you'd be the only one left. Surely she won't try to stop your wedding!"

Ed rolled his eyes. "Don't you even think it! I put your things on the back seat, there's still room for that suitcase."

"Thanks, Ed, I appreciate your help."

Marcy was only five inches shorter than her brother, but he reached up and patted her on the head, intentionally messing her curls. Of course, that drew a put-upon sigh from his sister. "What are big brothers for after all? We're really good at helping little sisters with all their problems in life, you know." He sighed, "I'm just glad you have a car, I don't have time to drive you to the airport."

Marcy looked daggers at her brother, shaking her head to get her hair back the way it was supposed to be, after Ed messed it up. "Listen, Bro, maybe you could have gotten by with that stuff when we were kids, but we're not now!"

Ed shrugged. "Almost had to come rescue you from Mom just now, didn't I?"

"No! I handled that job all by myself!" She almost stuck out her tongue at him, like she had done so many times as a little girl when he'd exasperated her. In fact, Ed glanced down at her mouth, perhaps expecting her to?

A few minutes later Charlie, Marcy and Ed heard plates hit the table. The noise was the only sound in the kitchen. Another sound was repeated three times then the refrigerator door slammed. Colleen was making much more noise getting food on the table than usual. Charlie hurried in from the living room, Marcy came through the utility room from the garage and Ed came in the back door from getting the paper.

At the table, Colleen was silent, but Charlie said the blessing over the food and said, "So, have you got everything in your car, Marcy? I heard you packing last night and here you are at breakfast this morning."

"Yes, Daddy, Ed helped me down with some things and I have everything in." She grinned at her dad. "You know I won't even have to send for a piano." A hiss came through Colleen's teeth at that remark. Marcy ignored it and said, "I found that map you had to get to Sandy's so I'm ready to go. I'll follow you out the drive."

Charlie looked out the window and said, "It looks like you'll have a good day to travel and girl...," he looked at her with love in his eyes, "...be sure you follow doctor's orders and take two days to get there."

"I will, Daddy. I'll take good rest breaks, too. I promise. I don't want a relapse so soon after he has released me."

"No, we surely don't want that!"

Charlie set his fork down, drained his coffee cup and set it down, looked at the clock and said, as he spread his hands, one toward Colleen, the other reached for Marcy. "Shall we pray?"

Colleen reluctantly set her hand in Charlie's while Marcy clasped his hand tightly then reached for her brother's. "Yes, please, Daddy," Marcy said.

Charlie watched until Colleen finally reached for Ed's hand. He'd placed it on the table immediately, but Colleen seemed very reluctant to accept it. Finally, Charlie said, "My Father in heaven, we thank You for another day that You have given us breath. We have so many things to thank You for, we could list them forever, but we do thank You for a beautiful day for Marcy to leave on her trip. We pray that You will give her a good trip, keep her safe in every way and may she arrive at her sister's home in good time tomorrow. Bless us as we stay here give her mama peace to let her daughter go. Bless Ed in his endeavors and myself as I leave for work. We pray for this day and thank You for all Your abundant blessings, amen."

"Amen," Marcy murmured.

Charlie let go of Colleen's hand, but raised Marcy to her feet. His eyes moist as he put his hands on her shoulders and leaned down to kiss her. After his usual peck on her cheek, he said, "Be safe, my dear and drive carefully. We will see you when we see you, Marcy. Call when you arrive, please?"

"I'll call, Daddy." Her eyes also moist as she stood on tiptoe to kiss him. "Thanks for everything. You're a great dad I appreciate all you've done for me. Have a good day at work."

Charlie picked up his lunch pail, it was very light so he opened it to find it empty. "Mama, no lunch today?"

She glared at her husband. "You're letting her go!"

He smiled at his wife, but anyone that knew him could tell that the smile didn't reach his eyes. He closed the box, then turned to his wife again and said, "I see. You have a good day, too. I'll see you this afternoon, Mama."

He set the lunchbox on the counter and left the kitchen, through the utility room and out the back door without looking back. Colleen stared after him, her mouth hanging open. It was the first time she could remember he hadn't kissed her as he left. She snapped her mouth closed and looked at her two children. The glare left her eyes instantly as she looked at them. Ed stood behind Marcy, as if to walk her out the door. Charlie's departure seemed to take all the fight out of Colleen she stood beside her chair, tears flowing from her eyes. Silently she shook her head.

Marcy came to her and put her arms around her mom. "I'm leaving, Mom. I'll see you." She leaned forward and kissed her mom on the cheek, but Colleen didn't move or speak, only accepted the kiss. Marcy nearly cried, it felt like she was kissing a wet fish, but she let her hands drop and took a step back.

Ed saw what had happened, he was disgusted with his mom and decided that enough was enough, so he said angrily, "Mom, you're doing to Marcy exactly what you did to Sandy! You wouldn't kiss Sandy goodbye, you wouldn't hug her. You didn't even wave to her. That's how you've been every time! It makes me totally disgusted ! Is that how Marcy'll remember you?"

"But I don't want her to go!" Colleen wailed.

"She is, Mom. You'll let her go without a kiss or hug?" He looked a long time at his mom and finally said, "Mom, I'm disgusted with you! You act like a child yourself!"

Finally, it seemed Ed's words registered, Marcy was indeed leaving. Colleen pulled in a deep breath, pulled the edge of her apron to her eyes and wiped the tears from her face. She let it drop and put her arms around her youngest. "Marcy, I love you so much. I can't bear the thought of you going so far away since you've been so sick."

Marcy snuggled into her mom's arms, then tipped her head back and kissed her cheek. After the kiss, she said, "Mom, you know Sandy's phone number, call any time. She'll be glad to talk and so will I. Fix Daddy a good supper, since he had no lunch. I'll see you sometime."

"Oh, Marcy," was all Colleen could say. Her hands dropped from around her daughter and picked up the end of her apron. Instantly, she was wringing it in her hands.

Marcy tried to ignore Colleen's actions. "Bye, guys, have a good day!" she exclaimed and escaped out the kitchen door.

Finally, Marcy was in her car, when she turned the key it started right up. Marcy was glad it hadn't been driven since she'd gotten sick. Quickly, she backed it from her spot in the garage and turned around before heading for the street. It was still very early, the sun hadn't moved high enough to shine over the house, but Marcy felt both happiness and sadness. She was on her own, but her mom was very unhappy. Ed had herded his mom to the back porch, while Marcy left the garage. Tears were streaming down Colleen's face again, but she stood in Ed's arm and waved, while he grinned and waved his little sister out of sight. He didn't try to force Colleen down the incline.

When Marcy reached the street, she had to stop for another car, but she pulled in a long breath then let it out. She felt like raising her fist in the air in triumph. "Finally, I'm on my own! Thank You, Lord!" she murmured. She looked back up the driveway. Ed had brought Colleen down the ramp, so Marcy waved. "Sandy, here I come! It's good to be alive!" She drove to the gas station on the Avenue to fill up her tank.

"Miss! You're driving!" the older man exclaimed.

"Yes! Can you believe it? The doctor finally released me and said I can."

"You're going someplace?"

"Yes! All the way to Georgia to see Sis."

"Ah, give her my regards."

"I will thanks and you have a good day."

"Oh, it's a beautiful day!"

Friday at four, the office door opened and Sandy was there with Jon on her lap. A wide grin in a darkly tanned face greeted her and two arms went wide then engulfed her. "Darling, you are such a sight for sore eyes. I love you so much, it kills me to leave you, especially now."

"We did fine, Honey, again."

"I know, but I miss you and Jon so very much out there." Ramon looked out the window close to the desk and let out a sigh, "You know how nasty it was yesterday, we were drenched, but no one complained, thank goodness."

Sandy's eyes sparkled, as Ramon continued to hold her. Since becoming Ramon's wife, she'd learned that a peck on the cheek was not how he wanted a kiss, so she gave him a good kiss and said, "I'm glad of that. It was nasty yesterday. I remember what Nancy's told me about that man on her first hike. Honey, remember that invitation you gave out back in February?"

Ramon moved to stand, keeping his hands on Sandy's shoulders, but he scowled and said, "An invitation I gave out in February?"

"Yes! Marcy's finally been released and she's coming down. She left early this morning, she'll be here tomorrow."

"Ah, now I remember! You'll have someone here when I can't be. That'll be great!"

Exasperated, Sandy said, "That wasn't what I was thinking, but I'm glad she's coming."

Chuckling, as they made their way from the office, Ramon said, "Let's see, someone new in town…. Who have you been thinking about for her?"

"Honey," Sandy chided. "This is my sister, the one who was a no-nonsense nursing student, who had her eyes on one goal, being a foreign missionary nurse."

"I know, but all that's changed. Doctor won't let her back for nursing school and he put a squelch on the foreign soil, too."

Sandy chuckled. "We'll have to see what happens. If you don't remember, Marcy Bernard is one determined young woman."

Sandy headed for their bedroom suite and Ramon followed her. He always took a shower when he came home, but Sandy wanted to be close to him every minute he was with her. Before Ramon stepped into the warm spray of the shower, he continued his thought, by saying, "How about Brad's grandson at the hardware store?"

Sandy shook her head. "Isabel says he's never darkened the door of the church since he's been in town. He sleeps in every Sunday morning."

Remembering Roger, Ramon chuckled and peeked around the shower curtain. "I guess he's your next project, then."

Sandy laughed loudly enough that Ramon could hear it in the shower. "Honey, you are something else! I hardly know the fellow and he has no reason to come here and except for gas I hardly ever go there. He's not your friend, several years younger than you and he doesn't need anything from me. It'll be a long shot to hound him like I did Roger."

Above the spray, he said, "We'll think of something. Maybe sic Marcy on him."

"Oh, my! Now that would be something!"

Happy to be home again with his little family, Ramon started whistling in the shower. Sandy smiled. Ramon did know how to whistle. He had changed so much since she'd come as his receptionist two years ago. He was a wonderful Christian man and a loving and attentive husband. She looked down at the sleeping baby, yes, he was a great daddy. The tune he was whistling was *Amazing Grace*. Yes, everything about their lives was amazing and only by the grace of God. She started singing the words to Ramon's whistled accompaniment.

Their latest customer walked out the door with a fresh cup of coffee. Natt had poured it for him and had taken his donation. Brad sat behind the cash register with his eyes closed, he had done the transaction for the man's hardware goods, but the man had waited for his coffee before walking out. Natt sat down in one of the empty coffee nook chairs and sighed, then looked out the big window at the perfect day outside. Here it was summer, the sun was beautiful and he was cooped up inside!

"What's the matter, Son," Brad asked. "Ya sound a bit down. Achally, it's a good day."

Still looking outside, Natt said, "Grandad, it's a beautiful day. If I'd kept on at school I'd be out for summer vacation and have a job where I'd be outside most of the time. I love being outside, it doesn't matter if I'm doing construction or being a life guard, it's all outside."

Brad chuckled, took a long swig of his coffee, looked over the counter at his grandson and said, "Yeah, gettin' a deep tan someplace so's the girls would look gaga at ya. I know." Brad chuckled again. "Been there, done that."

Still looking out the window, Natt said, "Grandad, it's not so much the deep tan or the girls so much as just being outdoors. I miss that a lot."

"Hmmm, had a thought. In a couple weeks my twin nephews is comin' for a visit. One's a career officer in some military branch and the other's been divorced a couple years, anyways, they're both single. I think your gramma said one of 'em said they wanna to go on a hike of a couple days and the other wants to visit. If that's so, maybe DeLord'll take ya both on a three day hike and the other one'll mind the store."

Natt's voice was noticeably more chipper, as he said, "Grandad, that sounds super! Has Gramma called about that hike yet?"

Brad looked up at the big clock that had been on the wall in the same place so long that the paint around it had faded. He pulled himself up from the chair, using the counter. "Seems it's my lunch time, I'll go ask her and if she ain't, I'll build a fire under her. We'll have you a long weekend out a this here store if it's the last thing we do. Now get off that duff a yours, here comes that DeLord fella hisself for gas, nope, it be Sandy in her van. Go be friendly, Son, I'll see ya after my dear wife feeds me lunch."

"Yeah, Grandad, I'll see you later."

Brad walked out the back door to walk across the street to his house, but since he had no customer in the store, Natt went out the front. He was bored to death and even with air conditioning in the store, he couldn't stand being cooped up inside for one more minute on such a beautiful day. If the driver of the van was Sandy, maybe he'd get to see how she worked that thing without using her feet. He'd been curious ever since they'd met her at that trailhead back on Memorial Day when his family came and they went on a hike.

He walked out as Sandy stopped at the gas pump. She was behind the wheel and a minute after she shut off the van she reached behind her to do something that Natt couldn't see, then backed away from the wheel. He walked slowly, watching as she wheeled herself across the van in the big empty space to the side door and before he reached the back of the vehicle, he heard the big door whining open. Soon he saw the grating inside the door move and finally it stopped in a horizontal position. He was at the corner of her vehicle when she rolled out onto it.

"Hello, Mrs. DeLord," he said, giving her a broad smile. "Ever since we met you at the trail where you were painting I've been curious how you worked that van. I guess you had to have it specially made for you?"

Sandy gave the young man a broad smile, as she reached for the control on the handle of the lift. "You're Natt, right?"

"Yes, Ma'am." he said, as she lowered the lift with herself on it to the ground.

She wheeled off and Natt stepped back a bit, while she said, "Natt, I'll give you an exclusive if from now on, you'll call me Sandy."

Natt laughed. "Hey, that's no problem. I'd rather call somebody by their first name, but first time, my grandad would have my hide, you know."

Sandy chuckled. "Yeah, southern gentlemen and all that." Moving away from the van, she waved her hand toward the lift and said, "Say, while I pump my gas, get on that lift, push that button and take yourself up. Inside take a look behind the wheel and see all the gadgets I must work to make the thing so I can drive it."

"Thanks, Sandy, I'll just do that."

Natt traded places with Sandy then did as she said and rode the lift up, it was a strange sensation to enter a vehicle by being lifted from the ground to the floor. Sandy went around to the pump and started filling her tank. He ducked inside and went to the empty spot behind the wheel and made a close inspection. It was amazing what all the labeled buttons were for. Still, there was an accelerator and a brake pedal in their normal place near the floor. He guessed the manufacturer had made this van especially for a paraplegic, but a normal person without a handicap could drive it, too. It made sense, but he'd never seen such a vehicle. He wondered if the other passenger seat could be removed, if that was for a normal driver. He looked around the rest of the van, instead of a seat behind the driver there was a wide open space so the wheelchair could be turned around. There was one seat in front of the cargo area.

Sandy finished pumping her gas, so Natt let himself down. He walked around the back and Sandy had her hand out with money. Natt absently took the money, but he said, "Sandy, I saw all the gadgets, but the first time I saw this van a man with perfectly good legs drove it."

"Yes, that's my husband, Ramon. You see, when he drives it we wave our magic wand and a seat appears and he sits to drive."

Natt's eyes sparkled as he laughed. "Sandy, I needed that, I've been in that store all summer and I'm about to go stir crazy. I guess there are things you must change for him to drive, but the first time, there by the trail, I couldn't imagine. I didn't know you or realize you were paralyzed and to see that empty spot where you always see a driver's seat gave me a jolt."

Sandy laughed. "I guess it would give you a jolt." Sandy had given Natt his money, but she felt a tiny nudge, since the young man didn't rush off. She always took those nudges as the Lord telling her to speak for Him, she would take that nudge. "Say," she said, "you live in one of Isabel's cabins, right?"

Nodding, he said, "Yes, I do, in number two. Believe me, it suit's me just fine and she keeps it clean as a whistle."

Sandy nodded. "When I moved here at first, that's where I lived, in her first cabin. She's a great lady and I love her. Do you eat your meals there or with your grandparents?"

Natt chuckled. "No, I've heard Grandad say a few times that I'd eat them out of house and home if I ate with them. I pretty much keep Alex up to date on his frozen dinner supply."

Sandy's face lit up, as she said, "Kind of how my husband used to do. Ramon's home for a long weekend, why don't you come for dinner on Sunday. Of course, we go to church in Blairsville, so it couldn't be until one o'clock, but would you?"

Looking at the lady in the wheelchair, knowing she was handicapped and remembering that she had a baby only a few months old, sleeping on the back seat in the van, he said, "Really? You're inviting me to a meal? Are you sure it's me you want? I mean, I'm a guy who doesn't get home cooked meals very often, you know." His grin spread. "Remember, I just told you Grandad thinks I'd eat them out of house and home."

Sandy smiled Natt had never seen someone so lovely as this lady when she smiled. "Listen, Natt, if it's because I'm in this chair, don't you think a thing about it. I've been in this thing all my life. It doesn't keep my hands from making the best spaghetti sauce in Vansville. You ask anybody, you'll see."

Natt nodded. "If that's so, count me in! Can I bring some Italian bread?"

"Sure, if you want. After dessert, you can plan to stay the afternoon and be in on my practicing. I'm giving a concert in Roger's church in a week."

"Great! I can't wait!"

"Okay, it's a date!"

Sandy took herself to the lift, did the routine and fastened herself down behind the wheel, while Natt moved slowly back to the store, counting the money that Sandy had given him for the gas. He pulled in a long breath not that it didn't have a few fumes from Sandy's exhaust, but now there was no reason to stay outside. No customers had come while he talked with Sandy the day was so beautiful he wished he could stay outside for the rest of the day. He looked at his watch, his grandad should be back from his lunch, which would make it time for his. He sighed; too bad he only had a half hour. Did the owner of the only hardware store in town ever play hooky? As far as he knew, his grandad didn't have a sign that said the store was closed because the owner was hiking in the hills.

He took Sandy's money in, the door closed behind him and the air conditioning cooled his skin. As he reached the cash register, Brad walked in the back door. As he came forward, the cash drawer opened and Natt sorted out the bills into their proper places then pushed the drawer shut. Brad walked slowly toward the front and said, "I talked to your gramma over lunch." He sighed, "'Course she hadn't called that hiking service, but she did while I was home. Their answering machine picked up so she left a message. We don't know any more'n we did, but now that we made that call I'm sure they'll call us back. Surely, they'd want more business any time they can get it."

Natt slumped into his favorite chair in the coffee drinker's nook and sighed, "Grandad, I talked with Sandy while she pumped her gas. She invited me to have dinner on Sunday at one. She says they go to church in Blairsville, but to come after that." He grinned at the old man. "I told her I'd seen her husband drive that van in for gas a while ago. All she did was grin and say they waved their magic wand and a seat appears for him to drive."

Brad chuckled. "Reminds me when I first met her. I was grouchy back then." He raised his eyebrows at the smirk on his grandson's face. "Listen here! Now I ain't like that now! You hear me, young fella?" Natt didn't answer, but pulled his hand across his face to hide his smile. Brad could be downright ornery if he wanted.

The old man huffed, "Anyways, she'd just moved to town, I didn't know her. She was single back then and drove that van in and bought gas, then she come in here and after she paid she asked me if she could put some advertisement in my winda up front there. I shrugged and said 'sure'." He shrugged and continued, "I 'spected her to give me this paper to tack up, or tape to the winda or sompin, but it was a little picture, said she was givin' piana lessons."

Natt scowled. "Piano *lessons*?"

"Yeah, gave me a start. Asked her how she did that. She said it was easy and moved her fingers back and forth, like she had 'em on a keyboard, you know?"

Natt chuckled. "So you never found out?"

"Yeah, I did, it was about Labor Day sometime, but Roger and Ramon got up a concert over there in his church. Ramon was the MC, always is, I guess she makes sure that he is. Achally, she's got some little black pouch she rigs up to the piana somehow. She plays better'n any piana player I ever did hear."

"She said I can stay the afternoon and listen to her practice, I guess she'll give another concert over there soon."

"Super! Gotta get there early, they never have 'nough chairs for one a her concerts. She is one spectacular lady!"

Natt stood up after all, it was time for his lunch. "Maybe I can ask about going on a hike while I'm there on Sunday."

Brad nodded. "Yeah, you might. Can't hurt nothin' ta try."

"Well, Grandad, I'm out of here for lunch! I'll see you… sometime," Natt said, with a smirk, "it's a great day, you know."

"Umm hum, none of that, boy!"

However, Brad chuckled as he watched Natt make his way out the front door. He was glad for the young man, he spruced up his life. So, his grandson had thought he was a grouch back a few months. Yes, he probably was. Yeah, he'd been a grouch for most of his married life, but now he loved the Lord and it made all the difference.

Marcy figured she'd be in lower Delaware when she should stop for the night. She planned to tackle the Chesapeake Bay Bridge and Tunnel in the morning. Maybe she could get some good pictures, if it was a nice day. She'd been a good girl and driven only two hundred miles before taking a pit stop. She'd always stopped at a convenience store and looked around the store, giving herself twenty minutes before she sat behind the wheel again and set off. She sighed, why was she being such a good girl? Nobody was with her, nobody would check on her. She'd even gotten a good sandwich rather than a few packages of snacks and lemonade instead of a soft drink. One of these days she was really going to splurge! After all, she wasn't in nursing school any more, so she could forget about those nutrition classes. Right? She sighed she really wanted to be totally well. However, at this point, according to Dr. Wright, only a miracle could heal her heart totally, there was too much scar tissue for her heart to be like it was before February. She knew her dad had prayed for a miracle, but so far, it hadn't come. She sighed, God was in control she must rest on that.

She drove a few more miles and the sign for the bridge/tunnel loomed ahead, so she looked for a sign for a motel that had a vacancy sign. Only a few minutes later she found one and pulled in. She pulled under the overhang, took her purse and walked in. She saw that on one side was a restaurant that boasted it was open for all three meals, which was good, that sandwich had been a while ago. However, the smells coming from that place made her stomach growl. She was glad she was still in the empty hallway, her stomach embarrassed her.

She pressed her hand on her stomach then turned in the door across from the restaurant and some young man, who looked like he should be a life guard instead of a hotel manager, stood up immediately behind the desk. He stood up, wa-a-a-a-y up! Marcy wondered briefly if she'd have a crick in her neck when she finally got her key.

NINE

Giving her a smile like she'd only seen on a toothpaste commercial, the motel manager said, "Yes, Ma'am, you looking for a good bed for the night?"

"Yes, I am, do you have such a thing?"

"Yes, Ma'am, one bed or two?"

"Umm, I'm sure one is quite sufficient." She wasn't about to tell him she was alone—what single woman wanted to broadcast she was alone? Surely he could look out his window and see that her car was empty, now that she was inside.

He turned and leaned over his computer, then clicked his mouse and skimmed down the page, then picked up a card and swiped it through a machine. As he handed her the key card, he smiled again and said, "Ma'am, I have just the room for you. All our rooms have inside entrances, so once you go through this door into the motel itself, turn to your left and it's down the hall two doors. Our restaurant is across over there and it opens at six o'clock and stays open until ten. We do have a pool at the back of the motel for patrons' use. Since your room is on the back, the patio door leads right out to it. I hope you enjoy your stay."

Marcy smiled at the young man. "I'm sure I will thank you."

The young man watched her silently as she went out the door into the hallway. Her smile changed everything about her. As she reached the parking lot and the evening sun caught her hair, it sparkled and put beautiful shadows in the dark curls. She was one spectacular young woman.

Too bad she was only here for one night. There weren't many women who came through these parts, by themselves, who were that beautiful.

She left the office and went back to her car she'd park it then bring in her suitcase before she went for supper, then she could stay in her room until the morning. She'd been good today, but she could feel her strength draining slowly away. Swimming in a motel pool didn't appeal to her besides, if she got her swimsuit wet it'd probably get things in her suitcase musty before she'd get a chance to hang it out. She'd never been a great fan of swimming pools, not with all those chemicals in the water. If there was a lake with a beach and a swimming dock, well, that was a different story. In a lake she could swim for hours and really enjoy it. Or the ocean… oh, yes, now the ocean was the best swimming in the world!

She found a parking space that was close to the main door into the motel, but wasn't a handicapped spot, took her small suitcase and went back inside. Marcy had always been so focused on her goal in life she never really examined herself in the mirror. Sandy had always been so beautiful, not just her face, but her personality, that people flocked around her. Ed was a personable person, too. He'd never lacked for friends and had been a class officer every year since junior high school. Marcy, as the youngest, felt like she was always playing catch up to them both, yes, she'd had friends, she'd even brought several home a few times, but they were girlfriends. However, when she came back inside with her pull-behind suitcase, the young man from the office stood propped against the doorframe grinning at her.

Much to her surprise, he said, "Hi, wondered if I could interest you in supper with me?" He nodded at her suitcase. "As soon as you get that to your room, of course."

Marcy knew no one had followed her inside, but she almost turned around to see who the man could be speaking to. She looked at him, her eyes wide. "You're asking me?" Her last word almost came out in a squeak.

"Yeah, is someone with you?"

"Umm, no. My suitcase, um, I need to take it to my room," she said, a bit flustered.

"Fine, I have an hour. Have supper with me?"

Marcy cleared her throat. "Well, um, okay, I'll hurry."

"Great! Thanks!"

Her heart beating double time in her chest, Marcy tried for a smile and just a raising of one side of her mouth occurred, but it would have to do. Quickly, she went passed the man and through the doorway made the turn down the hall to the room with the number written on her keycard holder. She felt flustered and tried to put the card in wrong, but just in time slipped it in the right way and the little green light came on. She opened the door and pulled the suitcase in behind her. She flipped the switch right inside the door and the light came on over the mirror. A glaring, bright light to show her all her faults. At least there were no black smudges under her eyes any more. That was a plus.

She set the suitcase up, let go of the handle and stared at herself in the mirror. Her hair was a bit messy from her travels all day, since she'd had the window down a few times when she was in the hills and mountains, but it did wave just a little. It wasn't a beautiful, soft blond like Sandy's, but your run of the mill dark brown. Her eyes were the normal brown, too, not blue like Sandy's. One thing she was glad of, she didn't have to use makeup to cover the smudges under her eyes that had been there for so long since she got sick. She was average and ordinary, what could a handsome life-guard-type man want to eat supper with her?

She shrugged, this wasn't a date, he hadn't asked her to go someplace with him. Besides, she hadn't been on a date since… since she couldn't remember when… since her senior year in high school, maybe. Yeah, back then she'd been shocked when some guy had asked her to go with him to some sport event their school was in. She couldn't even remember what the event was or remember the guy's name, for that matter.

After her eyes were fully adjusted to the bright light, she dropped her purse on the counter, found a wash cloth, wet it and washed her face she never used makeup, so why start now? Besides, she didn't have any. However, she scrubbed her face a bit harder than she normally did, maybe it'd put a bit more color into her cheeks. She found her comb and tried her best to pull the rats from her hair. When she had most of them out, she shrugged, "That'll have to do. What you see is what you get. I never pretended to be some raving beauty."

She straightened her top and looked back into the mirror. Satisfied, she picked up her purse again, and the keycard, left the light on for later and pulled the door closed behind her. All the way back to the front she wondered what on earth the young man could see in her. When she turned the corner into the office area, toward the restaurant the young man stood leaning against the door frame of the office waiting for her. He levered himself away and gave her his megawatt grin. Again this time, she thought he looked like a beach bum, all that was missing was the swimsuit and a surfboard.

Taking a step toward her, he asked, "So are you as hungry as me?"

Still a bit flustered, she could feel the warmth creeping up her neck, as she said, "I don't know, I am pretty hungry. Say, I think I'm at a disadvantage here. You know my name, you read it on my credit card, but I don't know yours."

The young man reached for the door into the restaurant. As he held it for her, he grinned and said, "Sorry about that. I'm Shelton. Thanks for accepting my offer of supper. I eat here all the time, but it's usually alone. You came at just the right time." Ah, so it wasn't because it was her and her great beauty, she was just a convenience.

He held a chair for her then took the seat opposite. Reaching for her napkin, Marcy spread it over her lap and said, "I'm pleased to accept, Shelton, thanks. Are you here full time?"

"Yeah, Dad and I own this place." The young man chuckled and signaled the waitress, who came bringing two glasses of water. "Actually, he has the money invested and I do most of the work. I feel like I'm here twenty-four seven. Some of it's okay, some, it's a bit much. He's trying to get me ready to take it over so he can retire. I'm trying really hard not to learn too fast, it's a daunting thought to take over such a big operation." He shook his head. "When you're on the inside, you see so much that you don't know and it seems each day there's more to find out."

Marcy nodded. "I can believe that."

The waitress came back and took their order. Shelton ordered iced tea, but Marcy held up her water glass. Even though she dearly loved iced tea, probably it would have caffeine and she couldn't have that ever again. When the waitress brought Shelton's tea, they were making small talk until she brought their steaming plates back and set them down. Everything on the plates looked and smelled very good.

Marcy looked at the young man as he picked up his fork and said, "Excuse me, Shelton, do you say grace?"

"Umm, no, but go ahead, if you want."

"Thanks," she said and smiled at the uncomfortable young man. "Dear Lord, thanks for this food we're about to eat. Bless those who have prepared it and thank You so much for bringing me safely this far. I pray for a restful sleep tonight and a good day tomorrow for the rest of my trip, in Jesus' Name, amen."

When she raised her head, Shelton waved his hand in front of him and said, "You do that all the time? Even in a public place like this?"

Marcy nodded and answered immediately, "Yes, I do. After all, God's the One who gives us life and health and the ability to eat. He's given us so much, we have no way of thanking Him enough, so it's the least I can do to thank Him for it all. I was really very sick for a long time it's good to be well again, so I thank God."

"I suppose."

Shelton picked up his fork and began to eat. Marcy did the same, but it seemed that someone had turned the air conditioning down quite a bit in the room. They ate their meal with very little conversation. Marcy had never been one to talk much with people she didn't know and she really had nothing in common with Shelton. Of course, she would be leaving in the morning, so what was the point? She had entertained asking him more about his work here at the motel. She'd never met someone who owned or worked in one. From what he said, there were many things he did she wouldn't know about. However, Shelton continued to shovel his food into his mouth. Now that she had prayed, he seemed anxious to be done with his meal. She swallowed a sigh she wasn't at home living with Christians now.

As she wiped her mouth from cleaning her plate, she said, "Mmm, be sure to tell the chef that his meatloaf was excellent! I enjoyed everything."

"Thanks, I'll tell him."

After a refill of tea, Shelton looked at his watch, wiped his mouth and said, "I guess duty calls, I'm back at the desk until we're full or it's time to close. Thanks for sharing a table with me, Marcy. I've got the tab on this, so don't worry about it. Enjoy the rest of your dessert and have a safe trip tomorrow."

Marcy picked up her napkin and wiped her mouth, wondering if she'd forgotten to wipe a smudge of the cheesecake from her lip, or maybe she should have taken a shower and changed clothes instead of just washing her face, but she shrugged inwardly, smiled and said, "Thanks so much, Shelton, it was nice to have company for dinner. I guess Friday is a busy night for a motel owner. Thanks, though."

Standing behind his chair he absently pushed the chair under the table and said, "Sure, no problem. Hey, have a good trip tomorrow. I'm off on Saturdays, so I definitely won't see you, so have a good one."

Marcy smiled again. "Thanks."

Now that she was alone, Marcy didn't want to stay in the restaurant, so she gulped down her last mouthful of ice water and wiped her mouth. Shelton hadn't left a tip, perhaps she'd better. She opened her wallet and pulled out a bill, then set it beside her dessert plate. She pulled her purse from the back of her chair, slung it over her shoulder and hurried from the restaurant. As she went by the office, she noticed that Shelton had another customer, so she didn't bother him, but went on to her room. She had to admit, even if it was only to herself; that she was tired. She'd gotten up several hours before she usually did and hadn't had a nap after lunch as she had been having for many months. She sighed as she closed her door behind her. Even before putting her purse down, she turned the deadbolt on the door. When she'd been in school she'd heard about women alone who hadn't.

She walked passed the bathroom into the place where the large bed was. Remembering the single size daybed she'd slept on downstairs at home for so long, then the full size bed in her room upstairs, she looked at the queen size bed and wondered how she would keep from getting pulled into Alice's rabbit hole. She put her suitcase on the rack, then opened it and pulled out her soft nightshirt. She opened the door to the tiny bathroom and breathed out a sigh, there was a nice big tub and as she looked more closely, she realized it had jets on the sides she could relax and let the warm water give her a massage. She would indulge.

During a long soak in the bathtub, her mind turned to what would become of her. Dr. Wright had told her nursing school was out and also the foreign mission field, the two things she had always planned on. Today, she had left home for Vansville because Ramon had invited her, but more than that, because her mom was smothering her. She'd prayed for guidance, ever since she'd come home from the hospital for what to do with her life, but nothing seemed to be coming of her prayers. How could she know what to do? The motor shut off on the jets, so she let out the cooling water and dried off, pulled on her comfortable nightshirt and went to the huge bed. She was sure she'd get lost in it.

It was still light out, after all, summer had just begun, but she hadn't brought any of the novels she'd read so many of during her many hours in bed. Of course, a motel room never had any reading material except a Gideon Bible. As she went by her suitcase, she pulled her own well used Bible from her suitcase and went to the large chair by the patio door. She hadn't taken time for devotions this morning, she'd read her Bible for a while before she crawled in bed. She read until there was not enough natural light outside to read by, then spent several minutes praying. It felt good to spend time with her Lord.

When she stood up from the chair she found the pull for the drape across the patio door. As she studied things a little, she realized there was one pull for the sheers and another for the dark drapes, so she pulled them both. She put her Bible back in her suitcase then went to inspect the bed. Even though it was summer, she was glad to find a light weight blanket made into the bed covering. She liked that.

After making sure the door was secure, she climbed onto the bed and snuggled under the cover. In all the time she'd been on bedrest she found that having the room cool and a blanket over her helped her sleep. Even now that she was better and not in bed all the time, she still slept that way. The curtain over the patio door wasn't tight, but let a little bit of light come in around the edges. It would be easier if she needed to get up during the night. She let a sigh escape and drifted off to sleep. Tomorrow was a new day, the first day of the rest of her life. She would use it as God let her. She was excited to see Sandy, Ramon and of course, tiny Jon.

It was still early Friday, the only day they kept the store open until eight o'clock. Natt sat in a chair in the coffee drinker's nook and tipped it back on two legs. Since there weren't any customers at the moment, he felt it was okay to ask a question he'd wondered about for a long time. Natt felt he had a really good relationship with his grandad, so he would ask.

"Grandad, didn't you used to keep the store open on Sundays? I'm not complaining, you know, I just wondered why you close it now."

Brad sat several feet away in his favorite chair behind the counter, ready for all the many customers to check out. He let out a sigh and took another swallow of coffee, before he said, "I sure did, Son. I shore did." Natt sighed, it was like pulling teeth to get Grandad to tell a story.

Taking another swallow from his cup and looking longingly out the window, Natt noticed that even though it was late afternoon, the sky was still a deep blue, with only a few wisps of puffy, white clouds. The sun was in a position that it sent a bright beam from one of the gas pumps into his eye, so bright he had to look away.

Natt said, "Not that I'm complaining, Grandad, since I'm glad for a day off each week, still, I can't imagine being in this place every day but five or six all year! Why did you decide to close on Sundays, when you'd had it open seven days a week for so long? You used to think it was important to have it open for the gas pumps."

Brad let out a sigh and took a swallow, draining his cup, before he said, "It's a bit of a story. You sure you wanna hear it?" Brad looked into the empty cup, perhaps hoping for a reprieve. Realizing that this was going to be a long discussion, Natt stood up and came for his grandad's coffee mug. Brad handed it over eagerly.

On his way back to the urn in the nook, Natt said, "Sure, why not? We don't have a customer now." He grinned at the older man. "Grandad, it can't hurt to tell me, you know."

"Well, you never know about that." He reached for the mug when Natt brought it back and took a swallow, even though it had come straight from the urn. The liquid had to be scalding, but no matter… maybe his grandad had an iron mouth and throat. After he swallowed, Brad let out a sigh, "Son, it's like this." Brad closed his eyes, leaning his head back against the top rail of the chair, settling in for a story, then took another swallow before setting his mug close by on the counter. "Like I say, it's like this. That Roger fella, when he come here wasn't much of a preacher."

"What do you mean? A preacher not a preacher?" Natt asked, totally perplexed and besides, what did that have to do with having the store open on Sundays?

Brad picked up his mug again, took a swallow, held the mug on his belly, then raised it to his lips, before he said, "Well, see, that praise team he had blasted ya out even with them doors closed and mine too. Everbody who come here for gas or whatever complained every Sunday." Brad nodded to the back of the store. "In fact, I kep watch on the clock and when it got 'bout that time, I'd skedaddle to the back. Joyce, she'd go, but me, I kep' the store. Even back thar that didn't help much, it was loud! They done that 'bout thirty minutes or so. When they'd get done doin' their thing, he'd get up and read outta some book for a bit then they'd blast ya out again. They took up the whole hour, nearly. Your gramma went ever Sunday real faithful, but she always complained about the loud racket, but she'd tell me about his readin's ever Sunday."

"That doesn't happen any more, Grandad. I'm in my cabin, it's only a couple blocks from the church and I usually sleep until after they get done and church lets out."

Nodding, Brad took another swallow of coffee and said, "No, it sure don't and Ms. Sandy had a lot to do with that."

That statement perplexed Natt. Shaking his head, Natt looked at Brad, hoping the old man wasn't nodding off and telling something crazy in his sleep. Seeing that he wasn't asleep didn't even have his eyes closed, he asked, "Grandad, she doesn't go to church there. It can't be she talked him into her playing. What do you mean?" *Grandad, you're not making sense,* he wanted to add.

Taking another long swig from his mug and resting it back on his belly, he slowly shook his head and said, "No, she's alays gone to church with Ms Isabel, but see, Ramon and Roger, they be good friends and got on her and set up this concert real soon after she came. You know that church building was the biggest place in town back then, so that's why they had the concert there. It was a right good concert, too, believe me."

Natt had all he could do to keep his mouth shut. How could this story about Sandy's concert have anything to do with Brad closing the store on Sundays? Rather than lean on the counter, Natt went back to his chair in the coffee nook and sat down. Maybe he didn't really want to know... Or maybe the old man was having another stroke. No he wouldn't think like that, Grandad was just telling a story.

However, Brad didn't know Natt's thoughts, so he took another swig and continued, "Them two guys are like peas in a pod, and bein's it was his church, ever time he came to see her for somethin' for a concert she'd be on him like fleas on a dog. He'd come over for sompin or they'd invite him for dinner. Anyhow, I heard one time he be over she played '*The Old Rugged Cross*' and he went outta ther house 'bout screamin'. He left their place on two wheels with that Jeep of his an' hightailed it back to his house. That time it was near Thanksgivin' over a year ago. Believe it or not, he got converted and did a sermon for Thanksgivin' instead of a talk." Brad shook his head, took another sip of coffee and said, "It shore was sompin, it shore was!"

Natt was scowling, then took a sip of his own cool coffee, before he said, "Grandad, the preacher got converted? Surely you can't mean that! A preacher's a preacher, isn't he? How does a preacher get converted?"

Setting his empty mug on the counter next to the cash register, he nodded emphatically, "Oh, yeah, somethin' happened, he ain't been the same man since! Sandy played that Thanksgivin' service and he preached a good message, I was there and heard it, but come Sunday, he calmed that music team right down, cut the time in half when they played and he preached some good stuff then, too. That's what Joyce said and I heard it from a bunch of others, too. It was no readin' that's for absolute shore!"

Natt was trying very hard not to get frustrated with the long story. "Okay, so how's that relate to you closing the store, Grandad?"

Brad sighed this was the part he wasn't too proud of. "Son, yur like a dog with a bone! Ya don't leave nothin' alone!"

Natt left his chair in the nook filled his cup and came to the counter. He leaned back on the counter, then leaned over and patted his grandad's shoulder. Giving him a grin, he said, "That's the journalist in me, Grandad. Come on, it doesn't hurt much. Actually, you're just answering my question."

Brad picked up his cup, saw it was empty, set it back down and sighed, "You don't know how much, Son."

Natt chuckled. "Well, I gotta hear it first to know, Grandad."

Brad pulled his hand from the cup handle, folded his hands across his middle, took a deep breath and said, "Well, I alays close on Thanksgivin' I have for years, ya know, 'cause y'all come up for dinner in the afternoon.

Joyce alays said it was the thing ta do, bein's it be a national holiday and all. Anyways, your gramma talked me into goin' with her that Thanksgivin' mornin' to the service they alays have, so I did. All them other years Joyce'd tell me he give a talk, somthin' 'bout Thanksgivin' but just a readin' or a talk on them pilgrims, so I figgered it wouldn't hurt none to hear a talk. So I went, sat there on the back row, ya know. Instead, seemed like he preached a sermon on stuff from the Bible and it was right at me and I didn't like it a whole lot, no, not a bit!"

"Uh huh." Natt turned away, with his grandad's mug and took it to the urn in the nook and filled it, then brought it back and handed it to the old man, who took it eagerly, but with the steam coming up, he only blew across the top. "Here you go, Grandad, your cup's full."

Brad took a long swig from his mug then set it aside. Rather reluctantly, Brad said, "Well, see, it was like this. Raylyn and Heidi was there for the first time. I hadn't seen her in years I don't think I ever saw her little one till that day, neither." Natt almost sighed out loud, here was another rabbit trail!

"Anyways, Roger, he took a shine to her right now. At first I thought it was her, got him to change, but I still didn't like him preachin', so when he had her out someplace that Friday, I did some stuff at his place, wantin' to scare him and run him outta town."

Natt was shocked, his grouchy, docile grandad? He could hardly believe it. Natt folded his arms across his chest. "Grandad! I knew you used to be a bad grouch, but run a guy out of town? You? I can't believe this, come on tell me more! Your story's hard to believe! On a Friday night you did stuff?"

Brad sat forward in his chair, grabbed his mug and took another long swig, then looked hard at his grandson. "Tell me, what am I now a good grouch?"

Natt let out a puff of air then shook his head. "Grandad, you're getting off the story! By the way, what did you do?"

"Oh, stuff." He heaved a sigh and took another long swig from his mug, then deliberately set the mug on the counter, but Natt stood close by, his elbows leaning on the counter, looking at him very expectantly. There was no smile on his face and Brad knew the boy would get on him, so he said, "I went in his house."

"Yeah, go on."

Brad took another long swig and held his mug. He looked into the mug, maybe hoping it'd make it easier. "…and blowd out the pilots on his stove then turned 'em burners all on and started his bath tub on a fast drip and closed the drain." He let out another long sigh, before he said, "Gave his dog somethin', cut his phone line and messed up his cow and chicken feed and, um, guess I broke a winda, too." Looking sheepish, he added, "Umm, ya know, stuff."

Agitated, Natt took a few steps around the counter and came back. "Grandad! He didn't get you arrested for all that?" Natt gasped, looking at the old man as if he had sprouted horns. This was not the old grandad he'd known his whole life! "Man, alive! You went in his house and did all that? And… and well, he didn't come back while you were there? Man alive! This is unbelievable! The dog? You hurt his dog?"

"I put a note on his desk at the church, too," Brad mumbled into his chest and wouldn't look at his grandson.

Natt was shaking his head. "Wow! I can't believe you're still on the outside! In Atlanta someone found out doing that much stuff, the guy'd get him arrested!" Natt saw that Brad's coffee mug was empty again, so for something to do to ease his agitation, he took it back to the urn and filled it up. As he brought it back, he held it out and handed it to Brad when he was close enough. "How'd you get in all those places, Grandad? I mean, don't they lock the church? You just went to his house and… man alive I can't believe it! You of all people! You went in his house – and his church? Man!"

Brad shook his head. "Nobody much locks doors around here and Roger lives on a country road, so his house weren't locked when I went there." He shrugged. "The church, I had a key, see I was the one who give him his key, but I didn't tell him I kep a spare. See, I was purdy ticked at the guy, you know?"

Natt shook his head. "Grandad, for crying out loud! It's too hard to believe you'd do something like that! Okay, so now you're gonna tell me why you closed the store on Sunday. Surely you know what it took you were the only one in the store until I came. I know it wasn't Gramma who talked you into it."

"Boy! I swear!" He took a long swallow and put his mug on the counter. He wiped his mouth on his sleeve, before he said, "It's like this. After I done that and nothin' happened, Roger didn't even come in! 'Course I wouldn'ta tol' him it was me, but I guess mebe he didn't know it was me. I called up Alex and told him we needed a town meetin' to get the preacher out. Well, he called the meetin'. 'Course, it hadda be in that church, there weren't no bigger place in town then, but everbody came, more'n I 'spected, includin' Ms. Isabel, Ms Sandy and Ramon. Even that rich guy, Casbah came, I mean, that church buildin' was packed out! Everbody, includin' Ms Isabel and Ms Sandy went on about that boy. Instead of kickin' him outta town, they give him a raise! I dun got out voted big time! And I, um, got outta there! Acourse, he kep preachin'. Joyce said he was good, too."

Brad sighed and shook his head. "After that, my conscience hurt me so bad I closed the store the next Sunday and went to church. Seemed like the boy preached right at me again! It weren't fair, but I run down front and Roger hisself prayed with me. I confessed, he forgave me and dropped the charges. That's why the store's closed and why I go to church now."

After some thought, Natt said, "Wow! So you think I should go to church? Is that what you're telling me?"

Finishing up another mouthful of coffee, Brad nodded and said, "Yep. It done me good ever Sunday, it'll do you good, too. Didn't you say you was goin' to Ms Sandy's for dinner on Sunday? I didn't get that wrong, did I?"

"Yeah."

"Be prepared."

When Brad didn't add anything, Natt let out a long sigh and looked at his grandad to see if he would say anything more. When the old man took another swallow instead, Natt pushed away from the counter, thinking he needed a cup of coffee now. Maybe he was in for another long story. He walked back to the nook and picked up his mug. As he held it under the spigot, he asked, "Grandad, prepared for what?"

"You'll see." Brad looked up at the clock on the wall, quickly set his empty mug on the counter and said, "Hey, would you look a that! It's time fer me to go fer dinner. Joyce'll have my head if I ain't there in five minutes. I'll see ya after a bit, since it's Friday." Brad winked at his grandson, put his hands on his knees and pushed himself up, then moved faster than Natt had seen him move in a very long time toward the back door. The old man never looked back and never stopped until he was outside. Natt watched the man nearly run from the store.

To the closing back door, Natt muttered, shaking his head. "Thanks, Grandad. Be prepared for what? She's serving spaghetti and I'm taking a loaf of Italian bread, what should I be prepared for?" He took his grandad's mug to the sink and rinsed it out, turned it upside down on the drain, then filled his mug and brought it back, then took the chair Brad had emptied. His grandad could be such a conundrum when he wanted to be. Natt took a long draw on his mug, there still were no customers.

On a sigh, Natt said, "And Ramon'll be there, what should I be prepared for?" A half hour later, his grandad came back to the store through the back door just as the front door opened and a customer walked in. Natt sighed there'd be no time to ask him anything more. Friday nights were busy, since it was the only night they stayed open late. Probably knowing Natt wanted to ask some questions, Brad hustled forward toward the man who came in. Acting as if he were the savior of the world.

Natt waved to Brad as he came toward the cash register, but he turned toward the front door and said, "Howdy folks. Grandad's here, he'll help you get whatever you need. He's got a full belly and I'm on my way to fill mine. Thanks for shopping here." Natt kept on walking and put his hand out to push the door open.

The man raised his nose and said, "Ah, I smell your good, fresh coffee! While my wife shops for her stuff, I'll get me a cup and have a seat and talk to Brad. Fella, you done real good putting this place in here for us guys."

"Thanks, sir," Natt said, as he opened the front door and stepped out into the early evening. As usual, it had been a lovely day and now, with the sun in the west, the warm breeze made for a terrific evening. It would be even better if he didn't have to go back and finish out a couple of hours more at the store. He sighed and walked toward his cabin. He wasn't all that hungry right now he felt more like walking in the lovely evening air. That was one thing about Vansville he really liked. On any given day the air you breathed was fresh and clean. He chuckled to himself there wasn't much else in Vansville, but clean air! His stomach grumbled, clean air could wait, a growling stomach; not so much!

Marcy woke to the sun streaming through the tiny slit in the drapes across the patio door. She sighed, she'd planned to get an early start on her second day of travel, she'd wanted to reach Vansville while it was still light, but obviously that wouldn't happen, since the sun was already well up in the sky. She looked at the clock on the bedside stand and sighed again. It was past the time she'd wanted to get up. She'd forgotten to set the clock and now it was nearly eight. Used to, when she was little and her parents had traveled, you could ask the front desk to give you a wake up call, but now that everybody had cell phones, there were no phones in the rooms, just an alarm clock. Oh, the joys of modern technology! Too bad she hadn't joined in as yet.

She scrambled out of bed and rushed into the shower. She'd had a bath last evening, but a shower this morning would get her on the move. She was glad for the blow dryer by the mirror, with her curls, she could blow her hair and it'd be dry and styled when she left the room. Ever since she'd been old enough to decide for herself how she wanted her hair, she'd kept an easy hairdo and with nursing school, short hair had been essential.

Almost an hour later her suitcase was in her car and she was in the restaurant for breakfast. The restaurant wasn't crowded. She'd eat a good breakfast then get one sandwich before she arrived at Sandy's, sometime this afternoon. Now that she wasn't in nursing school and didn't use near the energy, she didn't need as many calories as she'd needed then. She had lost a lot of weight during her illness, but now she was nearly back to her ideal weight and she didn't want to go over that. She knew if she did much sitting around she'd look like a balloon. She'd be sitting most of today, so a good breakfast and not much else today would be good.

A thought hit her, as she sat waiting for the server to come for her order, was Sandy doing all the cooking since having the baby? Now that it was summer, Ramon was probably back on the trail and that left Sandy to do everything! Maybe she should have thought of that before coming. She might be putting more strain on her sister than there had been. She shrugged. It didn't matter, she was over half way there and she wasn't going back to her smothering mother. She'd had enough of that! She wondered again why her mom had acted as she had. She still had Ed at home it couldn't be an empty nest syndrome, surely. She shook her head, she had no answer, but she was glad to be away from it. At least Ed had gotten her mom to wave at her, she hadn't done that for Sandy and she'd felt so bad for her sister.

She made her order, making a face when she had to order decaf coffee. Dr. Wright had made it very clear she could never drink anything caffeinated again. There were three things he'd said she couldn't have - caffeinated anything, go back to nursing school and be a foreign missionary. She guessed she could live without the caffeine, but ever since she was a little girl she'd wanted to be a missionary nurse overseas. Her dad's words came to mind, 'In all things God works for the good of those who love him…' It was so hard to believe that 'In all things…' meant all the changes in her life, all from some virus nobody else had gotten.

After eating, she went to the office across from the restaurant to return her key card, as the checkout instructions said. There was a man about her dad's age seated at the desk but she was the only guest in the office. It wouldn't slow her down to smile and be pleasant. "Good morning, Ma'am. Was everything alright?"

"Yes, I slept well, thank you. Here's the key card the man last night gave me. Thank him again for paying for my dinner. The food in your restaurant is very good. It's well prepared and there's plenty of it."

Acting a bit surprised, the man said, "My son paid for your evening meal?" He reached out and took the card from Marcy.

Marcy shrugged. "It was the man who checked me in last evening who invited me to eat with him and then paid for my meal. He said he and his dad owned the place, so I guess to answer your question, yes, it was your son."

The man stroked his chin, as he placed the card in a special holder and said, "Huhh, that's a new one. Never knew him to do something like that before. Sure, I'll tell him. Have a good trip, miss. Drive safe and all that."

"Thank you." Marcy smiled and left.

Without Marcy knowing the man's thoughts and he might be middle-aged, but he agreed with his son, the lady was one beautiful woman. It was too bad she wasn't here for a job interview close by he'd encourage Shelton to get better acquainted, not just have dinner. But, life went on, one day his wife might have grandchildren.

Only a few minutes later Marcy followed the signs for the Chesapeake Bay Bridge and Tunnel and found herself on the massive structure. The first pull-off was already full, so she drove on and found a place to pull off and left her car to get some pictures. It was a beautiful day, so the sun did an awesome job sparkling off the water. The sky overhead was a deep blue with tiny clouds perfectly defined in it. Off to the east was a great expanse of water, where the Bay eventually emptied into the Atlantic, but on the other sides there was shoreline, some farther away than other places. Dotting the expanse of water were boats, some large, some tiny. Some were motorized, others were graceful sailboats. She snapped pictures to her heart's content then stayed for a bit, breathing in the salty air.

She had always loved the ocean and every time she had the chance, she'd go to the shore. She sighed, she hadn't been to the shore in a couple of years her nursing program didn't give her much time off for the last two summers. Of course, this year there was a different reason than the other years. Ed and Marg had gone, but they didn't ask her to go, she wouldn't have gone with them anyway, she'd have felt like a third wheel.

She thought about her siblings. Beautiful Sandy went to Georgia in August two years ago. They married in October they hadn't met before she went. Ramon was a handsome man. How could he not be with his Mediterranean good looks? Ed and Marg had been going together more or less exclusively for all of Ed's higher education, but it had been an on-agin off-agin thing. He'd finally asked her to marry him and Marg insisted they have a formal church wedding with all the trappings. She was to be a bridesmaid and Sandy was to play and sing. Marcy sighed, now that she was damaged goods, with a bad heart, who'd want to marry her? She put a squelch on that thought. She wasn't coming down here to find a man! Besides, she'd planned to go to the missionfield as a single woman, probably stay that way for the rest of her life.

After taking several pictures, some she thought were quite spectacular, she climbed back into her car, waited for several cars and a semi to pass, then drove on, into the tunnel. She was glad to be in the slow lane, it took her eyes a few minutes to adjust from the bright sun to the dark tunnel. Others whizzed by her, but only minutes later, she had only gone a few hundred feet when traffic in both lanes ground to a halt. She scowled, what was the problem? When she was on the bridge traffic was moving well. Could there be an accident up ahead? The driver of the car beside her put his car in park and leaned back in his seat. It made her wonder if he had a

CB or some other way of knowing what was ahead. Did a CB even work under so much water and inside thick walls of concrete?

As she thought about it, she knew they wouldn't find out because any emergency vehicles would have to come in from in front of them, both lanes behind her were filled as far as she could see, which was back to the entrance. She could still see the little square of light where the traffic came down off the bridge. Soon the car in front of her let off on his brakes, but he didn't move. Obviously people were expecting to be here for a while. She also put her car in park and let off her brake pedal. A few minutes later she heard a faint siren up ahead. Unfortunately, she had been correct, there was a wreck up ahead and whoever was coming to answer a call had to wait for traffic to clear out in front of it so they could enter.

She looked at her dash clock then turned off her engine, as she realized several other drivers were doing. It was probably as good thing, it would cut down on any pollution in the tunnel. There were tunnels at General Hospital complex they had to have air circulated in all the time. As her car became quiet, she heard another siren probably a wrecker had come on the scene. Perhaps it would soon be cleared away and they could get out of here. While she sat with nothing to do, she looked at the walls and wondered how much water and dirt or rock were over and around the tunnel walls…

Her hands turned clammy. No, she wouldn't go there. She'd never liked tunnels she'd walk outside from the hospital to the nurse's residence if possible, just to avoid walking in a dingy, dimly lit, damp tunnel. Her friend had seen one of those gigantic roaches down there once. She'd stayed away from that place until it rained a week later. She'd kept her eyes straight ahead and wouldn't look at either the walls or the floor and she'd nearly run the whole way! Even in the wintertime she'd rather walk outside than in the tunnel. She made herself think about something else - anything else. She could do life very well without huge bugs, thank you very much.

There was a narrow walkway along one side of the tunnel and someone was coming toward them. Who would be so foolish as to walk on that little walkway in this huge tunnel? She started up and pushed the lever to open the passenger window because the man seemed to say something every few steps. After the window was down, she turned the car back off, then waited for the man to come closer. Hot, damp air poured into her car. It was so humid in the tunnel that she started sweating immediately.

When the man was at the railing by the next car in front of her, he leaned over the rail and shouted, "There's been an accident ahead. It involves a car and a semi. It'll be a while they have to get a semi wrecker from several miles down the road. Thanks for being so patient." Then the man walked on to say his speech to cars behind her. She watched him he even went as far as the first few cars still on the bridge.

"Great!" Marcy grumbled and reached for a napkin to wipe away the sweat. As soon as the man walked on, she started up and put her window back up. She left the car running for just a minute to circulate the drier air and take out the musty smell. "I hope it's cleared up before lunch time. I didn't pack any food and I'm supposed to stop for a sandwich."

It felt almost like a tap on her shoulder, but a voice in her heart said, *Marcy, did you bring your Bible along? Did you pray for those people in the wreck? Maybe somebody was hurt pretty badly and they need God's touch.*

Immediately, tears came to her eyes. At one point in her life she'd felt so close to her Lord and Savior, but recently, she'd set her Bible aside and instead had been reading some novels. How could she have put God on the back burner when He'd done so much for her? Marcy opened her door and stepped out, then opened her back door and found her Bible in her little suitcase. She hadn't bothered to read this morning, since she'd woken so late.

Actually, she hadn't read yesterday morning, either, since she'd wanted to get an early start. She sighed the Lord had put a stop to her forward motion here in the tunnel. If she'd taken the time to read at the motel, she probably would have missed this accident. About half an hour later she heard cars ahead of her start up, so she laid her Bible on the passenger seat. As soon as she saw the brake lights on the car two in front of her come on, she started her car. Only moments later, her car started cooling off, but there were a lot of fumes in the tunnel.

TEN

Soon the traffic was moving and before she reached the other end of the tunnel they were up to speed. She was glad she hadn't been the one involved. She never did see any evidence of the accident, not even glass on the pavement. The verse: "So what is your life, it is only a vapor that vanishes away." came to mind. They'd been stopped for nearly an hour, but now there was no evidence of anything that had happened. As she left the tunnel, traffic spread out, some moving much faster than she wanted to. Her stomach growled, her dash clock told her it was lunchtime. Even though her tank didn't need gas, she'd fill up and get a sandwich at a station soon. That stop hadn't been her choice, but obviously God had a plan. Maybe it was just so she'd stop and read her Bible!

Not long after she'd left the Chesapeake Bay her route turned inland and soon, she found herself in the hills that later became the Appalachian Mountains. She rolled her window down and breathed deeply of the clean, fresh air. Philadelphia didn't have air this fresh, not even after a drenching rain. She remembered Sandy had told her it was much more fun to drive the smaller roads and see the scenery than to take the interstates. She'd been doing that, since she must take two days to arrive and she was enjoying every mile. The weather had cooperated for her trip, she was glad for her air conditioning, but in the higher elevation the temperature was great.

She stopped soon after leaving the Chesapeake to get a sandwich her stomach reminded her that she needed something to fill it. As she'd started doing yesterday, she stopped at a gas station that had a convenience store so that she could do both things at once. This store even had a tiny restaurant. When she went in to pay for her gas, she found that the restaurant sold grilled sandwiches. When she entered the store it smelled good enough to get lunch. A grilled cheese sounded really good. She took a potty break, then climbed on a stool at the counter and ordered a grilled cheese and a root beer float. She hadn't had a root beer float since she'd been in nursing school. They hit the spot and she was glad she'd made the stop. After enjoying her float, she went back to her car for the next leg of her journey.

Later on in the afternoon, she looked at her gas gauge and realized she hadn't seen a gas station in quite a while and her gas tank hadn't felt the business end of a gas pump hose in a very long time. Thinking back, it had been a while since the last town. She loved wide open spaces, but all this forest and fields didn't fill her gas tank. The needle was almost on the E when she finally saw signs of civilization. It was a small town, but she saw a gas station on the street ahead of her. Letting out a sigh, she pulled in and stopped at a pump.

She sat a minute after she turned off her key, but this wasn't the gas station on the corner of her street and the Avenue where her friendly, neighborhood gas station man who knew everyone who came to his place. Nobody came hurrying out of the store to pump her gas. Of course, she knew that, but she missed old Harvey. It didn't matter what the weather was, he'd come outside with a smile and for those he knew, he'd start talking the minute he recognized you. He knew what kind of gas you took and started it even before you got out of your car. She stepped out of her car and turned to pull open the little door in front of her gas cap and a young man came out of the store. He walked up with a friendly smile.

Marcy didn't know what to do; did this guy pump gas? Did he come out to be friendly, but she had to pump the gas? She looked up at the pillar close by, but there wasn't a sign that said it was self serve or they pumped it. She saw it was the old fashioned pump where you had to go in the store to pay for the gas. She sighed did they even take credit cards? She glanced at the door of the store and was relieved to see the different credit card symbols. At least this little burg was that modern, glad she could put off paying for another month. Come to think of it, how was she going to pay for expenses when her savings ran out?

Marcy looked at the man, wondering why he stood there, doing nothing, but not saying a word, but he was staring at her. Her heart rate sped up, but not in a dangerous way. Before she hyperventilated, she turned away and gave the gas cap a twist, then haphazardly stuck the nozzle in the hole. Just so she didn't have to look at him, she inspected the nozzle and found how to keep the gas going without holding the lever.

When she had clicked the lever and gas was flowing in the tank, the man finally spoke. He cleared his throat and said, "Ma'am, I don't mean to startle you, but you look like someone I saw yesterday here at this pump."

Marcy scowled. "What do you mean?"

"Umm, do you have a sister?" His neck turned pink. "She drives a light blue van, only a couple of years old."

Marcy was very cautious, always had been, after all, she had lived in Philadelphia all her life. For two years, she'd been at General Hospital, which was downtown. Downtown Philadelphia wasn't the best place to live. Philadelphia meant 'The City of Brotherly Love' but that time in its life was long gone! The police sent gang war victims to General, it happened a lot. She knew not to give away any kind of information. She was not about to give anything away in some little burg in the middle of nowhere.

"I have a sister." She stared right back at the man, maybe he'd tried to intimidate her, but she wasn't about to take that!

"She drives a light blue van? Her name's Sandy, right?"

Puzzled, Marcy asked, "How would you know that?" Did Sandy go far and wide to do her paintings? Surely she'd buy her gas in Vansville unless she was painting somewhere, but she hadn't come to Blairsville yet… goodness where was she? The man continued to look at her, she couldn't imagine why.

"She was here yesterday and you look like her."

"I… what?"

The gas shut off, so Marcy turned quickly back to the nozzle and pulled it out of the tank, then stood holding it like a gun pointing at the young man. The gas cap still hung down against the car. With a scowl on her face she looked at him and asked, "What is this place, here in the middle of nowhere? Is it really a place? Does it have a name?"

"This is Vansville, Georgia, Miss."

"This... I'm in Vansville?" she asked, totally shocked. "I've come to Vansville? But it's not... well maybe it is." Babbling? Was she babbling?

Natt nodded. "Yes, didn't you expect it to be?"

Not remembering that she saw a sign at the edge of town, she said, "Well, no, I thought I'd come to Blairsville first."

Pointing from the way she came, he said, "You came the wrong way to go through Blairsville. You must have come through the country from the highway." He smiled, hoping to put her at ease. "It is a beautiful day for a drive in the country."

Marcy sighed, still holding the nozzle in front of her. She shrugged. "I guess I did. I'm not too good at reading a map I think I turned off the highway too soon or something. But I'm in Vansville now?"

Natt nodded, looking at the end of the nozzle. "Yes, this is Vansville. Miss, were you going to pay cash or with a credit card today?"

Marcy looked down at the nozzle she still held, shook her head and pushed it back onto the pump, then put the gas cap in its place, she felt her cheeks warm and hoped the blush didn't cover her face. This guy had totally blown her mind. Her map said she should come to Blairsville. Surely she hadn't, had she? Had she really turned off the highway before the proper exit? "Umm, I have a credit card! You took me so by surprise when you said I looked like someone. Yes, I'm Sandy's younger sister, Marcy."

Natt nodded. "It's good to meet you, Marcy, I'm Natt Thomas."

"Good to know you." Marcy reached back into her car for her purse, then straightened and asked, "So you do take credit cards?" *Well, duh, the sign's on the door, stupid.*

"Yeah, but you'll have to come inside for us to process it. We're a bit in the hicks for the gas company to get us new pumps that take cards outside."

Marcy chuckled a bit. "It's a good way to sell other things, by having people come in the store. I guess you thought of that, though."

Natt grinned, "Sure! That's a given, but we also have a coffee urn that's bottomless and you're welcome to have a cup for the road." Thinking about it he added, "Of course, since it's Vansville, I assume you're on your way to visit your sister."

Marcy made a face, as she turned to walk inside with Natt. "Don't even mention coffee! I love it! I used to drink lots of it a few months ago. Even in hot weather, it was my beverage of choice. However, I have a small problem and my doctor told me no coffee. Anyway, if you say this is Vansville, I think I'm almost to my destination, since I'm spending time with Sandy for a while. I'm sure she'll have a drink for me. Still, I need to pay for my gas."

Natt held the door for her and followed her in. "Grandad'll take your money or process your credit card." He stopped at the coffee drinker's nook and took a seat, since there were no other customers at the moment. Brad always worked the cash register. Since that was about all he did, Natt wouldn't stop him.

Marcy pulled her card from her wallet and held it out. She saw the old man behind the counter and exclaimed, "I know you! You're Brad. If you'd come out instead of him, I'd have known I was in Vansville."

Brad's eyes popped open he stood up and reached under the counter for his credit card machine. He grinned at the young woman and said, "Can't place your name, but you'd be Sandy's sister, no doubt about it."

"I am, I'm on my way there for a visit. I haven't seen her since Christmas when we came down for the week."

Nodding, Brad said, "Good, good. She be a bit covered up with that new baby, but that little guy's a cracker jack! He shore is a precious one!"

Concerned, Marcy said, "She's doing alright?"

"Far as I know."

"Oh, I'm glad to hear that! When I talked to her on Thursday, she never told me how she was, but that's Sandy for you."

Brad nodded. "That's for shore! Yep, that baby shore is somethin' to write home about, I'll give you that!"

Brad ran her card through his machine, then as he waited for the paper to print, he said, "She be doin' a concert next week for us here in town. You know. Did she ask you to sing, is that why you be here now?"

Marcy sighed, shaking her head. "I believe that's why the doctor put her in the hospital six weeks before she had the baby! She doesn't know how to say 'no' or when to quit!" Marcy took the pen Brad held out to sign the slip and added, "She's always been that way, for goodness sake! She has that baby, Ramon's back on the trails and she's playing a concert! It's good she sits down all the time or I'd tan her hide!"

Brad chuckled. "I agree, Miss, but you know your sister. That girl's a go-getter. Yah, we missed her sompin fierce when she were in the hospital."

Marcy pointed her thumb over her shoulder. "So that guy's your grandson? You got him working in the store with you?"

"Yup. Good lookin' ain't he?" He winked at Marcy, a grin covering his whole face.

From his seat behind her, Natt's face turned a bright red. Under his breath, he grumbled, "Grandad! Please!"

Marcy didn't comment. She signed the credit card slip and Brad gave her the receipt. She took it and turned to leave the store and realized Natt was sitting in the nook, so she said, "Thanks for telling me where I was." She shook her head and walked to the door. "Believe me, if I hadn't needed gas I'd have probably gone on by and gotten myself totally lost. I've done that before. This place is a bit different from Philadelphia where there's a street sign on every corner. Besides, the last time I was here was at Christmas, it looks a bit different from then."

From his seat behind the counter, Brad smiled back at her. "No problem, Miss. Have a good time with your sister."

"Nice to meet you, Marcy," Natt said.

"Yeah, good to meet you. I'm…ah… usually not that scatter-brained. But, hey, I've been driving all day."

"Yeah, it does something to a person, I know."

When Marcy had left, Natt came back to the counter. Brad grinned at his grandson and said, "I saw you out there makin' time with Sandy's sister, did you tell her you're goin' to Sandy's for dinner on Sunday?"

His neck still pink, Natt said, "Grandad! I never knew you to be a matchmaker! Besides, where'd she say she's from, Philadelphia wasn't it?"

Brad looked out the door, watching Marcy's car pull away. "Yeah, I bulieve she be from that big city, but hey, she's here now!" He nodded. "Yeah, she be a pretty young thing, too. She don't got nothin' on you jes 'cause she be from Philadelphia, you be from Atlanta and your dad's got a paper." Then he looked back at Natt, pushed his thumb into his own chest and said, "Who me? A matchmaker? Never thought of it!"

"Uh huh, your nose is growing, Pinocchio."

Brad looked at the clock, then out the door to make sure no hoards of people were about to descend on the store. With the parking lot empty, he winked at Natt and said, "Well, it's time to close up, it's about five o'clock. Time for shut down. You be comin' to church tomorra, Son? Ya know, that boy ain't much older'n you. He's a good man, what he says is good for the soul."

"Grandad," Natt sighed and since he sat in the chair closest to the door, he turned the lock and the switch on the door jam that turned out most of the store lights. In the semi-darkness he reached for the plug on the back of the coffee urn, "It's my day off, my chance to get out and not think about the store. I'll think about it. I may come, one of these days, you know."

Brad put Marcy's receipt in the drawer and the credit card machine away, as he said, "Okay, but Roger, he's a good man. You should come hear him." He hit a few keys on the cash register and the machine started going through shut down.

Natt let out another long sigh. "Grandad, I said I'll think about it and I will." *Not too hard and not too long, though.*

Brad nodded. "Uh huh. I know how I used to 'think about it' when Joyce'd plague me to go with her to church. I'd git right back at her, 'course, that's one reason I kep the store open on Sundays, sos she'd leave me be. You… you don't even got nobody to ask ya when it's time to get goin'. How's about yor Gramma calls ya in the mornin'?" Brad gave his grandson a wink, then turned back to the register and tore off the paper. He studied it a minute, then folded it and placed it in the bank bag under the counter.

"Grandad," Natt said, with a sigh and picked up the urn to take it to the back to clean it for the first pot on Monday morning. "I'll do the thinking without you sicin' Gramma on me. One of these days I'll come."

Grinning, Brad stood up and headed for the back door. His hand on the knob, he said, "Yeah, that's zactly what I'd tell her."

Any other words Brad might have said were drowned out by the water splashing into the urn back in the sink and then gurgling down the drain. Natt grumbled to himself, "That old man is something else! I swear!" He hurried, the water splashed into the urn, he swished his cloth around in it and dumped out the brown water. It was too nice a day to be cooped up in any building, especially in his place of employment. Summer days and especially summer Saturdays, were meant for laying out at a pool somewhere with friends.

A pretty, dark haired girl came to mind.

Marcy's steps were light as she headed for her car. She was in Vansville! She'd be at Sandy's house in minutes! Thank goodness that young guy came out, or maybe she'd have recognized Brad when she went in to pay, but she didn't realize she'd come to Vansville. She'd truly thought she'd come to Blairsville first. How did she get off track so that she came to Vansville first? She drove down the street that now looked familiar from when they came at Christmas. She knew DeLord's house was the last one before heading out of town. She scowled, she'd gone right passed it to the gas station and hadn't recognized it. Well, that was easy to figure! She'd seen the gas sign and she'd been worried she'd run out of gas for miles.

A car was approaching, so she turned on her signal and waited for the car to pass, then made the turn onto the parking lot. She knew better than to pull in front of the garage door, so she turned and parked in the slot right beside the building. She shut off her car and sighed she'd made it all the way from Philadelphia in good time and didn't feel any worse for wear. In fact, she felt great! She stepped out, then opened her back door and reached in for her smaller suitcase. As she closed the back door, the office door opened on the house and a smiling lady in a wheelchair and a grinning man filled up the doorway. Marcy looked a little closer and saw that in the man's arm was a baby dressed in blue.

"Marcy! You made great time! Get yourself in here! We're so excited you're here!" Sandy exclaimed and held out her arms. "We've been waiting for you and of course, Jon wants to meet his Auntie!"

"Hi, Sis, it's great to see you! Hi, Ramon and you have Jon!"

"Yup, we're all here and it's great to see you! You're all better?"

Marcy nodded; a wide grin on her face. "Better enough that the doctor released me on Thursday. I'm so glad to be shed of that place, you can't believe."

Knowing what she'd had to go through to get away, Sandy chuckled. "Are you talking about the doctor or Mom?"

She let go of her pull-behind suitcase and threw her arms around her sister and they kissed each other on the cheek. After smiling at Ramon and patting Jon on the back, she kept one arm around Sandy and said, "Now that you mention it, perhaps both. I had the Chief of Staff for my doctor and he was great, but Mom…" Marcy shook her head. "She tried her best to keep me, even yesterday morning. Would you believe, she grabbed my suitcase to try to keep me and didn't make Daddy's lunch!" Marcy looked perplexed. "Surely it's not the empty nest syndrome! I mean, Ed's still there. She never made a peep when I left for nursing school."

"Yes, but Ed's a guy. You know that'd be different for Mom."

"Yeah, that's true, but let me tell you…."

Ramon backed up and Sandy pulled her arms from around Marcy and pulled the lever on her control panel for her chair to back up. As it hummed, she said, "Come on in, girl! It's a beautiful day, but it's a hot one and it's cool in here. Ramon's always telling me we don't need to cool all outdoors. So how long can you stay?"

"Say," Ramon asked, "You got more stuff to bring in?"

"Yes, another suitcase and a box, there on the back seat."

"Great, I'll get them!" He handed a sleeping Jon to Sandy, who laid him on her lap, then continued to back up into the office. Ramon went out the door, but Marcy grabbed her suitcase handle and followed Sandy inside.

After Ramon was outside, Marcy exclaimed, "Sis, I'm free as a bird! I can stay as long or as short a time as I want or maybe it's until you guys get tired of me."

Sandy laughed. "We'll see about that! Sis, it's so good to see you. I'm so glad you came, we'll have ourselves a great time."

"Since you got here in good time, I guess you didn't get lost?" Ramon asked, as he pulled the suitcase inside. Knowing how often Marcy drove and this was the first time she'd driven here. To hear Sandy talk, Marcy wasn't much on directions, public transportation was her forte.

Marcy made a face. "I guess I should say no, but I must have made a wrong turn somewhere, because if I hadn't needed gas I probably would have. I came right past here and didn't recognize your house, but I needed gas so I stopped up at Thomas's. That's when I found out I was in Vansville."

"Did you meet the owner?" Ramon asked, tongue-in-cheek. He moved down the hall ahead of the sisters with the box and the suitcase.

Marcy scowled at her sister. "Well, sure, Brad took my credit card. He was behind the counter, like he always is."

Sandy shook her head, a huge grin on her face, as if she knew a secret. "He's not the owner now; it's Natt, his grandson."

Marcy nodded. "Yeah, I met him." What was that tone of voice she'd heard from both her sister and brother-in-law? *Natt, the grandson, your age, remember?*

They were going single file down the hall, when Sandy said, "He's coming for lunch on Sunday after church. Why, that's tomorrow!" *What a concept!*

Exasperated, Marcy said, "Sis, why is that? Don't you have enough work with Jon and now me? Good grief!"

"Sis, spaghetti sauce isn't hard to make."

"Well, I know, but still...."

In the living room, Marcy let go of her suitcase and took a step up beside her sister. She looked sternly at her and shaking her finger, Marcy said, "You know what? I think you're matchmaking. You, sister dear, should leave such things alone! I'm here to visit I'm not here to be part of any matchmaking scheme! After all, I just got off bed rest, for crying out loud!"

With a straight face, but her eyes twinkling, Sandy said, "Sis, would I do that? Why, you're my no nonsense, foreign missionary!"

Not loosing a minute, Marcy glared at her sister. "Mmm, I'm also your **single, unattached,** not able to go abroad, sister."

Grinning at Marcy, Sandy said, "Well, there is that..."

Marcy heaved a big sigh and decided that the subject desperately needed changing, so she said, "Sis, do you have something decaffeinated I could drink, I'm really dry. Natt offered me some coffee, but I couldn't have it."

"Sure, come on in the kitchen. I was about to get supper when Ramon said he thought he saw your car go by. Of course, he couldn't understand why you went by..."

Marcy made a face and said, "Mmm, that would be when I came in town and didn't realize I'd reached Vansville. Natt came out and told me point blank that I was actually in the town of Vansville. I didn't recognize anything about the place before that. Actually, I was too focused on getting to a gas station. I don't even remember seeing the sign with the town name and population. All I remember was that gas sign up ahead and I aimed my car for it."

"Hey, that's okay, Sis. It's a lot different from Christmas time and this is the first time you've driven here on your own."

Marcy still shook her head. "I know, but your house isn't that far from the road, why didn't I recognize it?"

Sandy shrugged. "Couldn't tell you."

"Well, I don't know, either," she huffed. "That virus zapped my heart, but I'd swear it didn't affect my brain..."

Ramon had taken Marcy's suitcase and the box into the guest room on the way down the hall, but he caught up. When he was on a trail he couldn't hold Jon, he wanted to as much as he could, so he took the baby back from Sandy and placed him on his shoulder. The little guy was so comfortable with his daddy, he never woke up. However, Marcy noticed his little hand curled around his daddy's neck, even though he didn't wake up. It sent her heart throbbing. He was such a perfect baby!

They had crossed into the kitchen when all three of the adults heard a sound from the youngest member of the group. Ramon pulled the baby from his shoulder and saw the remnants of his face scrunched up, as Jon filled his pants. Shaking his head, Daddy said, "Uh oh, I think your son gave us a present. I'd better go check it out right away."

Sandy sniffed the air. "I believe you're right, Honey. He sure knows how to pick the most inopportune times to give us presents."

Ramon turned to go back down the hall with his little bundle, but Marcy looked at the little boy in his daddy's arms. Now that he wasn't holding the baby on his shoulder, she could see his face, his eyes were open now. He was absolutely precious. She could see some of each of his parents in the baby. Her heart turned over, how she loved children! Pediatrics had been one of her most favorite courses in nursing school. Softly, she said, "Umm, could I maybe do that? I'd love to hold Jon, if you don't mind?"

Ramon turned around and with a grin, said, "Hey, don't let me stop you from having the pleasure of smelling your nephew's latest present." He handed Jon to Marcy and continued, "Go in our room and on into our bathroom. His changing table's in there with all the paraphernalia you need to keep tiny bottoms clean, dry and fresh. Go for it, Auntie!"

Marcy grinned back at her brother-in-law. "Thanks, I'll do my best for this little guy." Smiling, she held out her hands eagerly.

She took the baby from him, cradling him in both hands. She smiled at him he was wide awake and looked at the new face solemnly. Marcy bent, bringing the tiny body to her face and blew a raspberry on his neck. Ramon and Sandy had wondered how Jon would act his first time with Marcy, but the baby's face burst into a grin and a laugh worked its way from inside. They looked at each other and grinned, Jon and Marcy would soon be fast friends; that was obvious.

Without looking back at her sister and brother-in-law, Marcy started down the hall. Looking at the baby, she whispered, "You, little guy, are precious! We'll get you cleaned up in no time, though then you'll smell fresh as a daisy." Marcy made a funny face at the baby and whispered, "Whew! You sure know how to make a smell!" Of course, Jon didn't know what she said, but he giggled at her and Marcy's heart turned over. God had taken away the missionary nurse, she was damaged goods could she even have children? Marcy put a stop to that negative thought. There was no need to think about that question or an answer now.

Marcy followed Ramon's directions and soon walked through the large bedroom, then into the super large bathroom. Ramon had built the suite especially for Sandy and her wheelchair. Of course, Marcy saw the changing table with all the necessities for cleaning and drying tiny bottoms.

She lay the baby on the table and said, "Okay, little guy, here we go! We are about to make you the freshest smelling baby in all of Vansville." As she unsnapped his wet romper she shook her head. God certainly had loused up her plans... Even though they'd been good plans, plans she'd hoped would glorify God. Had He zapped her with Rheumatic Fever because they weren't His plans? *"Oh, God, I'm sorry,"* she whispered.

While she pulled off the romper, Jon looked at her, stuffed his fist in his mouth and started cooing. Before Marcy undid his diaper, she took a deep breath. "Whew! You are ripe! We're about to remedy that this instant!"

With Marcy out of the room, Ramon said to Sandy, "So, what do you think about that sister of yours?"

Looking at the empty doorway where she had last seen her sister, Sandy said, "I don't know how much weight she lost while she was sick, but she's still thin. That Rheumatic Fever must have been really hard on her. It's taken six months for her to get back enough that the doctor released her! She must have been **really** sick!"

Ramon shrugged; a gleam in his eyes. "I guess you'd know, but she looked pretty good to me. I'd never guess she'd lost weight."

Sandy sighed, "You men have no concept of the finer things."

Putting his arm around his wife, he gave her a wink, before he said, "Maybe not, but hey, two good looking sisters…"

Sandy gave her husband a big smile. "Maybe I'm glad I asked Natt for dinner tomorrow after all. It can't hurt."

Ramon chuckled and squeezed his wife's shoulders. "Darling, you're the best! I'm so happy that you're my wife."

Grinning happily at her husband, she stretched up as far as she could. Ramon knew that sign and quickly leaned over for a kiss. As soon as they finished the kiss, she said, "I'm happy being your wife, too. I'd recommend the state to anyone! I love you."

"Mmm," as he brought his face close for another kiss, "I love you, too, Sweetheart." Before he straightened up, he claimed her lips. After a loving kiss, he whispered, "Darling, you are the best thing that's ever, ever happened to me! You not only introduced me to our Savior, but you've made me a better man."

After their kiss, Sandy took out the pan she wanted to fix supper in and Ramon opened the refrigerator to pull out a pitcher of lemonade. He'd heard Marcy ask for a decaffeinated drink and this was the only thing they had in that category. "Love, if Marcy can't have anything but decaf, we'd better put that on the list. We have lots of coffee, but no decaf and you have several boxes of tea, but no decaf."

"That's right. I'd forgotten that she said she couldn't have anything with caffeine in it. I'm glad I got that box of lemonade the last time I was in Alex's. I guess it's something about the caffeine that bothers her heart?"

"Yes, I think I'd heard that people with heart conditions can't have that stuff." He looked up at the clock over the sink and saw it was nearly five o'clock. "I tell you what, while you get supper going, I'll run to Alex's and get some decaf coffee. I know she loves coffee and she'll want some in the morning."

"Great! You know if you don't get it tonight, we'll have to wait for Monday. Thanks, Honey, that's a perfect idea."

Ramon ran out the door, then rushed down the street and ran the few steps from the corner to Alex's door, because he saw the man walking the aisle toward the sign in his window. Alex turned the sign in the window, but before he could get to the door to lock it, Ramon pushed it open and sighed as Alex turned toward him. A drop of sweat ran down his neck.

"You're out of breath," Alex observed and turned away from the big window facing the street. "I've never seen that happen in all the time I've owned this store and you've lived in that house. My goodness, young fella, I thought your hiking keeps you so in shape, it's hard to believe you'd be winded like this."

Pulling in a deep breath, Ramon said, "Alex, I ran from my house to get here before you locked up. Marcy just pulled in and we have nothing decaffeinated to give her to drink. Except water, of course. Monday's a long ways off to relegate her to just what comes from the well. Got any decaf coffee or tea?"

Pointing to the aisle where he kept his drinks and drink supplies, he said, "Sure! It's all on the same aisle as your leaded stuff. Go find what you need."

"Thanks, Alex."

"So Marcy's come to visit? She all better now?"

"As better as she'll be, I guess. The doctor's released her and said she could drive down, but she's a bit thin and well, we haven't really seen any signs, but she only arrived just before I came. Still she said she'll never be able to have caffeine again."

"Wow! For your family that's a cryin' shame."

"Yeah, I know! I guess both Sandy and Marcy cut their teeth on leaded coffee, their dad likes his strong enough to walk."

Alex chuckled. "You aren't far behind that, Son."

"Mmm, well, the trail does that to me."

Alex rang up his purchase, then hit more keys and said, "Well, young man, you're my last customer for the day. You walk out the door and my door's locked. You take care and we'll see you again. Have a good Sunday."

"Thanks, Alex, have a good day off."

"Oh, don't worry about that! Wife told me grandkids are coming tomorrow."

"Sis, why do you keep going to Blairsville to church if what you say about Roger is true?" Marcy asked the next morning as she sat with Sandy and Ramon at breakfast and chewed on a mouthful of toast. "You told us when we came for Christmas last year that he was preaching good sermons now, he was a true pastor and the people loved him. He built that ramp just for you and yet the only time you go there is to play concerts. If he's so good and he and his family are such great friends, why don't you support him?"

Scowling, as if she hadn't thought along those lines before, Sandy said, thoughtfully, "It's not that easy to pick up and leave where we've been going for so long, really, Sis. Isabel goes there, there's Sunday school, which they don't have here. They ask me to substitute for the musicians occasionally. Actually, it's all kind of complicated."

Marcy took another bite and washed it down with her decaffeinated coffee, but then she said, "I understand, Sis. I know it's hard to change. Mom and Dad tried that church closer to them then decided they liked the one they'd been going to. It's even that one that treated you so badly when you did that concert and Daddy had to carry you in all the time. Still for you, it's at least a half hour drive to Blairsville and now with the baby you must get up nearly at dawn even now in the summer to get ready. Isabel's daughter's here who can drive her to church, so that isn't a need. Maybe if you went here to church you guys could be a help to Roger by being Sunday school teachers perhaps. Think of all the children who are your pupils, where do they go for Sunday school? If you went here don't you think you'd get to do more than substitute occasionally for the musicians?"

Sandy sipped her coffee and looked at her sister. "You may be right. I started going to Blairsville because Roger didn't preach the Word and he does now. What I've heard, he's really good. At the time, Isabel was driving herself, but now Ruth goes with us. Still, it's only been a couple of months since Ruth moved here for good."

Marcy finished her coffee, then nodded and said, "Exactly. I don't think I'll go with you guys today, I'll stay here and take my daily walk to church and back, since it's a beautiful day. I can start your spaghetti sauce when I get home. That's something I know how you do and I can do that to help."

"Thanks, Sis. We'll give this some thought."

Only a few minutes later Ramon placed the baby's car seat on Sandy's lap and took them to the garage to the van. The three rode up together on the lift and Ramon fastened Jon's infant seat on the bench while Sandy fastened herself in the passenger spot. Ramon climbed behind the wheel and left for Isabel's, where he would pick up both Isabel and Ruth, then leave town for Blairsville for church. It happened that way most every Sunday.

It was a good ways, they did have to get up so early now with Jon and it was a bit out of the way to go to church in Blairsville, since the church was downtown. Roger was his best friend here in town, he'd invited them to come several times, but they only went in the evening. Maybe they ought to do more thinking about it. Most of all, what Marcy said about Sunday school hit home in Ramon's mind. Sandy did have fifty piano students. There was no Sunday school at Vansville church, where did all those kids go to Sunday school. Anywhere?

Marcy watched them go and waved them off, then took her mug, filled with another dose of unleaded coffee along with her Bible onto the back deck that Ramon had built in the corner made by the new bedroom suite and the back of the kitchen. Since there was no Sunday school at the Vansville Community Church, she'd have over an hour to have devotions. She hadn't read much in her Bible in the last two days. In the Chesapeake Tunnel had been the last time. That surely hadn't been anything but reading, she hadn't pondered what she read.

For a while she sat in the comfortable captain's chair, her Bible closed on her lap and savored her surroundings. She'd been here in Vansville twice before, once for Sandy's wedding had only been for two days. It had been nearly two years ago! That had been in October, but still really warm. They'd stayed in Isabel's cabins and it had been hectic, hardly a minute to sit and be quiet. Their mom had been so opposed to the wedding happening at all, she, Ed and their dad had their hands full just trying to keep her away from all the preparations. The words she said were 'wet-blanket' enough, she couldn't imagine what havoc she would have created! She was glad the pastor had been warned not to ask if there were any objections! She didn't know Ramon's mom that well, but as she understood it, that woman had been deathly opposed, too.

The last time here was at Christmas. There had been a bit of snow on the ground – white snow – not like the stuff that took on the soot of Philadelphia. Sandy had been practicing for her Christmas concert, including trying to sing some of the songs and longer pieces. It was very easy to see how much trouble she was having, trying to get enough breath with the baby pushing on her diaphragm. She remembered not long after she'd asked for the time off, Ramon had called and asked if she'd sing the songs Sandy wanted to sing at the Christmas program.

Somehow, Ed and her dad had found out what Ramon had asked and coerced her into singing all the songs that Sandy had been expecting to sing. Because she wasn't a musician and couldn't read music, she'd had to practice a lot to feel comfortable with the music she was to sing in Sandy's place. They'd come early and then stayed until after Christmas, but it was too cold to enjoy much outside. Really, this was the first time she could look off at the hills and mountains and truly appreciate God's handiwork all around her. He truly was an awesome God. She loved Him. He had saved her from her sins; He had made her His child. Tears sparkled in her eyes. She had been so sick, but He had brought her back to health. She would praise Him!

She sat so quietly that a bluebird flew from a nearby tree limb and sat on the railing close by. She had her hand on the mug handle, but she didn't dare move. As she sat watching him, he threw his head back and let out a song that truly thrilled Marcy. "Father God," she murmured, "thank You so much for sending this little bird. I praise You for everything!" She swallowed a sigh, "Yes, even Rheumatic Fever. You have something else for me, I know. Thank You." She sighed, as she finished her prayer, "Father, I really would like to know what it is You have for me. You took away the possibility of being a nurse and of going overseas six months ago, surely You've figured it out by now, haven't You? Would it be so horrid to let me in on Your plan?"

As she continued to sit quietly, another thought hit her. Yesterday, she'd stopped for quite some time on the bridge to take pictures, to enjoy the views and the salt air. The sun had been warm, since she'd lost weight, warmth felt good. The thought hadn't occurred to her before, but if she hadn't stopped for those few minutes would she have been in front of that accident that happened in the tunnel or would she have been involved?

That was a sobering thought, it had obviously happened not long before she entered the tunnel. She took a sip of her coffee, wow! God really did have His hand on her!

The town of Vansville was different in every way from Philadelphia. When she lived there, she could always go to the gas station or the grocery store to get filled up or pick up something she'd forgotten, that big city never slept. It also treated Sunday like any other day, businesses were open with few exceptions, but Saturday evening at five o'clock when Alex closed the grocery store and Natt closed the hardware store, Vansville pretty much rolled up its sidewalks until Monday morning. The only thing open on Sunday was the church. A long time ago that was the way it was in America, but not any more.

Some time after the bluebird flew away, Marcy finished her coffee and read three chapters in her Bible the church bell in the steeple of the one church in town began to ring. Marcy looked at her watch, she had only ten minutes to walk four blocks she had better get on the move! She was glad she only had to grab her purse from her bedroom and head out she'd dressed after her shower. She'd dressed in a cool outfit, not something to draw attention to herself, who was there to impress in this little town? Actually, she never dressed to call attention to herself that was something she'd learned at her parents' knees.

Marcy went back inside and set her mug on the drain board after running a bit of water in it. She wondered if Sandy and Ramon locked their doors, but they hadn't given her a key, so she decided to lock the front door, but leave the back door so she could get back in after church. She kept her Bible in her hand, grabbed her purse from the bedroom and hurried out the front door and pushed the lock before she pulled it closed. She pulled in another big breath of the sweet morning air. There was no pollution that she could tell. The church bell rang again.

Others were walking up the steps to the walk into the church as she arrived. Alex, the grocery store owner and his wife were ahead of her and Brad and his wife were crossing the street. She waved at Brad and wondered briefly if his grandson lived with them and came to church, but he wasn't with them. She didn't wait for them, but kept on toward the door. It didn't really matter what their grandson did, she was only visiting. Perhaps while she was here God would show her what He had planned for her life. Being away from her mom would surely help her think more clearly. She'd be able to see God's signs better.

Roger Clemens stood at the big double doors greeting all those coming inside. He spoke to Alex and his wife, but when Marcy reached him, he exclaimed, "Marcy Bernard! How good to see you! Are you all better now?"

Marcy smiled at the young man and said, "Yes, thank you. Actually, as well as can be expected, which means there're some residual scars on my heart. The doctor released me on Thursday and said I could drive, so here I am for a visit. I'm sure glad to spend some time with Sandy and Ramon and get to know Jon."

"That's great!" His grin was a mile wide and his eyes twinkled, as he said "I don't suppose you have a song up your sleeve you could bless us with this morning?"

Giving a sigh, Marcy shook her head and looked inside at the praise team on the platform. She said, "Roger, I haven't sung since I got sick. I don't know how my lung capacity survived. I don't read music, I had to practice and practice those songs Sandy wanted me to sing at Christmas." The praise band started a number and Marcy said, "Umm, I pretty much have to sing with a piano. I sure never sang on my own!"

ELEVEN

Placing his hand on her shoulder, he winked at her and said, "We'll hold off on that for another week or two. The longer you're here, breathing this good air and eating Sandy's good food, you're bound to get those lungs working again in fine mode. You have such a lovely voice we need to hear it again."

"Roger, you're just like the preacher back home," she grumbled. "He won't take no for an answer no matter what the reason!"

Roger chuckled and patted her shoulder. "One of the things they teach you in seminary."

"Mmm, I'm sure," Marcy said, skeptically. "I think it's something desperate preachers lay awake at night working on."

Chuckling, he patted her hand, as she took another step. "Hey, now, how could I do that? I didn't even know you were in town until now. Besides, Lenny's the cause for being awake at night, but that's almost behind us now."

Marcy went on in the sanctuary, but she heard Roger say to Brad and his wife, "So you didn't persuade that grandson of yours to come yet again? He didn't go home did he? I know Atlanta's not that far."

"Roger," Joyce said, "he's a tough one. He's been to college, you know."

Totally serious, Roger said, "Joyce, I know how college can take the fire of the Lord out of you, it did it to me years ago, but I'll bet something or someone'll put that fire back in that boy one of these days."

"Pastor, I sure hope so!"

Marcy found an empty chair and sat down. The first thing she noticed was that the music the praise team played was much more subdued than she remembered. Another thought registered: *So Brad's grandson didn't go to church and Sis has invited him for lunch....hmmm.*

Marcy wasn't too interested in the praise songs the band played, the church she and her parents went to back in Philadelphia had a piano and organ that played mostly the old hymns and only one or two praise choruses and those were mostly in the evening, but she really enjoyed Roger's message. She had no point of reference for when he changed from doing readings to preaching a sermon, but since the last time she'd been here, which had only been last Christmas, his sermon today had more depth and it was great. She was very glad she came. She hadn't realized how relevant a young pastor could make his sermon. She liked the pastor at the church in Philadelphia, but he was white haired and had grandchildren.

As soon as Roger said his dismissal, Heidi was out of her seat. "Miss Marcy! Miss Marcy!" She came running down the center aisle with her arms wide. "You come to church today! You stay long time?"

Marcy squatted down and hugged the little girl. She grinned and kept her hands on the little girl's shoulders. "Hi, Heidi, you've grown so much since I was here last! My goodness, and you have a new brother!"

The child gave her a huge smile and pressed her hands down her pretty dress. "I know, I be four now." She turned to look at her mommy. "Yeah, I got a new brother, he be good boy! You stay long time?"

Marcy shook her head, wishing she knew the answer to that herself. "Honey, I don't know. I came to visit and we'll see what God has for me."

"Daddy say you been sick. You all better now?"

Nodding, Marcy said, "I'm as better as I'll get for a while. My doctor doesn't think I'll get all the way well, ever."

Fiercely, the little girl hugged her again and said, "Miss Marcy, we pray real hard you get *all* better real soon!"

Marcy felt her eyes getting scratchy, so she blinked, she wouldn't cry in front of this beautiful child. "Thanks, Honey, I know God hears prayers like that."

Heidi skipped off, so Marcy looked around as the church emptied. Several people recognized her and welcomed her, but there were few young adults and no families. Heidi and her baby brother were the only children in the service. They had to be in the service, there was no program for children. Raylyn had to keep Lenny quiet for the hour or take him to Roger's office, there was no other choice. Sandy had nearly fifty children piano students, did any of them go to Sunday school and if so, where? It wasn't at Vansville Community Church.

Roger was about to close the front door when he looked around and saw Marcy still behind him. He turned and smiled at her. "So, you like my church so much you're going to hang out here, Marcy?"

She smiled and started walking down the aisle toward the double doors, but she said, "Roger, you don't have Sunday school."

Waving his hand around, he said, "Marcy, what you see is what you get. We have a pretty good sized auditorium and it fills each Lord's Day, but except for the little room through that door, which is my office, there is no place to hold Sunday school. There aren't even any restrooms here. I wish I knew how to remedy the Sunday school part, but without rooms or enough interest it can't happen and surely money for such a project would have to come from somewhere." Marcy walked passed him and he pulled the door closed. "I've thought about it, but that's as far as it's gotten."

On the little stoop just outside the big door, Marcy stopped and said, "I said something to Sandy about that this morning. She has fifty children as her students. One, of course, is Heidi, but do the other forty-nine go to Sunday school somewhere?" Earnestly, Marcy said, "Roger, your church really needs kids and youth to survive beyond this generation. Your sermon was good, but with only adults the church'll die!"

Nodding, Roger let out a long sigh and looked around at the not too large area surrounding the church, before he said, "I know you're right, Marcy. I wish there was an easy remedy, but there's not, not that I can see, but it's worth some thought. Thanks for bringing it up. Are you staying around or just here for a visit?"

"I really don't know. I only arrived last evening, so I'll have to see. It was a good sermon today, Roger. Thanks."

The young man's face lit up, as he said, "Thank you, Marcy. I'm glad you're better and that you're here."

She nodded. "Believe me I am so glad to be better. You can't believe! Bed rest at home with my mother is not fun!"

Roger nodded. "You know, I think I've heard something like that before from a lady who looks an awful lot like you."

Marcy nodded. "Thank goodness it was only six months for me, for her it was a life time! I can't imagine how she stood it for twenty-five years!"

Roger nodded. "I'm glad she survived, actually, I think she did more than survive. Your sister is a gracious lady."

She preceded him down the steps as he made sure the door was closed behind him. It was still a beautiful summer day, but at high noon, the sun shimmered off the asphalt street. Marcy looked around at the grass around the church. It was only on two sides, there were streets on the other two sides. "How much land does the church own, Roger?" she asked.

"Not a whole lot. I think the line, both on that side and the back is only half of the green that you see. I know Alex, Brad and Derek are influential men in the community, but I have no idea how to go about finding out what we'd need to have Sunday school rooms built. It'd be a major project, that's for sure."

Marcy nodded. "We'll have to think about that."

Roger watched Marcy walk down the steps to the sidewalk and turn toward DeLord's house. She was very different from her sister, not nearly as bubbly or outspoken, but much more intense. However, she and her sister both shared their intense love for their Lord. Marcy had the much darker German heritage than Sandy, too, but she was a lovely young woman.

As Roger stood watching Marcy walk away from the church he realized he stood nearly in the same spot he'd stood all those Sundays ago. At that time he'd stood empty, wondering why his life was such a sham. Thanksgiving was almost upon him, he felt no Thanksgiving, no reason to give a Thanksgiving message. Today his life was full, full to overflowing. He'd just preached a sermon inspired by the wonderful Presence within him. God had truly blessed him.

He also went down the steps and turned to his Jeep. Heidi was in the back seat loving on her baby brother and Raylyn sat in front smiling at him as he came closer. His heart turned over, how he loved his family! Yes, Marcy had a good point, Heidi was getting good Christian training from her mommy, but it wasn't the same as Sunday school. As she said, maybe not right in Vansville, but very close by there were children and their families who needed to know God's love for them and that His love was shown for them by Jesus' death on the cross. He would never forget when Sandy played *The Old Rugged Cross* that time, it had changed his life.

As Roger opened the driver's door to his jeep, Raylyn asked, "Honey, what was it you and Marcy were talking about?"

Roger sat down and closed his door, stuck the key in the ignition and said, "She's concerned that there's no Sunday school and no rooms to even have any. Outside here, she asked where the property lines were. That's something I'm not even sure of and I sure don't know who to ask about that, either."

"She is something else! You know, I think you'd better keep an eye on that girl, she'll have a Sunday school going in no time at all."

"Daddy, how Miss Marcy do that?"

Roger chuckled at what part of the conversation Heidi had zeroed in on – how literal a four year old could be. "Munchkin, Mommy's not saying Miss Marcy'll have Sunday school so fast, but she thinks Miss Marcy'll have some thoughts people here in Vansville will have to listen to because she thinks having Sunday school is really important."

"Uh huh! Sunday school be real 'portant! I liked my Sunday school teacher back in Mishgan lots and lots."

"I know you did. We'll have to think about it, won't we?"

"Yes, Daddy, we do." *Maybe sooner rather than later,* Roger mused to himself.

Marcy took her time walking back to DeLord's. The service in Blairsville started about the same time as the one here, but there was travel time to figure in. The sun was out in all its glory and mountains or no mountains, it was hot. She went in the back door, then through the living room and unlocked the front door. She was glad for the central air that kept the house comfortable. She took her Bible and purse to her room and changed to shorts and a cool top, since Marcy wasn't used to the heat in Georgia. The clock in the living room was playing part of the Westminster chime, so she hurried to the kitchen to start the spaghetti sauce. Their mom made the best sauce and both Sandy and Marcy knew her secret, so Marcy took out her sister's huge frying pan to start the delicious sauce. That was something she could do for her sister.

She also found a pitcher and made tea to pour over ice later. She'd noticed that Ramon had gone to the grocery yesterday and gotten both decaf coffee and tea. She smiled maybe she'd see if she could wean Sandy and Ramon off caffeine. *Mmm, maybe elephants fly, too.*

She was so grateful and so very happy to be here. She sighed and looked out the window to the back yard, with the green, green grass. Maybe she did need this time to recuperate for a while, not just physically. She smiled, as she stirred the sauce, she needed to remember to be content; God would show her her path in His time.

The sauce was bubbling nicely when Marcy heard the garage door opening at the other end of the house. Her family had returned from church. For some strange reason the Sunday when she was on strict bedrest popped into her mind. She laughed. Soon the door from the garage opened and Sandy called, "Hi, Marcy, it smells delicious, thanks for starting dinner. I'll be out to help in a couple of minutes. You know..." Sandy grumbled, as she came closer, "...if you make dinner, I won't be able to take credit for that delicious sauce."

Marcy lifted the lid on the water pan and it was boiling well. Completely ignoring Sandy's last comment, she called back, "No hurry, Sis, I'm about to put the spaghetti in the boiling water. Where's your bread? Do you have some?"

"Natt said he'd bring some," she said, merrily, as she went through the door into their room. "He should be here about one o'clock, Ramon can cut it or whatever."

Ramon followed his wife into their room, but winked at Marcy before closing the door. "See you in a bit, Marcy."

"Oh, yes," Marcy grumbled to herself, "We're having company - some **unattached, my age, male** company. Oh, yes, don't mention that he **doesn't** go to church. We must find that out by going to said church." Marcy didn't bother to say any of this very loud, Ramon and Sandy were both behind the closed door to their bedroom.

Sandy's chair came humming into the kitchen and the smile on her face rivaled the sun. "So was Roger good today?"

"He really was. You told me about that praise band of his and how loud they used to be, but they weren't *too* bad today. Still, it's not like the church at home, they didn't sing one gospel hymn or any of the ones I really like."

Sandy pulled some salad fixings from the refrigerator and put them in the sink, before she said, "I know. At least he's toned them down and won't let them take over the service, but they rarely do any of my favorites, either. There isn't one hymnbook in the place, I've checked. Did Natt Thomas come?"

Marcy smiled. "Nope. Roger asked the Thomas's, but Mrs. Thomas made an excuse."

Her eyes twinkling, Sandy said, "You need to get on him, Sis."

Putting her thumb into her own chest, she looked her sister in the eye and asked, "Mmm, I do, huh? Thanks Sis, thanks a bunch. I met the guy yesterday for all of ten minutes. I didn't really know who he was until I was about ready to leave the store and today you tell me **I'm** to get on him. Hmm, what's wrong with this picture?"

"Why, nothing, nothing at all!"

"Mmm, right!"

Her tongue in her cheek and pulling a door open in a lower cabinet, Sandy said, "But didn't the great commission tell us to start in Jerusalem then work out to Samaria, then to the uttermost part of the world?"

Agreeing instantly, and nodding to Sandy's back, Marcy said, "Mmm hmm, that's what it says and just where would *my* Jerusalem be?"

Turning so she could look at her sister and grinning broadly at her, Sandy said, "Why, here in Vansville, of course! Isn't that where you are, Sis?"

"Mmm, Sis, I sure am. You've been here how long?"

Ramon stepped into the kitchen with his son. "Hey, she's been evangelizing her Jerusalem! Remember, I wouldn't have anything to do with religion before she came and Roger needed his heart rearranged. She's done that."

"Oh, yes, I understand that," Marcy agreed heartily. "But I only came yesterday and found out today that this grandson you're speaking of doesn't come to church."

The church bell woke Natt. He opened one eye, saw the sunshine and closed his eye. He had just snuggled down under his covers and heard his air conditioning kick on when the church bell rang again. Thank goodness for a double bed, he pulled the second pillow over his head and closed his eyes for another nap. About a half hour later he woke up, threw the pillow off his head and turned to his back, then looked at the clock. One day soon he'd get up early enough to meet his grandparents at the church. He would, he really would, he'd promised them and also that preacher that he'd come. He sighed, it just wouldn't be today the bed was too comfortable.

He lay in bed for another few minutes then finally, with a sigh, sat up on the edge of the bed. Barefoot and with only his sleepwear on, he padded to the kitchen and fixed a mug full of coffee and found a Danish, then went in his bathroom to take a shower and shave. He hated shaving on Sunday, it was the only day he didn't usually have to do anything but loaf around and he liked it that way. However, today he'd been invited to Ramon's house for a spaghetti dinner and he must show his better side…if he had one. After all, Sandy and her sister… wait a minute! She'd invited him for dinner when she knew her sister would be there? Of course she hadn't told him that maybe she hadn't known when she invited him. Hmm, maybe she had…

He stuffed the last mouthful of his Danish in his mouth and chugged down the last half of his coffee and pulled out a clean polo shirt to wear with his slacks. "The pits!" he grumbled. "The woman's stuck in a wheelchair, has a new baby, now her sister's come to visit and she's invited me for dinner." As an after-thought he added, "And Grandad told me to be prepared! I am not too sure that this is the best way to spend a Sunday afternoon." No matter, Sandy had insisted that he come and he said he'd come with the bread. He'd gotten the bread last evening just before the store closed. What would he do with a loaf of Italian bread if he didn't take it to eat with spaghetti?

He emptied the last of the coffee into his mug, grabbed up the last Danish and walked out his door onto his porch. He put the food on the little wicker table that sat between the two chairs that matched all the other wicker furniture that Isabel had on all the porches of her cabins. He looked down the street a block or so and saw the people leaving the church building. He looked from the street out to the small meadow, intent on enjoying the day for a few minutes and sipped his coffee he slouched down in the chair, sliding his ankle over his other knee. He took a deep breath it was loaded with pine scent. Vansville was nothing like Atlanta, the town was so small that nature was so close he could hear the birds chirping from where he sat.

Taking another mouthful of Danish and another swig of coffee, he savored the day. Maybe he could even hear the stream back behind Duncan's house gurgling over the rocks. Life here was slow compared to the city and at times he missed the faster pace. At other times he could easily do without all that hustle and bustle, horns blowing and sirens blaring. He guessed the last siren he'd heard was when the ambulance came for his grandad. He always locked his door, but it was only habit, he knew Ms Isabel didn't lock her door if she was staying in town.

He kept looking at the church, even after it had emptied, but the preacher's Jeep was still there. A minute later, one lone woman walked down the steps. He squinted and realized it was none other than Sandy's sister. He looked up and down the street, Sandy's van wasn't there and her sister started walking the other way toward the DeLord house, then he remembered that the light blue van always came onto Isabel's parking lot each Sunday and picked up Isabel and Ruth. Hmm, so sister didn't go with them today, but she had gone to church. He sighed, he'd better be careful at their house today all these people went to church…. Would they get after him? Maybe that's what Grandad meant to be prepared!

He swilled down the last of the coffee and set the mug back on the table, then jumped up from his chair, hurried off the porch and sprinted down his walk. He would be in another place when the blue van came back! Once he reached the end of Isabel's property he slowed down to a fast walk, he had a lot to think about.

However, he didn't want another lecture from Isabel about sleeping in and not going to the Lord's House on the Lord's Day. He had survived one too many of those lectures, besides, yesterday he'd gotten one of those lectures from his grandad! What was it about this place! Did everybody go to church in rural Georgia? Was he the strange one, since he didn't go to church? The only answer he heard was the gurgling creek, much closer, but still out of sight. His pace slowed as he left the buildings behind.

His question made him wonder what his family would be doing today. He shrugged, that wasn't hard to figure out, his family were true creatures of habit. His dad had gotten up when he heard the Sunday paper hit the door and brought it inside, then made a pot of coffee. While he drank two cups he'd read the paper cover to cover, then he'd get dressed. He didn't have time to read the paper any other day of the week, in fact, he pretty much wrote the paper in Atlanta.

Probably yesterday he'd made arrangements to meet two friends at the country club and they'd spend the late morning and all afternoon playing golf, then shooting the breeze in the back of the Pro-shop over a beer or two. His mom would sleep until his dad left then she'd pamper herself with a makeover that would start in the whirlpool in their gigantic hot tub and was meant to last a week. His brother got up when his dad did, but never leave his room because he'd get snagged by his TV that housed his latest video game hero. He'd sit there yelling at those animated characters until his noise finally roused his sister. Once she was finally up she'd work on looking as slovenly as any teenager could, then bury her nose in a novel. What was wrong with that? That's how his family spent Sundays. As far as he could tell none of those things hurt anybody. Danny had only recently taken over his place with the video games.

Natt sighed Atlanta was too far to go for a one day visit.

When he was in the woods behind Roads' house, he sat on a large rock that sat precariously beside the creek. He leaned over and put his hand down in the cool water and let the rushing stream tickle his fingers. It was a beautiful end of June day, there was a nice breeze murmuring through the pines. It was a good day to be alive. To tell the truth, he didn't really miss those video game characters.

With the water rushing through his fingers he breathed deeply, moved his shoulders and let the tensions of the week roll off his back. Really, Vansville wasn't a bad place to live if you didn't care about having excitement in your life. He guessed Sandy's concert next week would be the biggest excitement in town since he'd moved here in January. Maybe for his family, his grandad getting clobbered by the limb was another bit of excitement, still that was lame.

The van crunching on the gravel parking lot in front of Isabel's house off in the distance made him look at his watch. He had about forty minutes to get to DeLord's house. He must stop in his cabin and get the loaf of garlic bread he'd bought at Alex's store yesterday, but he didn't have to go yet. He sure didn't want to seem too anxious to see Sandy's sister! Really, he didn't want to see her, especially if she went to church! He didn't know much about Sandy DeLord, but if she'd gotten her husband and the preacher converted…well, keep him out of that!

Twenty minutes later he left the rock, shook off his hand and went back to his cabin for the bread. He looked at himself in his bathroom mirror and decided he looked good enough for Sunday dinner, but since he'd been outside, he went to the bathroom and ran a comb through his hair. After all, he was a civilized man wind blown hair didn't make the best impression.

He picked up the long loaf from his table and looked at it. How did you carry a long loaf of bread through town? If he carried it by the end of the wrapper near the ties it would drag the ground. Surely you didn't sling it over your shoulder like a pick-ax! However, if he carried it by the middle he'd probably squash that part of it and the thing would be hanging down on both sides of his hand. He sighed, found a plastic bag with handles and stuck it in. It's a good thing he ran a hardware store, not a grocery store!

He was not looking forward to dinner, but he picked up the bag and realized that the top end of the loaf rested against his arm. Maybe that was a good way to carry it. He sighed and opened the door, time to face the music. Out of habit, he picked up his keys from the table, pushed the lock on the door and walked out. Vansville was small enough he knew where the DeLord's lived without having to ask. On the sidewalk he looked down the street. Now that church was over, there wasn't one car parked between Isabel's and DeLord's! Could life get any more simple and uncomplicated?

Sandy had rinsed the spaghetti and turned it into her large bowl in the kitchen and Marcy placed the last paper napkin beside the fork on the dining room table when someone knocked on the door. Since Ramon sat in the kitchen holding Jon in his arms, Sandy called, "Come in, Natt, the door's open!"

The front door opened and Natt took a step inside. The instant he turned the knob and the door opened, his stomach gave a rumble, the aroma was the best he'd smelled in many months. He'd never been in this house before, but he noticed how large the room was and how wide the traffic lanes were, obviously that was because of Sandy's chair. He wondered what it was like being married to someone who couldn't leave a sitting position in a wheelchair. Ramon had to be some kind of guy. He'd never known a person in a wheelchair he wondered how he would be with someone like that. As he turned to close the door, he saw Marcy standing in the archway between the living room and the dining room. His mouth grew dry, he had to swallow.

"Hi," she said. "It's good of you to come."

Natt couldn't figure out why, but he could feel heat on his neck. "Hi," he answered and wondered how he could be a former journalism student and the present owner and major salesman of a major store in town and not be able to think of anything more profound. Not only that, he felt his ears burning!

He held up the bag and said, "I have the garlic bread, should I take it to the kitchen?"

Marcy had her mouth open to answer, but Ramon called from the kitchen, "Natt, bring that stuff out here. Sandy just handed me the knife to cut it and the plate's sitting here on the table. We'll have that stuff ready in a second."

"Gotcha! On my way!" he answered.

Natt nodded to Marcy, but she had turned back to the table and didn't look at him again. He couldn't think of anything else to say to her, so he walked a wide circle around her and headed for the kitchen. Where was the nonchalance he'd felt yesterday when he'd talked with her at the gas pump? He sure felt tongue-tied today! In the archway between the dining room and the kitchen he said, "Sure, Ramon, it's ready to slice, or maybe get a minute in the oven. Alex didn't say if it needed heating or not, but it does need to be sliced. It sure smells good in here!" Good grief, men didn't babble, did they?

Natt sauntered into the kitchen, still holding the handles of his plastic bag. Ramon sat holding the baby but the big bread knife lay on the table beside him. Sandy was at the sink letting the cooked spaghetti slither into her bowl and Marcy came and stood in the archway behind Natt. Ramon stood up, came around the table, held out his arms to Natt and said, "Here, hold Jon for a minute while I cut your bread."

"Wh-what? Y-you want me to hold it?" Natt choked out, his eyes growing huge. "Last baby I held was my brother eight years ago. Mom wouldn't let me hold him much." He set the bread on the table and half-heartedly raised his hands, but the look on his face was priceless.

Ramon's grin stretched across his face, as he placed the baby on his hands. His eyes twinkled he had no trouble figuring out how uncomfortable the young man was. "Come on, Man, babies don't break. Jon's used to anything. He lays on Sandy's lap all the time and listens to the hum of her chair. You can do it. Here, just hold him in your arms and support his head."

Natt didn't bring Jon to his chest, he didn't move, only to look down at the infant resting on his arms. The fearful look intensified as his eyes sank down to the little bundle resting on his hands. "I'm not so sure," he whispered.

Seeming to pay the young man no attention, Sandy said, "Marcy, did you pour the tea yet? I heard you put the ice in the glasses." After putting the spaghetti bowl in her lap, she added, "Girl, you have just about taken over my job!"

"I was on my way to the fridge, Sis."

"Great! As soon as Ramon slices the bread, we'll be ready. I heard Natt's stomach growl a few minutes ago, I'm sure he's hungry." Natt didn't say anything, but he could feel his cheeks start to burn from Sandy's comment.

Activity moved around Natt. Sandy set the cover on the bowl of spaghetti on her lap and headed for the dining room. Ramon pulled a cutting board from the cupboard, then pulled the bread from the wrapper and started slicing the bread, while Marcy pulled the pitcher of tea from the refrigerator, went to the kitchen table and began pouring the tea over the ice in the glasses on the table. However, Natt and Jon were like an island. Natt looked down at the baby and Jon very solemnly looked back at Natt. The baby's eyes were wide open, but there was no expression on his mouth. Natt couldn't seem to look anywhere but at the baby. He had no idea what to say or do in the situation he was in.

Ramon finished cutting the bread, threw the wrapper in the trash then picked up the bread plate to follow his wife into the dining room, leaving Marcy the only other one in the kitchen. Neither of them spoke, when Jon scrunched up his face, his eyes closed, and a loud noise came from the other end. It was like a firecracker going off, Natt danced in place, looked up at the only other person in the room, the panic spreading exponentially over his face. "What - what was that? What did I do?" he gasped.

Marcy laughed, set the pitcher on the counter, turned and held out her hands. "You didn't do anything he just filled his pants and needs a change. If you'll set the tea pitcher in the fridge and take the glasses to the table, I'll change him. Umm, be sure to wash your hands first."

"Oh, thank you!" Natt's gratitude was heart-felt, as he quickly handed the baby to Marcy. "Umm, sure, I'll do that."

Natt washed his hands at the kitchen sink, while Marcy disappeared from the kitchen. Concentrating on what he was doing, Natt set the pitcher in the refrigerator, but didn't see the tray sitting beside the glasses, so he picked up two full glasses and headed into the dining room with them. He set them down at the top of two of the places then went back to the kitchen for the other two. Sandy and Ramon shared a silent smile behind Natt's back. If the young man had been uncomfortable before, he was totally unwound now. Only minutes after Natt reappeared with the other two glasses, Marcy came from the other direction carrying a sweet smelling, cooing baby in her arms.

Marcy set Jon in his infant carrier that sat on a stool between his mommy and daddy and said, "So, we're ready to have dinner, we're all clean as a whistle."

Still ill at ease, Natt looked at his white hands and said, "I need to wash my hands! Is there a bathroom close by?"

Ramon nodded, his eyes twinkling, he'd heard Marcy tell their guest to wash his hands before bringing in the tea. "Yup, down the hall, first door."

While he was gone, Marcy took the seat at right angles to her sister and said to both of them, "You two are something else! That poor guy! He's uncomfortable being here with all of us then you make it worse by shoveling Jon off on him!"

Chuckling, Ramon gave his sister-in-law a wink and said, "We're leaving it up to you to make him feel at home."

"Me!" Marcy squeaked. "No way!"

"Sure, why not? He's your age, you know."

"Brother-in-law..." she chided.

"Yes?" Ramon said innocently.

Natt came back to the dining room, but had to move around the table to the empty seat. He looked at Ramon, obviously bypassing Marcy and said, "Sorry."

"Not to worry," he said, nonchalantly. "Besides, babies have their own timetable. Just now Jon decided he had to make a stink."

Sandy smiled at Natt, seeing his discomfort and held out her hands to Ramon and Marcy. Ramon, of course, took her hand, as Sandy said, "Natt, we always say grace before meals and we hold hands around the table. Please join us, won't you?" If he had been uncomfortable before, it ratcheted up another notch, because it didn't take a rocket scientist to see whose hand he must hold. Natt bit down on his tongue and hoped it would keep his cheeks from turning crimson. He knew his behavior with the baby had told the other three how inexperienced he was with babies.

Ramon held Sandy's hand and laid his other hand on the table toward Natt. Marcy also took Sandy's hand then tentatively put her hand on the table between herself and Natt. Reluctantly, Natt took Ramon's hand then looked at Marcy's small hand resting on the table. His eyes went around the table, first at the faces watching, then at the hands. A minute later, he cleared his throat and laid his right hand across Marcy's, but didn't fold hers into his.

Ramon decided that was good enough, so he began praying, thanking God for the food. Ramon raised his head immediately and Natt's stomach growled loud enough for the others to hear. Embarrassed, Natt quickly lifted his glass and took a long drink of iced tea. Paying no attention, Ramon reached for the large bowl of spaghetti. "Ah, my favorite meal. Well, I'll have to qualify that. It's my favorite meal when my wife makes spaghetti. Natt, you'll have to help me decide on this one. Marcy fixed the sauce, I never tasted hers we'll have to check it out."

As he passed the bowl to Natt, Marcy said, "Brother-in-law, I think I need to put you in the same box as my brother! I make good spaghetti sauce! Sandy and I have the same mother and we both know her recipe."

Scowling at the young woman, Ramon said, "Tell me, why do I go in a box with Ed? You know we've only been together a few times. He's a nice guy, though, so I guess that wouldn't be too bad a deal."

Still scowling at the young man, she exclaimed, "Because you're the third biggest tease in the country! Right behind my dad and my brother. I swear!"

Ramon looked at Sandy perplexed. "Darling, am I a tease?" He took a big helping of sauce drizzling it over his huge pile of spaghetti and handed it on to Natt. "Eat up, man! You got a hard afternoon ahead of you, listening to my wife practice for her concert." He shrugged and grinned at the young man. "My sister-in-law's a wild card one never knows how things'll turn out with her around."

Marcy huffed, "Brother-in-law, there you go again!"

Natt already had his mouth open, so when Marcy finished speaking, he blurted out, "I...I do? Grandad told me Sandy's good, she's played in Atlanta."

Ramon shrugged. "She has, but it's been a while, the baby, you know...."

Natt looked at the sleeping baby, content in his infant carrier. He'd never heard Sandy play he didn't know she'd been in the hospital for six weeks. He looked from the baby to Sandy, who by now had received the spaghetti bowl from Marcy and was putting some on her plate. The baby, of course, was sleeping and Natt had no idea what to think. What in the world did Ramon mean by saying Marcy was a wild card?

Before he could say anything, Sandy said, "Sis, are you up to singing at the concert? There's a piece you could sing, if you will."

Her fork poised above her pile of spaghetti, Marcy said, "Sandy, all the singing I've done since I got sick was a little in church this morning with all the others who sang. I have no idea what my lung capacity is now. I sure didn't sing too loudly this morning. Roger asked me to sing in the service, but I turned him down really fast. I even reminded him that I don't read music." She shook her head. "He's something else!"

"Well, sure he is!" Ramon exclaimed.

Stirring the sauce into her spaghetti, Sandy said, "We'll have to practice that this afternoon. Surely you can work into something."

"Yeah, you did good at Christmas, you know."

Marcy sighed and shook her head, "Sis, it's no wonder Roger didn't have a chance or Ramon, either."

Natt looked from Marcy to Sandy to Ramon and asked, "A chance at what? What do you mean by that?"

Ramon grinned at the perplexed young man. "Sandy is nothing if not persistent. I guess she's had to be with her mom the way she is."

"That's good, is it?"

Ramon took a large mouthful of spaghetti, chewed and swallowed, before he said, "My friend, before Sandy came to Vansville I was not a Christian, I had no use for God or the church. I'd never been to church as an adult in fact, I couldn't remember ever going to church. My mom had no use for church, still doesn't. However, Sandy came as my receptionist and every chance she had, she reminded me I was a sinner and needed to accept God's gift of salvation through His Son, Jesus. Before the summer was over certain things happened, events occurred and I became a Christian.

"Not long after Sandy came, my friend, Roger and I persuaded Sandy to play a concert for the town. The church was the only place big enough to hold that many people, so Roger had to come here several times to make some arrangements. At the time, he wasn't very much of a Christian and Sandy started in with him. It wasn't long before Roger got right with God and now he's a great pastor." He waved his hand between the two sisters, and said, "Maybe you get the picture, Sandy's persistent. Marcy doesn't think she has much of a chance of getting out of singing at this concert in a few days." Ramon grinned at the lady across from him. "But then, Marcy's persistent, too."

In the softest whisper, Marcy said, "Brother-in-law…"

"I see," Natt said, rather softly. Maybe he was getting the picture. Maybe he understood why his grandad told him to be prepared! Without saying anything else, Natt lowered his head and studied his spaghetti.

Marcy was silent, but she wondered what Natt was thinking. It was very obvious by the look on his face that he was having some thoughts maybe they were second thoughts about even coming to this house. Natt had been looking at Ramon as he spoke, but as he spoke his reply, he quickly dropped his head and took the plate of bread slices Ramon held out to him.

Natt took a thick chunk of bread and handed the plate to Marcy. Disgusted, he noticed that his hand shook as he held out the plate. He swallowed and willed more strength into his hand, he was a man, after all, things like babies who filled their pants on his watch, a persistent lady he didn't know well and a very pretty girl his age didn't make a ninny out of him! So his hostess was persistent, he'd been studying to be a journalist, that was their middle name! They'd taught him to take things in stride at the university.

Sandy ate daintily. After everyone had eaten several mouthfuls, she said, "Natt, you told me the other day or maybe it was your grandad that you now owned the store. That wasn't what you'd planned to do with your life, was it?"

Ah, now he was back on safe ground, he could answer this. "Oh, no, definitely not. Dad's the Editor in Chief of an Atlanta newspaper and I was planning to be a journalist. He said he had a position on his staff waiting for me. I was a junior at the university there in Atlanta and on the school paper staff as one of the regular writers. No, when Grandad had his stroke on New Year's we were here. When Mom and Dad came back from the hospital that night they asked me to run the store for my vacation, so I did. Before Grandad was released from the hospital, we all knew there was no way Grandad could come back and do what he did before he had the stroke. We all decided that I was the best one to help out. I agreed to both of those plans, but I never thought it'd be a permanent position."

After another mouthful of the delicious spaghetti, Natt continued, "However, as time went on Grandad didn't come all the way back. It was obvious that he'd never be able to take on the load by himself and Gramma...." He shook his head and added, "I've come to terms with this, I'm okay with it now, but it's sure not what I'd planned to do with my life."

Ramon nodded. "Marcy's kind of in that same boat. She was in nursing school and she planned to be a missionary nurse, overseas, but right around the time Brad had his stroke, Marcy came down with Rheumatic Fever and had to drop out of nursing – the doc told her it was a permanent drop-out." He looked over at Marcy and said, "Unlike you, she's still wondering what she'll do with her life."

Natt looked at Marcy and asked, "You said you're from Philadelphia, didn't you?" When she nodded, he asked, "If you're not sure of your plans why are you in this Podunk? What's here to spark your career?"

"*Not* my mother," she answered succinctly.

"Ah, I see."

"Yes, well… at least she's not here! It's too far away for her to just run over."

Marcy felt much more comfortable talking with Sandy, so she looked at her sister and said, "Something else that's not there are these beautiful hills and mountains! I sat on the deck after you left for church and just soaked up the beauty. While I sat, a little bluebird came and sang to me. I really enjoyed having my devotions out there this morning."

"A bluebird?" Ramon asked. "Wow! They're such a shy bird I'm surprised he came so close to the house and you."

"Yes, it was a bluebird. He hopped around a while and showed me his red chest. I loved hearing his song, too."

"Oh," Natt said, after he swallowed, "Did Gramma call and leave a message about a hike the other day?"

"Yes, she did," Sandy answered. "She only mentioned two people who'd like to go, but we only schedule hikes for five or more people. It doesn't matter how long the hike is for, but we're pretty strict about having five people."

"Hmm, it was Grandad's nephew and me who were wanting to go. Maybe I'll call back to Atlanta and see if I can round up a few of my friends from school. They're off for the summer, maybe there's a few of them who'd want to go. I'd sure like to get out of that store for a few days. Summer is when I try to find out-of-doors jobs. At least other years I've had jobs that kept me out-of-doors."

Ramon scowled and picked up another hunk of bread. Pushing it into his mound of spaghetti, he said, "I thought you said Brad couldn't run the place by himself. I know every time I come in he's sitting in that same chair, maybe even dozing. Does he get up and wait on people like he used to?"

TWELVE

Natt also felt much more comfortable talking to Ramon, so he said, "Yes, that's true. Grandad doesn't even remember to turn on the gas pumps after he opens the store. Lots of times I open the Laundromat, too, because he forgets it's part of the complex and he does doze a lot. Pretty much, he runs the cash register and that's about it except when I'm on lunch. He told me the other day that his twin nephews are both coming. One of them wants to hike, but he thinks he can talk the other one into running the store for a few days."

"Ah, that makes sense. I often wondered how store owners could do that day after day and not go stark, raving mad cooped up like that."

"Maybe Grandad can, but not this guy," Natt said, emphatically then stuffed the last hunk of bread into his mouth.

"How rugged are the trails?" Marcy asked, trying hard not to act too enthusiastic, but she knew she'd really like to get out in these hills and mountains. Sitting out back on the deck, enjoying the view had wet her desire this morning.

Ramon shook his head, seeing right through her thinly veiled question immediately. "Most of them are up and down hills and a few are in the foothills of the mountains. Maybe by the end of the season you'll be strong enough to hike, but since the doctor's just released you I wouldn't want to chance it, Marcy."

Marcy made a face and let out a long sigh. "Thanks," she grumbled. "You read my mind, Brother-in-law."

The handsome man grinned and winked at her. "I kind of figured that was why you asked, Marcy. I think you're here to rest, but not with your mom hanging over you."

"Mmm, but you know I don't want to be treated like an invalid."

Sandy laughed. "No chance of that, Sis. Say, Ramon has another hike going out tomorrow morning. Usually while he's gone I drive around to find some scenery to paint, since I take Jon with me, that'll leave the other front seat for you. How's that?"

"That'd be great, Sis!"

Sandy smiled. "Cool! How about you getting dessert? It's in the fridge."

"Sure, not a problem." Glad to get away from the confusing young man who sat beside her, she jumped from her chair and hurried into the kitchen. She let out another sigh, she had avoided looking at him, but she hadn't seen him looking at her, either. She opened the refrigerator and pulled out the strawberries and whipped cream Sandy had prepared for dessert. She found bowls and put them all on the tray Natt hadn't used for the drinks.

After dinner, Marcy insisted she fill the dishwasher, while Sandy went to the piano to start practicing. However, Marcy seemed to have no energy, even after such a good meal. As soon as she finished filling the dishwasher and getting it started, she went to her room and lay down. Both Sandy and Ramon could tell that she wasn't feeling well; the usually vivacious young woman could hardly drag herself from the kitchen down the hall to the bedroom. There was a small click as the door closed, then silence behind the door.

Natt watched Marcy go by, but he already sat in one of the comfortable chairs in the living room, enthralled by Sandy's playing. She had chosen another new piece to play after the intermission, it was another classical piece written by one of the masters of the eighteenth century and of course Natt had never heard it. He watched as Sandy's fingers flew across the keys, her back working rhythmically on the little black pouch attached to her chair. He was amazed, just as he'd been on the trail with her painting. He had never seen anyone with such talents, but who had such a positive attitude and was paralyzed in a wheelchair. He determined he'd have to quit whining about being in the store every day.

So he was unhappy about not being a journalist, but he still had his health and all his limbs worked. In fact, he wasn't really doing badly as a store owner he was making lots more money than he ever had at other jobs. Other than the fact he felt cooped up in the store, he really didn't mind the job. Ordering supplies was tedious, but he really had fun talking to all the customers who came in and he'd made friends with several of the suppliers. Something else he realized, many of his profs had regularly told their classes to be antagonistic to get their stories. He knew, here at the store, he didn't have to be antagonistic with his customers.

While he sat listening to the wonderful music, he remembered what his dad had mentioned back on Memorial Day. He'd been inspired by Sandy and had spoken about her on the way back to Vansville. He'd asked Grandad what Sandy would do if someone interviewed her and he put an article about her in the Atlanta paper. A smile worked its way over Natt's face, he could ask and if she consented, he could be the one to interview her! He was sure if he did a good job his dad would print his article in his paper. What a super idea! Maybe he didn't have to give up journalism completely, not if he could help it! His mind came back to the sounds of the piano when he recognized the one finger rendition of *Twinkle, Twinkle, Little Star.*

Later in the afternoon, Sandy raised her hands from the keyboard, but Ramon was on his feet, held the baby in one arm and took the black pouch from Sandy's chair and laid it on the music rack on the piano. Before Natt could think of something to say, Sandy whirled around and said, "Say, Natt, we always go to Roger's church for his evening service. Since it's nearly time; why don't you go with us? Besides, if you do, you'll be able to say you're one of the few who've ridden on my lift into the van."

Natt had his mouth open, but Ramon said, "Hey, that's a super idea! You won't have as far to walk to Isabel's cabins from the church it's only a few blocks from the church, not across town like it is from here."

Natt couldn't very well tell them he had other plans, what other plans were there to have in the little town of Vansville on Sunday evening? Everybody knew the town rolled up its sidewalks at five o'clock on Saturday evening. "Umm, yeah, I guess I can go."

"Great!"

Marcy's door opened, but no one saw her, so she stood and listened to the short exchange from her two conniving relatives and their poor unsuspecting company. She sighed and shook her head. No, people her sister set her sights on didn't have much of a chance! She was surprised that Sandy had noticed when she felt bad after lunch and hadn't insisted she come in the living room to practice anyway. No, Sandy was great! If it had been her mom, she would have taken her by the arm, right from the table and nearly dragged her to her room! Probably she'd have pulled her up from the table during dessert and trundled her off to bed. She was sure Sandy noticed how ill she felt, but unlike her mom, Sandy let her make her own choices and didn't comment about how she felt.

As Marcy thought about it, she hadn't gotten one of those weak spells in a very long time. Could it be that the drive down had taken more out of her than she'd realized? Maybe it was the extra heat. It was hotter here than in Philadelphia. Actually, it could have been the change in altitude Vansville was in the mountains, not on sea level. It didn't matter, she'd felt weak, but now that she'd taken a nap she felt better.

She walked into the living room and said, "I guess I'm about ready to go with you guys to church. So you do go to Roger's church in the evenings?"

"Yes, we started back when the weather was bad in February, going each Sunday. We had gone once in a while in the evening before that. Only one guy from the praise team comes on Sunday night and between the two of us, we supply the music for the songs. There's a lot more singing on Sunday night and Roger has a Bible study, instead of a sermon."

"So there's a Bible study in the evening. Does Isabel come?"

"No, she and Ruth still go back to Blairsville."

Marcy shrugged. "I guess her friends are there."

Sandy nodded. "That's what she says."

The ladies found their purses then the four went down the long hallway to the garage. Ramon followed Sandy holding the infant seat until he'd closed the house door into the garage. Then he placed it on Sandy's lap and took the key to the outside passenger door of the van. When the lift was on the ground, he said, "Okay, here's how we'll work this. Sandy and I'll go up first and while I get Jon buckled down, Sandy'll send the lift back down and you two can come up on it. Marcy can close the door while

Sandy gets locked in. It's a piece of cake and we'll be on our way." Ramon winked at Natt. "Good to have you going, man."

"Umm, thanks."

Both Natt and Marcy stood watching the passenger door slowly open, then, after it was all the way open, the lift moved from its closed position to finally reach the floor. "Wow!" Natt said, "I bet if you had to do that outside in the rain a body could get pretty wet waiting. It looks like it's got only one speed, snail."

"You got that right!" Ramon answered, as he stepped on the lift with Sandy. "When Sandy was my receptionist before we were married, she lived at Isabel's cabins and this garage was my office. She got pretty wet several times when hurricane rains came up the coast. When we got married, that was the first thing I did was make this into a double garage so she could load and unload in the dry." Ramon grinned. "Actually I don't mind a bit having to get in my truck in the dry, either."

Natt chuckled. "I can imagine."

As the lift went back down, everyone heard the church bell ring and Sandy said, "Hurry all you can, guys. I never know until we get there if I'm to play for the service or not."

"We're on it, Sis," Marcy said, stepping on the lift.

When they arrived, all was quiet, so they let Sandy off and she started up the ramp. Roger met her and as Ramon closed up the van they heard Roger say, "Sandy, Gil called just before we left the house and said he couldn't make it, would you be kind enough to help us out?"

Sandy smiled and said, "Sure, Roger, when'll you buy hymn books so people can find the hymn and sing along? Some of those second and third verses really have a message, you know."

Roger sighed, a smile on his face for the lovely lady, "Sandy, between you and your sister, you'd have us going way over budget. I'm not sure where we'd get money for two projects like you're both suggesting."

As Sandy headed for the side aisle, she looked back and asked, "What would those projects be, Roger?"

Roger had to raise his voice as Sandy moved away, "You're suggesting hymn books and Marcy told me we should start having Sunday school."

Sandy turned and looked across the seats toward the back door and grinned. "Excellent idea, Roger! We'll put that on the agenda."

"Mmm, sounds familiar," he muttered to himself.

Roger turned back toward the door, shaking his head. Marcy was there, with Natt behind her, then Ramon with the baby. "Marcy, you've stirred up a hornet's nest! Raylyn asked what we'd been looking at when we stood on the stoop for a while this morning. Of course, Heidi was in the seat and heard me. Now she's all fired up about having Sunday school."

Marcy gave the young pastor a radiant smile. "See, what did I tell you!"

Without answering her non-question, Roger turned and said, "Why, if it isn't Natt Thomas! How is it you're here and with these guys?"

Natt's mouth was open, but before he could answer, Ramon said, "He came to the house for Sunday dinner, stayed to hear Sandy practice and of course, she finished just in time to come to church, so we brought Natt along. He won't have as far to walk home this way." Ramon gave Roger a wink behind Natt's back.

"Fantastic! It's good to have you, Natt. Come on in, all the seats are free. We don't hold any open specially."

"Yeah, thanks," was all the young man could say. It wasn't hard to see the red working its way up his neck onto his chin. Except to come to church for the Christmas Eve service here at this church, Natt had never been in any other church building. To say he felt out of his element was to put it mildly.

Ramon turned at the back of the seats, but Marcy led Natt up the center aisle. She turned into the second row, with Natt walking reluctantly behind her, while Ramon also turned in the same row from the other side. Ramon stopped at the end seat and set Jon's infant seat next, then Marcy sat in the third seat. Natt looked around, but quickly sat down next to Marcy, the church was filling up quite fast and he felt conspicuous. He guessed it had been Christmas Eve, with a late night service when he'd last been in a church and it was in this little church. His parents never went to church. Like a kid, his head had been filled, remembering the stacks of presents under the tree, he hadn't heard a word Roger said.

He was a bit chagrined, perhaps he should listen to the message tonight, after all; he was an adult. Thinking about tomorrow at the store didn't seem like much of an option. Sandy started to play, he noticed she didn't have her little black pouch, but the sound was still great. He decided to give his dad a call and run his idea by him maybe he could do it after the concert. Actually, he'd invite his family up for the concert. He'd never heard classical music played around his parent's home, but then, CDs and tapes were nothing like hearing a concert first hand. Sandy DeLord had talent coming out her little finger. Soon after they sang a few hymns Roger stepped to the podium and opened his Bible for the evening Bible study.

After the service, the man who had been the foreman of the ramp-building project stood back, letting all the other worshipers go ahead of him. Finally, when only Ramon, Sandy, Marcy and Natt were left, he came up to Roger and asked, "Say, Pastor, what's this I hear about Sunday school? I even heard little Miss Heidi talkin' about it."

Roger pulled in a breath and took the man's hand, before he said, "Corky, at this point, it's just wind blowing through the trees. I know it's something we need, but as things stand, it's something to dream and pray about. We don't have any rooms and no space to put any or any resources to put any up."

The older man nodded. "Now that I'm retired, I got a bit of time on my hands. I think I'll be looking into that, you know. I got family who needs to hear some things from that Good Book. They're not far from here this'd be a good place for them to come."

Marcy's eyes were shining, her smile spreading across her face. She forgot she'd come with anyone, as she raced up beside the two men. "Really? Oh, that would be terrific!"

Corky looked at Marcy. "You'd be Ms Sandy's sister, aren't you?"

"Yes!"

"You're here to visit for a while?"

"I sure am!"

Holding out his hand to her, Corky said, "How'd you like to be my right hand helper in comin' up with somethin'?"

Marcy was almost dancing, as she grabbed his hand. "Mr. Corky, I'd be thrilled! Sunday school is so important! And…and any church needs a Sunday school."

The older man laughed and said, "It's just Corky, but I forgot your name since you was here back at Christmas."

"I'm Marcy Bernard, I don't know much about building stuff, but I'd be glad to give you any help I can and lots of encouragement."

Giving Marcy a big grin, Corky said, "Wanna meet me here tomorra about one o'clock or have you got something on you can't get away from?"

"Sure! I'll be on the spot!"

Roger, Ramon, Natt and Sandy all stood around the two. Sandy, her eyes sparkling, exclaimed, "Corky! Are you serious?"

The older man nodded and smiled down at the vivacious woman. "I sure am, Ms Sandy. I got a couplea grandkids needin' to come hear the good news. They live a few miles out from here but they don't go no place on Sunday. I've tried to get their Mom and Dad to come, but they don't see no children here, so they don't come."

"Well, that better stop!" Sandy and Marcy exclaimed together.

"I know!" Corky exclaimed. "And I'm just the man to change things!"

Natt watched Marcy. She was a beautiful young woman. He'd thought she was a pretty decent girl when he'd met her briefly at the store on Saturday and he'd been encouraged when she said she'd come to visit her sister. He'd seen her come from the church this morning, but hadn't revised his thoughts about her then. At Ramon's house for dinner, he'd had a few second thoughts, but he still thought he'd maybe pursue something casual with her. However, as she became so enthused and animated talking about Sunday school, he decided she wasn't someone he wanted to get better acquainted with. After all, he was perfectly content with his life the way it was. If it was good enough for Mom and Dad, it was good enough for him. Right?

When Marcy still stood beside Corky, her eyes shining, Natt decided it was his chance to escape. There was space between her and the last seat into the aisle and he took one long step to reach it. From there he took several more long steps toward the doorway leading to the foyer. He'd almost made it, when Roger realized what the movement was and whirled around.

"Hey, Natt!" he called. "Hey, don't run off!" Roger took several long strides, too and was beside Natt before he made it through the inside door. Holding out his hand, he said, "I see Sandy and Marcy prevailed on you to come to church tonight! Welcome! I sure hope it won't take as long to get you here again, Man!"

Scuffing his foot on the carpeting in the foyer, he didn't look up at Roger, he also saw his hand, but didn't reach up to shake it. Instead, he mumbled, "Umm, yeah, Pre… umm, Roger. Maybe so." Reluctantly, Natt raised his hand and gave Roger's hand one shake before he dropped his hand again. "Yeah, I gotta go." He still wouldn't make eye contact.

Roger put his hand on Natt's shoulder and said much more quietly, "Really, Natt, I'm glad you came. We'll look for you again."

Natt shook Roger's hand from his shoulder, stepped away, then raised his head and his eyes mere slits, he said, "I don't think so." A deep scowl spread over his handsome face and sparks flashed in his eyes. He stuffed his hands in his pockets, as he continued, "My folks don't think church is worth two nickels, they never go, I've never been at home. They relax on Sunday and do stuff they think is fun that they can't do when they work. Why should I take my only day off each week to get dressed up and come sit in some stuffy building with a bunch of people mostly my grandparents age for a couple hours? It's stupid! Besides, this way you can save my seat for some other unsuspecting soul. So long, Preacher!"

As Natt pushed open the outside door, Roger's face showed how stunned he was. He had to swallow before he could say, "Natt, I'm really sorry you feel that way. We talked about it tonight we talked about what *you* do with Jesus, during *your* life. That's the most important decision *you* can ever make in your life. It has nothing to do with your parents, but everything to do with where *you're* headed." Roger's last sentence reached Natt through the wooden door that closed behind him. Roger sighed, he was pretty sure the door was thick enough Natt hadn't heard his last few lines. Eternity was a very, very long time.

Sandy always seemed to be in tune with what was happening in someone's soul. She was enthusiastic with Corky's pronouncement, but only seconds after Natt started his mad dash for the door, she turned and watched. Corky and Marcy were in enthusiastic exchange, but Sandy was aware of Roger and Natt's every word. As she watched the outside door close and Roger turn back into the auditorium, she moved around Ramon and rolled down the aisle toward Roger.

She smiled at the dejected young man and said, "Roger, he goes on our prayer list tonight! It's a good thing he's so accessible at the store. We'll have him in God's hands in no time at all, you'll see."

Roger gave Sandy a sad smile. "I'm glad, Sandy, he'll go on ours, too. My parents are good Christian people and they prayed for me for nearly seven years before you brought me back to the cross. Natt doesn't have God-fearing parents who'll pray for him. It looks like we're on our own with this guy."

Sandy reached out and took Roger's hand. "Roger," she chided, shaking her head, "we are not alone! God is on our side, with Him we are a majority! Let's start now." She bowed her head, so Roger followed suit and Sandy said. "Father, we've seen and heard what Natt just said. We know we can't move his heart to You, but You're the Author of the impossible and we know You can bring that young man to Yourself. We pray You will start that process right now. Thank You in advance, in Your Son's precious Name, amen." Sandy raised her head and looked earnestly into Roger's eyes. "Roger, a verse of Scripture comes to mind.

> 'Now to Him who is able to do immeasurably more than we ask or imagine according to His power that is at work within us, to Him be glory in the church and in Christ Jesus throughout all generations, for ever and ever! Amen.'" (Eph 3: 20,21)

Roger took his hand from Sandy's and placed it on her shoulder. He looked down at the beautiful woman, gave a sad smile and said, "Thanks, Sandy, you always know what to do and what to say. I appreciate it."

"Roger, you said what needed to be said to Natt. You planted the seed, but God's the only One who can make it grow and produce fruit. Now, about Sunday school…"

Roger had to laugh. "Yeah, about that…"

Monday morning, Natt walked in the store right behind his grandad. He'd opened the Laundromat on his way by from the cabin and now went straight to the switch that turned on the gas pumps. Before Brad could say anything, Natt disappeared into the back, picked up the big coffee urn, put it in the big sink and started water into it. It was big enough he could measure out the grounds and fill the filter while the water ran. Brad, of course, headed for his favorite chair behind the cash register. If Brad didn't say anything about his visit at DeLord's or his reluctant time at church, he wouldn't bring it up, but he sure had a lot to think about from his time in that church house!

However, much to Natt's surprise, Brad stopped at the cash register long enough to punch the keys to open it up, but didn't even move to sit down. He followed Natt to the back room, then leaned on the small counter beside the sink. Natt didn't even have to think what was on his grandad's mind it was there in his eyes. Quickly he looked away, but Brad asked, "So how'd it go at Sandy's yesterday, Son?"

Trying not to show his agitation, Natt shrugged and said, "All right, I guess. She and her sister make good spaghetti. I enjoyed a home cooked meal. She did practice after that and I agree with you, she's awesome!"

"Heard you went to church with 'em. That's good, Son."

"Yeah, Grandad, sorta couldn't help it."

His eyes twinkling, he said, "Ahh, they he'pt ya make your decision to go?"

"Absolutely!" he said, a bit vehemently.

Brad put his elbow down on the counter next to the sink and as water splashed into the urn, he said, "So what's the deal, Son? Why you all worked up about it?"

Natt let out a long sigh, was he that transparent? He shook his head, working on measuring out the coffee into the filter. Finally, he took another breath before he said, "Grandad, what's so all fire powerful about going to church? And what's the deal about that Book Roger reads from? So I know we talk about Baby Jesus born in a manger at Christmas and we celebrate Easter in the spring because this same Jesus grew up and died on a cross. It's supposed to be important, too, but I don't get it. At Ramon's house, they held hands and bowed their heads and said some words before we started eating. They talked a bit about Roger's sermon. Last night, Sandy played that piano while people sang some songs I'd never heard then Roger got up and talked about stuff from that Book.

"That girl, Sandy's sister, is all fired up about something called Sunday school. None of this makes sense to me, Grandad. What's the deal about church? Why do people bow their heads and say some words to Somebody they can't see? Mom and Dad don't do stuff like that. Dad reads the paper and plays golf, Mom pampers herself all day on Sunday. Nobody at home goes to church, it doesn't hurt them."

The twinkle had left Brad's eyes, he looked at his grandson very seriously, as he said, "Your folks don't go to church, do they, Son?" Brad had a twinge of conscience because he really knew why. "You never been but when you come here?"

The water had reached the line, so Natt shut it off, placed the filter basket inside, as he said, "Yeah, that's right. We hear church bells ring all over the city, but Dad and Mom pay no attention. They're on easy street, Dad's the editor of Atlanta's biggest paper, Mom's an exec we live in a big house. I didn't get a scholarship to cover costs at the university because Dad and Mom make too much. Don't tell me church makes you rich, I know better. Every week, like clockwork, they do the same things, just like you guys go to church. Us kids, we sleep in, study, read, play video games, whatever. They don't much care what we do.

"In the dorm, there was this kid who was just plain weird, he got all dressed up and went to church every week. He asked me to go with him, but, hey, no way, Jose! I didn't want to be weird like him! But when I was there at Ramon's house, he said Sandy got him to become a Christian and Roger, too. And at his church, he said that Book he had everybody read from was super important, maybe like it was life and death."

Natt, still acting agitated, took the urn from the sink and headed for the coffee drinker's nook. Brad followed him and took a deep breath, he'd never really bared his soul to anyone, especially to his grandson, but Brad said, "Son, I didn't always act like it was, but it is life and death! Jesus, that Baby we celebrate at Christmas, came for only one reason."

"Yeah, so?" Natt shrugged nonchalantly. He plopped the urn on the table a bit more vehemently than he needed to. The water splashed up into the grounds, but Natt didn't notice, he plugged the cord laying on the small table into the coffee maker and it started to wheeze. Natt spun on his heel to look at his granddad. The look on Brad's face gave Natt pause, he'd never seen such a look before from his granddad.

Brad nodded and slid into one of the chairs. Looking his grandson in the eyes, he said, "It says in that Book, the Bible that He's God's Son. When He came to earth as a Baby, He didn't have a human father his

Father is God in heaven. He lived a perfect life for thirty-three years, but because He did, people didn't like Him and nailed Him to that cross."

Natt took a napkin and wiped up the few drops of water on the sideboard that had slid off the side of the urn. "Okay, I know that. Besides, Roger talked about that last night. Actually, I guess you were there and you heard him. I suppose it something sensational that He didn't stay dead, I guess we celebrate Easter because He's alive."

Brad hardly acknowledged what Natt had said, but continued very seriously, "But you know, long before we were ever born, God knew about us." He pointed between himself and Natt and said, "He knows every thing about everybody, Son. He knows what we think. You know, He knew what was in my heart when I went to Roger's that night and did all that stuff. But you know, He loved me, even then. Yes, Jesus came as a Baby, but there was only one reason He came to earth and that was to die on that awful cross. He never sinned, but when He died on that awful cross, God, His Father, heaped all the sin, even mine and yours on His Son that day. Jesus became our sin sacrifice."

Natt's eyes turned to saucers, as he looked at Brad. Absently, he picked up the urn's lid and set it on the top. Turning he gave Brad his undivided attention and said, "Wow! Grandad! How do you know all that?"

Looking earnestly at his grandson, he said, "It's in that Book that Roger talked from last night. I know Isabel has one in your cabin. She always keeps a Bible in every cabin, someplace where people'll find it. You should get it out and read it. Don't start at the beginning, but say, start in John, the book of John in the New Testament. It'll tell you so much. It tells ya all about why Jesus came and who He really is."

"I'll give it some thought, Grandad."

The urn finished wheezing and Natt filled Brad's cup and handed it to him. Brad reached for it, but he didn't take a swallow. He shook his head and said, "Natt, my boy, don't just give it some thought, read the words! You want to live forever in a beautiful place? You can, but only if you let Jesus take away all the bad stuff in your heart. I know you ain't done no real bad stuff like I did there at Roger's, but you know you done bad stuff. The Bible tells how bad stuff keeps you from heaven. God's way to go to heaven is to let Jesus take it all away. It's the only way."

Natt scowled. "That's so, Grandad?"

Brad took a swig of the fresh coffee and said, "I swear it, Son. It's all there, you need to find it and read it for yourself."

Natt looked down at the mug in his hands and said, "Yeah, I know where Isabel put that Book, I put it in a drawer someplace, but I'll pull it out. I'm sure I'll have time one day soon to read where you said."

Brad grinned at his grandson, stood up and headed for his favorite chair behind the cash register. He put his mug on the counter and plopped down on his chair. Looking at his grandson he took a swallow of coffee and said, "You do that, Son. Tonight, take that Book out to one of them wicker chairs on the porch and read the book of John. You'll learn an awful lot in that book." After another swallow, Brad said, "Oh, yeah, I'll ask ya tomorra if ya read it!"

They still had no customers, so Natt filled his own mug, brought it with him and leaned against the counter close to where Brad sat and said, "Umm, thanks. You know anything about Sandy's sister, Grandad?"

"Not a whole lot, just that she's all fired up and oh, so serious. Sandy laughs and says she's lots older than her, not in years, but well, thoughts, I guess."

"Oh, yeah, she's serious, all right! She gets a bee in her bonnet and she's like a dog with a bone. She was onto this Sunday school stuff with the preacher like… well, you know, but I was thinking more about why she's here. Why'd she leave Philadelphia?"

"She's been real sick. She's not all better yet, so maybe that's why she's here, sorta resting up before she goes back, you know?"

Natt took a swallow of his coffee, it was too hot to drink, but he wondered how Brad could drink it down like he did. His cup was nearly half empty. He swallowed quickly and said, "Ramon said she had Rheumatic Fever. Got sick about the time you had your stroke. She was a nursing student."

"Yeah, now I recollect. Doctor told her she can't do that no more. Sandy said she wanted to be a missionary overseas, but that's out, too. Mebe she's here to find herself."

A shudder went down Natt's back, as he said, "I think I need to stay away from her! If she's like her sister, and Ramon said she was, I could be in trouble!"

Brad chuckled. "You never know, she could be pretty harmless and she is your age."

"Mmm, she isn't harmless, but I do know she is my age, Grandad." Natt looked down at his grandad, the sparkle was back in his eyes. "Grandad, you aren't matchmaking are you?"

"Who me? Son, I don't know the meaning of that word! That's your gramma."

"Mmm, Grandad, I hate to tell you, but I think your nose is growing!"

Brad chuckled. "No, my nose ain't growin', but Son, I'm real serious when I say to read that book of John. You see, it's easy to say, Jesus was a good Man, but He was lots more'n that. Jesus is God. He made a way for us to go to heaven we can't if He ain't taken our sin away."

Natt sighed. He took another long swallow of coffee. "Grandad, I promise I'll read in that Bible tonight. I'll tell you about what I read tomorrow. I promise. Believe me; what you're saying is something I've never thought about."

"Good. I'll listen."

Monday morning was busy around the DeLord home. Ramon was heading out on a short hike and Sandy's two lady friends were coming for the morning, which meant that Sandy's star piano student was coming. By seven o'clock, Jon had his breakfast and Sandy was bustling around the kitchen, while Ramon packed his backpack to overflowing. Marcy was awake, there was too much activity in the house for her to sleep, but she hadn't found the energy to pull herself out of bed. It made her wonder how she'd ever gotten up early morning after morning in nursing school. The day she'd left home was the last time she'd gotten up so early.

Marcy knew Ramon and Sandy were being as quiet as they could be, but Sandy's chair had a distinct hum that carried through the closed door. Finally, Marcy let out a long sigh, pushed the sheet and blanket off her and swung her legs off the bed, then sat up. She sat for a few minutes and looked out the window. She had a corner room and enjoyed looking out at the majestic mountains that were right now bathed in the glorious sunshine of early morning. If she looked closely she could see wisps of ever changing and moving mist gliding between some of the trees close by.

Knowing that Ramon's hikers came so they could leave by eight o'clock, she pulled on a bathrobe and hurried into the bathroom for her shower.

Finishing quickly in the bathroom, Marcy threw on some clothes and ran into the kitchen just as Sandy put the eggs, bacon and toast on the table. Ramon was already sitting at the table holding his son and talking quietly to him. The baby looked like he was hanging on every word that came from his daddy's mouth. It made a perfect family scene and Marcy wanted to back out to let the family get on with their day.

However, Sandy smiled and said, "Marcy! I wondered if you'd make it before Ramon left. Come sit down and eat with us."

Marcy shook her head and scowled. "Sis, I should let you be together, since Ramon's leaving in only a few minutes."

"You're being silly, Sister," Ramon said, "Take some of those eggs and pass what's left along, would you?"

Marcy sighed, picked up the serving dish of eggs, took a spoonful and passed it along to Ramon, who had put the baby in his seat, then reached for a slice of toast before he took the egg dish from Marcy. "My darling, what's on for your day?" he asked.

Sandy smiled the smile she reserved for him and said, "After you leave and we clean up around here, Jon and I'll spend time in the office. I know that phone rang several times over the weekend. About ten, Raylyn and her crew, along with Nancy are coming for a couple of hours. They'll stay for lunch." Sandy smiled at Marcy. "I guess Marcy and I'll wing it after that."

Marcy shook her head. "I'm to meet with Corky after lunch."

"Oh, I forgot about that! Sure, I'll have to think up something till you're home."

"So all your trails are hilly and hard?" Marcy asked, enjoying her breakfast, surprised because she hadn't really felt hungry when she brushed her teeth.

"Most of them are, but remember, along with walking trails you're carrying a twenty or so pound backpack on your back, along with a one man tent hooked on the bottom. You could get soaked to the skin if a storm comes up and we all sleep on the ground. I've never had a hiker who carried a mattress along."

Marcy made a face at her brother-in-law. "Thanks, Bro, I really needed all that info. I know you're trying really hard to discourage me, but one of these days I'll be all strong and well, just you wait! Besides, Heidi said, she's gonna pray for me that I get **all** better."

Ramon was shoveling his food in his mouth, but after putting one last mouthful in, he grinned at his sister-in-law. "I know, she's a great kid. She loves Jon and he loves her and Lenny, well, if his legs were up to it, he could walk on water as far as she's concerned. Since you're the youngest of us, I'm sure you'll get along famously together, you, Jon and Lenny, oh and Heidi, too." Ramon grinned at his sister-in-law.

He stood up immediately, lifted his coffee mug from the table and went to the carafe. As he filled the huge mug, he said to Sandy. "Love, have fun with the girls. Don't spend too much time in the office. Remember our calendar's full until Labor Day." He grinned at her and leaned over so they could enjoy a long kiss.

Marcy huffed at the insinuation, she had her mouth open, but before she could think of a retort, Sandy said, "I know, but I hate not to contact those that have called in. I will stop when they come, don't worry about that, Honey. Heidi is too cute to miss and being in the office doing paperwork, is not what I want to do when she's here."

"That's great, Sweetheart!"

Ramon took his mug of coffee and headed down the hall toward the office, but Sandy lifted Jon from his seat and followed after him. Soon, they disappeared into the office and that left Marcy alone in the kitchen. She noticed that all the dishes and plates were empty, so she quickly cleared the table, rinsed the dishes and loaded the dishwasher. She heard car doors slamming out in the parking lot, so she hurried into her room to dress for the day. Not really knowing Sandy's routine, she decided to spend some time with her Bible now, since it sounded like Sandy would leave her alone for maybe an hour or more.

As she pulled some shorts and a top from her dresser, she grumbled, "Men are such a trial. That brother-in-law is just as bad as my brother."

After dressing in her cool shorts and top, Marcy took her Bible, a notebook and a glass of juice to the deck behind the kitchen and spent some time with her Bible while Sandy stayed in the office with Jon. The next time Marcy was aware of anything, she heard car doors slam on the parking lot. She looked at her watch and was amazed that it was ten o'clock. She closed her Bible and headed back inside, left the glass in the sink and her Bible in her room, then headed for the hall. She didn't know Nancy or Raylyn too well, but she adored Heidi.

All the ladies met in the dining room. Sandy went to the kitchen and started some coffee through her coffee maker, then came in to take Heidi to the piano for her lesson. Of course, Nancy reached for Lenny and Raylyn gladly let him go. "He is getting so big, Raylyn!" Nancy exclaimed, as she bounced the baby on her knees.

"I know and he eats like there's no tomorrow!" She chuckled. "I think that's how he takes after his daddy. That man loves to eat."

"So, Marcy," Nancy said. "Are you sticking around? Do you have job prospects? If you go back to Philadelphia will you have something to do?"

Bouncing Jon on her knees, she said, "I don't know, Nancy. Actually, I came for some different scenery and to get away from Mom. I'm sure Sandy's told you how she is. We all thought it was just Sandy, but Mom hovered over me the same way. I just *had* to get away!"

"So all your plans are on hold?"

Marcy sighed, "I wish I could say they were only on hold, but Dr. Wright informed me rather strongly many more times than once that finishing nursing school is out and with a damaged heart, I'm sure I can't pass a physical any mission board would want from me."

"That's a shame! How far along were you in your training?"

"I'd finished two and a half years of a four year program."

"Hmm, have you ever drawn blood or started IVs?" Nancy asked.

"Yes, actually I have, why?"

"Our phlebotomist has given two weeks notice he's leaving soon after the Fourth."

"And you don't have anyone who can do it?"

Modestly, Nancy shrugged and said, "I can do it in a pinch, but Dr. Stan keeps me pretty busy when he's there and when he's not, I'm in charge. Besides, I'd rather not if I don't have to. Could I put your name in as a person of interest?"

"Can I let you know on that? I had a weak spell yesterday, but that hadn't happened in several weeks. Maybe it's the change in altitude and I'll adjust, but for right now, I think I'd better hold off on that at least a little while."

"Not a problem, like I say, the man's not leaving quite yet." Nancy kissed Lenny's head, then smiled at Marcy. "Why don't you come to the clinic tomorrow. Tuesdays, Dr. Stan's not there, so it's not quite so hectic and I can show you around."

Marcy grinned. "Yes! I'd love to do that! Could I come about ten?"

"Sure! That'd be great!" Nancy chuckled. "Bring your walking shoes; remember the clinic is the biggest place in town."

Marcy chuckled. "Okay, but you know that clinic would fit inside General many, many times over and I used to run up and down those halls every day."

"I know, I'm sure it's larger, but the hospital I trained at in Atlanta was huge. Lots of times I threatened to buy some skates to move down the halls."

Marcy laughed. "Yeah, some of us said stuff like that, too."

At lunchtime, Natt waited for Brad to come back. As soon as he did, Natt left for Alex's grocery. As he walked in, Alex said, "So, I see you made it to church last night, fella."

Natt made a face. "Yeah, sorta got my arm twisted into going, as a matter of fact."

Alex scowled. "How's that?"

"The other day Ms Sandy invited me to come for Sunday dinner…"

"Ah, her famous spaghetti dinner. I remember you bought a loaf of bread."

"Yeah, that's right. Anyway, she invited me, so I stayed the afternoon and listened to her practice for her concert. Wouldn't you know, she didn't stop until it was church time, so I got roped into going with them."

"I see. Roger's a good preacher, you know?"

Natt stood in front of the big freezer eyeing some of the selections and said, "That's what they say. I wouldn't know a bad or good one, really."

THIRTEEN

Following Natt as he went to the deli to get his favorite sub for lunch, Alex said, "You know, I been going to that church a lot of years. The old man retired from there seven or eight years back, but before he left he got a bit senile. He'd been a good preacher until that happened. That Roger was fresh out of seminary when we called him. We thought we were getting a good deal, since he was young and single, but you know, he didn't do much. First Sunday he came I sorta wished we hadn't called him. He had some big book he brought with him and he'd find some reading he thought sounded good. Wasn't long after he started he got some people could work some instruments, so he got them together. Those folks called themselves a praise team, but boy! could they make a whale of a lot of noise, but the words were muffled and even though they put them on the wall, they didn't say much. All in all, I felt empty, didn't get much from God in those days. Couldn't see the point so I didn't go near as much."

Back at the counter, Natt said, "So what happened, Alex?"

"Ms Sandy got after him, before she married Ramon, even. I guess they had to get things coordinated for her concerts or something. Anyway, Roger and Ramon are good friends, so one day right before Thanksgiving a year or more back, she played him *The Old Rugged Cross*. I guess it slapped him up side of the head. God got hold of him and he's not been the same since. He's a fireball now and I've never seen that old book he used to read from since then, just his Bible. You know Jesus as your Savior, Son?"

Natt scowled, slapped down the correct change for the sub and headed for the door in a hurry. "I guess not, Alex." He'd thought about doing some shopping to fill his empty refrigerator, but that could wait for another day. Grandad had done a number on him this morning; he didn't need old Alex doing it too! Natt took his sandwich and hurried out the door, then walked down the street. Grandad was bad enough to hound him, now Alex... He felt his hand wanting to make a fist – around his sandwich – he sighed and relaxed his hand.

There was a pleasant breeze that cooled off the hot noontime, but since Natt loved the outdoors so much, he crossed the street and went to the steps leading up to the church and sat down. He unwrapped his sub and took a bite, but that didn't keep him from thinking. He didn't know *The Old Rugged Cross*. He guessed he'd have to find out what that was. Yeah, that preacher did seem all fired up about God, but he'd told him one time he'd been just like him. Maybe he'd give him a call soon. If he read from that Book his grandad wanted him to, he'd be a busy man. And here he was, bored with Vansville!

Since Brad took his lunch early and Natt took his after Brad returned to the store, he still sat on the church steps when Corky drove up. Only minutes later, before Natt could wrap his waste paper together, Marcy walked briskly up the sidewalk and they met in front of Natt. They both stood on the sidewalk blocking him in on the steps of the church and Natt wondered how he could get away. After all, his lunch break was about over.

Marcy was dressed in shorts and top, nice but not the dressy outfit she'd worn to church the day before. Natt could appreciate a good looking woman right along with the best of them and legs like that could turn a guy's head easily enough, but this one was all fired up about church.... and Sunday school, whatever that was. He wanted to escape, big time!

Corky looked down and said, "Say, you here to help on this Sunday school business, Son? We could sure use some help from the younger generation, you know."

"Oh, no! Not me! I was just finishing lunch." He quickly crumpled the wrapper from his sub, jumped up, looked at his watch, then holding in a sigh of relief, he said, "Actually, my lunch break's over now, I need to get back to the store. Grandad'll be needing me soon."

He looked up, right into Marcy's face. Her eyes twinkled and her lips twitched, but she said, "I know you'll be overwhelmed this afternoon with customers."

Natt looked away quickly, dusted his shorts off and took a step between Corky and Marcy. He took another step, looked back at Marcy, grinned and said, "Oh, you never know! Few months ago we were the only place around that had ice melt, they flocked in then."

Marcy watched the young man cross the street and called after him. "I'll keep that in mind and be sure Ramon knows that. He's got a big parking lot, winter comes early here in the mountains, I'm told and I've heard it's kind of hard sometimes." Natt raised his hand and saluted, then disappeared into the store.

Marcy remembered that at breakfast before Ramon had to leave that Sandy had prayed for Natt. She remembered vaguely last night while she and Corky were making arrangements to meet today that Sandy had buzzed after Roger... who had run after Natt. After the door to the hardware store closed she remembered Sandy and Roger bowing their heads. Maybe they'd prayed for Natt then. Maybe he was someone who needed her prayers. Sandy had said this was her Jerusalem, now that she was here. But Natt Thomas? The verse came to mind "*...and you shall be my witness...*" (Acts 1:8) Was this really her Jerusalem? Natt Thomas?

Corky stood watching the young woman beside him. She was pretty, not nearly as outgoing as her sister, but she seemed nice. She had watched Natt cross the street and called after him, he wondered if they might make a good match. Nodding after the young man, Corky asked, "So, you know Natt?"

Marcy shook her head. "Corky, I met him on Saturday when I came to town and needed gas he came out of the store and introduced himself. I found out after I got to Sandy's house that she'd invited him for dinner yesterday. We all talked, but I didn't learn too much about him. After dinner I had to lie down and I slept all afternoon. When I got up, Natt was still there and it was time for church. Ramon and Sandy sort of hogtied him into going along. That's the sum total of how I know Natt Thomas."

"Seems nice enough."

Still shaking her head, but looking across the street at the closed door, she said, "Corky, if he's not a Christian and Sandy and Ramon don't think he is, he's on the wrong side of the fence for me. Right now, I think he needs my prayers way more than he needs anything else from me. So what is there to do about getting Sunday school started here in this town? I know the potential is here, maybe it's hiding."

"Probably is."

Marcy turned to look at the small church, the only one the town boasted of having. It was tiny, compared to the churches in Philadelphia, but seemed about the right size for Vansville, unless people from the country started coming. If there was an active Sunday school, this building wouldn't hold all the families that could potentially come.

What was she thinking? She was a visitor, a recuperating visitor. Dr. Wright told her she was well, but she had a weak heart, too weak to go back into nursing or go overseas as a missionary. "*...Beginning in Jerusalem...*" Would she be here long enough to do anything? It took months to build buildings, didn't it?

Marcy sighed, that Jerusalem was becoming a broken record in her brain. How many times had Sandy or Ramon mentioned it since yesterday? Now she was hearing it in her own brain! Maybe God had brought her here to do more than recuperate away from her mom. Still looking at the church building, she sighed, then looked back at Corky who stood next to her, he'd heard her talk to Roger about starting a Sunday school and he'd come up to talk to her last night.

Finally, she asked, "So Corky, what's your thought on this? There's not much space and there's no place inside, except maybe for one class."

Flinging his arm toward the back wooded area, he said, "Miss Marcy, there's all them woods back behind. I been told Derek Casbah owns some acres back there somewheres, he's a member here and probably would give the church a good price on more land. I know for a fact the county schools is plannin' to build a new addition on a couple of school buildings and got some decent portable classrooms to get rid of. So, puttin' up some classrooms for our Sunday school ain't gonna be no problem at all. Jes' need to figger out what's comin' down."

Giving the man her biggest smile, Marcy said, "Corky, why did you ask me to meet you here if you knew all this already?"

Chuckling, the older man said, "'Cause I knew you was fired up about startin' Sunday school. You know Ramon's Derek's son-in-law, right? Or sompin like that."

"Yes, but they don't get along all that well. Besides, Ramon and Sandy don't go to church here."

"Not yet, give 'em time."

"You think if there was Sunday school here they'd come?"

"Worth a try, ain't it?"

Marcy nodded, but the ex-potential-foreign-missionary-nurse looked at Corky and said, "So, will you talk to Derek and the schools?"

"Tell you what. You talk to Ramon, I'll get them classrooms." Corky winked at the pretty girl. "Keep your eye on that young fella over there, too."

Marcy's neck felt instantly hot, but she said, "Corky! I'm only a visitor to Vansville! I told you, he's on the wrong side of the fence."

Looking shrewdly at the young woman, he said, "You gonna leave tomorra?"

"Well, no…"

"You got time to work on him." He patted her on the shoulder. "Besides, you leave, there won't be no Sunday school."

"Thanks, Corky, I needed that." *"You are my witnesses…. In Jerusalem…."* Marcy sighed as Corky opened the door to his truck.

For June, it was hot, even in the woods and high hill trails Ramon was leading his group through. Last night, they'd camped on the high plateau where the small spring-fed pond was. It had been refreshing to filter the cold water through their filtering devices so they could have cold drinks for their supper. No one yet had braved swimming in the pond, it was just too cold. Maybe during July and August that would happen. Ramon and Duncan had made this pond a stopping point for many of their hikes this year it was one of their favorite places to camp.

Not only was the water source excellent, there was plenty of wood, but today Ramon's group would be getting back to the parking lot. They'd been gone three days and Ramon was anxious to get back. Sandy and Jon held lots more appeal than strangers who only spent three to seven days on a trail with him. He couldn't abandon hiking, after all, that was their source of income, other than Sandy's piano lessons and her paintings, but he sure wished…

They'd had beautiful weather all three days and the hikers were in high spirits, since they were on the downhill stretch. These were five friends who'd kept up with each other since their college days, but had drifted apart after graduation, but each year they tried to link up for some time together and this year they'd chosen to do their togetherness on a hike in the beautiful hills of Northern Georgia.

Ramon had listened as they'd talked about their many high powered accomplishments and wondered how his life would have been different if he'd gone to college. He probably wouldn't recognize himself today. Of course, at the time, he couldn't have afforded to go to college. His mom had married Casbah, but that didn't make him rich. Right away, he'd antagonized his step-father, so he'd been more than poor.

From their comments, they'd been out of college about five years. All five men were married, but none of them had children and two of them adamantly said they were not going that route, not now, not ever. Ramon felt sorry for them, if they stayed the course, they would never know the joy or satisfaction of watching a little person, who had come from his own body grow into a strong, productive individual. Second only to his wife, Ramon loved his son. He felt it his highest responsibility to nurture and lead that little life on his way to heaven. While he thought about it, he realized even that part of his life had changed so dramatically. Back five years ago, he was leading hikes, but he had no use for God or His Son, his Savior.

Ramon took the next step and the men gathered behind him. "Hey!" one said, "we made it! Camping isn't like a condo, but this was great! Let's be sure to get together again next year."

"Sure will! I'll be in touch!"

Soon, remotes made car horns beep and trunk lids go up, then moments later slam down. Only seconds after that, car doors slammed and powerful engines hummed to life. Moments later, Ramon was alone on the parking lot, holding his backpack straps in his hand.

However, when the taillights left, he whirled on his heel and headed for the door that led him to his wife and baby. He opened the door and a lovely voice said, "Honey, you're home!"

"Yes, I'm happy to be here, too, Love." He dropped his backpack immediately and reached for her, his smile lighting up his face. "I never get enough of you, my darling. When I'm out there, I wish I was here."

Throwing her arms around his neck, she lifted her face for his kiss. "It's great you're here now! Hurry and get your shower! We have company coming!"

After a kiss, Ramon pulled back and scowling, said, "Company? Marcy...?"

"Oh, she's not company! Actually, it's one of Brad's nephews. He wants to be a hiking guide. He's coming for supper to talk and see if it's something he can do."

"Great!" Ramon lifted his nose. "Marcy's fixing spaghetti?"

"Yes, she's about taken over the cooking."

"That's good; you have so much on your plate."

Only a few minutes after Ramon left their bedroom after his shower, there was a knock on the front door, so he went to answer. A stranger who had a smile on his face stood on the other side. Ramon held out his hand and said, "You would be our company for supper?"

"Yes, I'm Eric Thomas, Brad's nephew and you'd be Ramon DeLord?"

Nodding, Ramon said, "Got it in one! Come on in. My wife says you're wanting to be a hiking guide? Come on, have a seat, I haven't heard the signal that supper's ready, so let's talk."

"Yes, that's great. I did my stint in the military and I'm wanting something to do with my life. Actually, I think I need a bit of R & R and something to do that's not quite as high power as the military for a while. Being outdoors is in my blood. Well, maybe I should qualify that – being outdoors, but not under so much pressure will suit just fine. Your wife told me you work things through your computers, so I brought my laptop. I hope that's good. What's the cost or whatever to be a guide?"

"You're familiar with this area?"

"No, not really, I've only visited my uncle on rare occasions."

"Our only requirement then, is that you shadow two of our guides on a couple of hikes until you're familiar and feel comfortable with us, our requirements and the terrain. With your laptop, you can get the trails down quickly. I'm sure you'll want to get your own equipment, but as you travel with us you'll see what we use."

"So perhaps I could go on your Fourth of July hike as a prospect?"

"Super! Mine goes for six days, since the fourth is on Wednesday. Will that work?"

"Perfect! Can my cousin, Natt go along?"

"You mean Natt Thomas?" When Eric nodded, Ramon said, "Sure! At this point, my group is only five people, so that's perfect."

Eric lifted his face and sniffed. "Great! Mmm, it sure smells good in here."

Ramon grinned. "That's my sister-in-law's spaghetti sauce and it sounds like things have been reaching the dinner table while we've talked, so let's go eat."

Eric, another big man, with a military physique, also grinned. "I'm with you on that! Lead the way, I'm right behind you!"

When they reached the dining room, Sandy was there smiling. Eric did a double take, seeing Sandy in a wheelchair, but didn't say anything. Sandy, with her usual smile, said, "Hi, I'm the gal you talked to on the phone, I'm Sandy, Ramon's wife, this is Marcy my sister and that's Jon in his infant seat, but he's already eaten."

Since Sandy held out her hand, Eric stepped forward to shake it and said, "I'm pleased to meet you, Sandy." He looked up from Sandy to Marcy and said, "It sure smells good!"

Marcy smiled. "Thanks, our spaghetti sauce is our mom's secret recipe."

After the blessing, Ramon said, "Girls, looks like we've got another guide-in-training starting this next weekend!"

"So, Eric'll be going on your hike with you?"

"That's the size of it." He looked at Marcy across the table and said, "Natt's going too."

Before Marcy could say anything, Sandy exclaimed, "That's great! He'll get to go on that hike he's wanted to take. You'll be taking them?"

"Yup. Last I heard, mine was a group of five."

Sandy looked at Eric and smiled. "You think hiking's your cup of tea?"

After chewing and swallowing a large mouthful of the delicious spaghetti, Eric said, "Yes, Ma'am, at least for now. Maybe off in the future I'll want something else, but right now, I'll be happy to be in God's out-of-doors."

Sandy was always quick to pick out a Christian, so she said, "You're a believer?"

Eric was enchanted with this lady who spent her life in a wheelchair. He'd seen many disabled people in his travels, but none as happy and joyful as Sandy. "Absolutely! I've loved the Lord for a long time, but the military and Afghanistan brought Him and me lots closer."

Sandy grinned at Eric. "I'm glad you're taking Natt with you. Ramon became a believer on a hike another of our guides also became a believer because of a few experiences on his hikes. Maybe Natt'll see his need." Sandy gave Eric a conspiratorial grin and continued, "The hike you'll be on is with two pastors, their wives and a seminary student. Actually, he may feel overwhelmed. What do you think?"

Eric chuckled. "Yes, you might say that. So it really doesn't matter the kind of group you take? It's not just youth groups?"

Ramon shook his head and answered, "Oh, we have our share of youth groups, but no, anyone who is interested is good."

Eric nodded. "I'm excited to take this on."

After dinner and more good conversation, Eric left for Thomas's house, where he and his brother were staying. Eric walked into Brad's house, it didn't smell near as inviting as the DeLord's, but this was where he was staying. The TV was on and his brother sat with Brad and Joyce watching. "So, how was the store today? Did you three sell out the place?" Eric asked.

"No, actually, we had a good group of customers, but Uncle introduced me to the workings of the cash register and Natt got me acquainted with the coffee machine and the books. Seems those are what run the store. And you, you're all signed up as a guide?"

"That I would be! Natt and I are going on the Fourth hike with Ramon. I have to go on one more hike with another guide, along with studying their hike program on my laptop and I'm off and running. I'm excited."

"You'll stay here, with us?" Joyce asked.

"Now, Joyce," Brad said, before Eric could answer. "You know Natt has his own place. Maybe Eric want's his own place, too. I kinda know Natt's a bit partial to Isabel's cabin."

"You mean Isabel rents out cabins for more'n a night or two?"

"That she does. By the month, achally."

"If it won't hurt your feelings, I'd just as soon get my own place I haven't lived with somebody in a long time."

Brad studiously looked at Eric as he said, "Oh, it won't hurt ours none. Natt nearly ate us outta grub before he moved out."

Joyce nearly hissed. "Bradford! He didn't either! If Eric wants to live there, it's fine, but if he wants to live here, it's fine, too."

"Since we won't be leaving on the hike until Wednesday, I'll look into that tomorrow."

"You do that, Son. I know Natt's right pleased with living there. Another of Ramon's guides started out livin' there when he came on board. 'Course, he weren't married when he came. Now him and Nancy live in their own house, back behind." He winked at his nephew, "Ya never know about things like that 'round here."

Chuckling, Eric said, "Uncle, I'll keep that in mind."

It was the Wednesday before Fourth of July. The DeLord's house was bursting and it was only seven in the morning! Three hikes were going out today and when all the guides left at the same time, it was an unspoken rule that the guides and Duncan's wife met at the base of operations for breakfast. Poor little Jonathan watched all the activity from his infant seat. There was so much going on as he silently watched the big people move around him. It was too noisy with much too much going on to take a nap.

As everybody sat down for breakfast, Jon's daddy picked him up and he grinned at his daddy. That was one face he knew and one shoulder he fit on really well. A little fist reached for the ear closest to him, but Daddy turned his head, opened his mouth and pulled the little fist between his lips instead. Jon's grin grew even wider and a happy coo came from his mouth. Ramon made a big noise as he blew a raspberry against Jon's fist and Jon giggled. Jon and Daddy were special to each other. Ramon didn't put the baby back in his infant seat until all the bowls were empty and Auntie had filled all the mugs again. With all this activity, Jon knew something was up.

The table had been groaning with food, but there'd been many chairs pulled up to it. Besides Ramon, Sandy and Marcy, Duncan, Nancy and Neal had been there. Eric and Natt had rounded out the bunch. Natt felt uncomfortable when Eric said grace, he hadn't known his older cousin was a Christian.

It was already hot, even before eight in the morning. The sun was blazing down from a clear, cloudless sky, today was a day for lazing in a swim suit next to some water, or staying in a nice air conditioned building. Any place to keep cool. However, three hikes were going out onto trails in the hills around Vansville. Natt would have his outdoors stint, away from his store and Eric would get his first taste of guide-in-training for DeLord's Hiking Service.

Nancy Roads looked forward to some fun time on Saturday with Sandy, Marcy, Raylyn and Heidi, because both Ramon and Duncan were leading holiday hikes and the girls were going to Clemens farm for the day. However, Nancy sighed, today was just another work day. The clinic had been open for a year now. The Friday of this weekend last year was the day that a frantic Ramon had brought Sandy in as their very first patient to discover that she was pregnant. They'd come and broken the ceremonial tape even before all the dignitaries had arrived.

After breakfast, Nancy said goodbye to Duncan before he vanished with the other guides into the office, since she had to be at the clinic by eight o'clock. The hikers usually passed her on the road as she went to work. The hiking service had grown over the last couple of years. To think that three hikes would go out today, with another guide-in-training going along! Before Sandy came to town, Ramon had been the only guide leading hikes, now there were three, almost four and they were busy most of the time. Everyone knew that Sandy had been the catalyst.

Nancy parked her car at home, ready to walk the short distance from her home to the back door of the clinic to start this day. She grabbed her purse and her insulated lunch bag from the passenger seat, slammed the car door and headed for the back of the building across the field. It was an impressive building, the biggest one in Vansville. She had to hurry she'd glanced at the dash clock just before turning off her car to see the time was only minutes before eight. She must not be late! Dr. Stan could be late if he was so inclined, but she would not be. Quickly, she pulled open the back door and hurried inside. She let the door close behind her, even though her eyes hadn't fully adjusted to the darkness, but the blessed coolness was a great relief. All was quiet at the front of the clinic obviously no patients had come in the front door.

Jon hadn't had much for breakfast, his daddy was leaving on an eight o'clock hike and his mommy and auntie had fixed breakfast for eight people. Poor Jon had been set in his infant seat after a diaper change, but with barely enough food to keep tears at bay. His poor little tummy wanted to be filled! Now it was time for him to have breakfast, then his bath and wonderful clean clothes. Marcy and Sandy made quick work of the dishes and Sandy filled the dishwasher cup with detergent and started the machine. As she picked up the baby from his infant seat and headed for her bedroom, Marcy hurried into her room for her Bible.

It was another sunny day she would have devotions on the back deck. She picked up her Bible from its place on the nightstand and headed back to the kitchen and the back door. She ran her cup of decaf coffee through the microwave to warm it up, then stepped onto the deck and closed the door behind her. The heat hit her like a brick wall. She still wasn't used to this kind of heat, so much hotter than in Philadelphia. Of course, Philadelphia had the ocean not far away that helped with the temperatures. She pulled in some of that hot air then turned toward her favorite chair. If she sat very still she could tolerate the heat while she had her devotions.

Over the past days, a colorful bluebird had been coming to sit nearby, usually, he gave her a beautiful serenade, which made her day so much brighter, but today he didn't come. Marcy was disappointed. She looked around, wondering if he was sitting somewhere else, he wasn't, not even singing from a nearby tree. Letting out a sigh, Marcy sat down in the chair to get the best breeze, took a sip of coffee, then started reading. She loved this time of day, Vansville was never a noisy place, but morning seemed even more quiet. Since the back deck was on the west side of the house, the sun didn't heat it up until afternoon.

As she read it seemed like a voice spoke to her, *Marcy, Ramon's gone again, this time for almost a week. Corky told you to talk to him about his step-dad and the land at the church. When will you do that? Will you wait again?*

She pulled in a breath. "Oh, God! I forgot again!" *Why not call him yourself at the bank?* "Yes, I will!"

After her devotions, Marcy hurried inside and found Sandy and Jon in the office, where she figured they'd be. "Hi, Sis, do you know what bank Ramon's step-dad works in?"

Scowling, Sandy said, "Yes, it's First Bank, but why do you need to know? We have our business account there, but we don't go there much to deal with him."

"When I met with Corky that day about Sunday school rooms, he said he thinks Mr. Casbah owns some of the land around the church, so he thought I should talk with Ramon about finding out about it. Since he's gone, I thought maybe I'd talk to the man myself."

Sandy looked up at the clock and said, "Get your purse while I shut this down, you and I'll make a trip into Blairsville, visit the bank and then make a day of it in the 'big' city."

Marcy chuckled. "I know you've been itching for an excuse to go to Blairsville!"

Sandy's eyes danced. "You got that right!"

Marcy grinned. "I feel good today I'm up for a shopping day."

"Great! You've put on a few more pounds you're starting to fill out your old clothes, so I think it's about time you got some new ones."

Marcy sighed, "Sis, don't even mention those pounds! I was hoping not to put on too many more and you know how easy it is for me."

"So far, Sis, you're looking great, so don't worry about it."

"I know, but I'm not running around General anymore, putting on pounds means I'm not getting enough exercise."

Sandy laughed. "Shopping's a great start!"

Heading for her room to get her purse, Marcy said, over her shoulder, "Mmm, yes, I know, especially with you and those wheels."

Sandy grinned. "Could be worse, could have Mom along."

Marcy shook her head. "Don't even remind me!"

Soon the sisters were in the light blue van with Jon sleeping on the back seat. When they were in downtown Blairsville, Sandy found her handicapped parking space behind the bank. They went inside and up to the desk to the side. Sandy gave her a grin while they crossed the foyer and Marlene asked, "Sandy, do you need to see Mr. Casbah?"

"Yes, if he's available."

"I'll see." She picked up her phone, hit a key and started talking. When she hung up, she said, "He says he's at a good stopping place so go on in."

"Thanks, Marlene," Sandy said, with a smile.

Sandy had Jon on her lap, her hand holding him in place, but his arms and legs were in constant motion, his brown eyes wide open. Sandy started her chair and Marcy walked along beside her. "It must be nice to know people in high places," Marcy sighed.

"Derek and I get along much better than he and Ramon. I'm not sure why that is."

Marcy said to herself, *You don't know a stranger, that's why.*

Derek met them at his door. "Hello, ladies, what's on your minds today?"

Sandy smiled and said, "Derek, I just came along as the driver, this is my sister, Marcy, she has something to ask you about."

Derek's eyes left his step-daughter-in-law and looked at the pretty girl beside her. Both girls were pretty, one dark, the other much lighter, but both very attractive. "And what would that be, young lady?" He stepped back into his office and said, "Come on in, let's talk."

Marcy swallowed, she wasn't sure, now that she was here looking at the distinguished older man what she should say. She pulled in a deep breath and followed him into his spacious office. "A week ago I said something at church about needing Sunday school. I don't know his last name, but Corky said you own some land close to the church and maybe you'd, umm, know how we could, umm, get some land so we could put up some portable classrooms so we could start a Sunday school."

Smiling at the uncomfortable young lady, Derek said, "Well, let's talk about that."

Derek went behind his desk, Marcy moved to a chair in front of it, but Sandy's chair began its familiar hum. She closed the door behind her. All this time, Jon lay on Sandy's lap. He'd fallen asleep, so used to the hum of his mommy's wheelchair. She pulled up beside her sister. Derek looked from Marcy to Sandy and gave them each a smile. "It's obvious you two are sisters. Would you be younger than Sandy?"

"Yes, Sir, I'm Marcy Bernard, I used to be from Philadelphia, but I'm here for now."

Derek rubbed his chin. "So Corky thinks I own some land around the church." After several minutes, he stood and went to a file cabinet. "There are several plots of ground I own in Vansville, but I'll have to refresh my own memory as to where they are in relation to the church. Of course, my home is outside of town… Let's see what we find in this topography map."

He pulled out a large, loose-bound book and took it back to his desk. "If I do, this thing'll tell me in a few minutes." As he began to thumb through the pages, he said, "So what's the thought on Sunday school or rooms to hold Sunday school?"

Marcy pulled in another breath and said, "Corky said, a school close by is planning to build an addition and has some portable classrooms it wants to get rid of. He said he knows he can get some, if I'd find out about the land. Sandy and I both think Sunday school is one of the most important things that's connected with a church and Vansville has none."

"Yes, you're absolutely right, Miss Marcy. If it hadn't been for Sunday school back when I was a kid, I'd be just like my wife, dead set against God. I'm just sorry to say I let my roots get neglected for too many years."

Derek turned one more page and said, "Ah, here's what I'm looking for." After looking at the page for several minutes, he turned the book around and pushed it closer to Marcy and Sandy. The page held pencil lines, obviously several were representing streets and at one intersection was the outline of a church. "This is what I thought. I didn't think I owned any of the land close to the church." Pulling a pencil from its holder, Derek tapped the picture of the church and said, "That church was started back in the twenties by Brad Thomas's grandad. That Bradford, gave that corner acre to the town to build that church, but the rest of the land around that acre stayed in the Thomas family. The land along Main Street was sold off in parcels, but the land behind, that faces that other street, still belongs to Brad Thomas." Derek looked up at Marcy and smiled. "Sorry you wasted your time coming here, but I'd say the man you need to talk to is Brad Thomas. You know him, I guess?"

Marcy smiled at the older man and said, "Yes, he's the guy who sits behind the cash register and dozes at the hardware store."

Chuckling, Derek said, "Yes, young lady, you got it in one!"

Thinking about the guy she didn't really want to see too much of, Marcy sighed and said, "I guess we'll have to do that, but thanks for your time, Mr. Casbah."

"You're very welcome, but Sandy and Ramon call me Derek, it wouldn't make me mad if you do the same." Derek stood up with his hand out, so

Marcy took it and gave it one shake. She still felt a bit uncomfortable with the white haired man.

Marcy smiled. "Thanks, I'll remember that."

As he walked them to the door, Derek said, "Say, wasn't it you who sang so well at Christmas in Sandy's concert?"

Sandy saw in Marcy's eyes what Derek couldn't, so she said, "Yes, Marcy sang at the Christmas concert in my place and she did a great job, Derek. Since then, she's had a bad bout with Rheumatic Fever. We're still working on getting her all healed up and getting her lung capacity back so she can sing again."

Placing his hand on Marcy's shoulder, he exclaimed, "Wow! I'm glad you're up and around, Marcy! I understand Rheumatic Fever is nothing to play around with."

"Thanks, Derek. I do feel more than a hundred percent better. No, it's not! After six months of recuperating, I must agree it's nothing to play around with. I appreciate your time and helping me find out who owns that land."

"You're most welcome. I'm sure I'll see you at church, perhaps next Sunday."

Marcy smiled. "Yes, I'll be there."

Back in the van, Sandy said, "Maybe you'd better wait until after the holiday to talk with Brad about the land."

"Sister, dear, I think I see right through your procrastination attempt. You, sister dear, are wanting me to wait until Natt is back. As a matter of fact, when we return to Vansville, if the store is open then, I want you to stop and let me out. I plan to have this all talked out *before* that grandson of his gets back from that hike."

"But Sis, how can you reach your Jerusalem if you do that?" Sandy exclaimed, her eyes twinkling, as she glanced over at her sister.

"I'm not the only one who's Jerusalem is here in Vansville."

"No, that's true still, it's good to spread things around. You know it wasn't only Peter who led people to Christ back then, John did right along with him."

"Mmm, hmm, I know that. I still think I'd like to get that task over with. Sometimes the old man's a bit gruff."

By supper time, on the high plateau, Natt was ready to call it quits with the hike. It had been a strenuous day of putting one foot before another on fairly rugged terrain. He didn't realize how out of shape he'd gotten walking around town and in the store. Maybe it was even longer than that, he'd spent hours in the stacks at school, eaten three squares in the college cafeteria and only walked between those buildings and his dorm. However, he knew that he was committed, it was not an option to go back now, they wouldn't get back to DeLord's place until Monday afternoon and that was many hours away. With a sigh of relief, he let his backpack slide from his back and turned to take the tent from the bottom of it.

He was here because his cousin had gotten him the place, but he didn't know the other five hikers and his cousin was in training to be a guide, so he had to stick close to Ramon. Of course, he'd met his cousin, but he didn't know him too well, either. If ever Natt felt like a man without a country, this was as close as he could come. He felt closest in age to the other single young man, so with his tent in his hand he walked over to him.

"Hi," he said, "I guess we men get to put up tents?"

Tony grinned, unhooking his own tent from his pack. "Yup, that's what I'm told. You're Natt, did I hear somebody say?"

"Yup and you're..?"

"I'm Tony. What do you do? I guess you're related to Ramon's helper is that it?"

"That's my grandad's nephew, so I guess that makes him some sort of a cousin to me. Eric's wanting to be a hiking guide, so he's in training and Ramon said I could come along. I'm the manager of the hardware store in Vansville, but with all this nice summer weather I wanted to get away from the store for a while. My grandad and I run it, but Eric's brother came too, so he's working the store with Grandad while I'm gone. What do you do?"

The young man, dressed in hiking shorts, a stretched out T shirt and hiking boots, grinned and said, "I probably don't look the part, but I'm a seminary student in Atlanta. I have one more year then I'll take a call to pastor a church somewhere. Those two men in our group are both graduates from the same school. They were seniors when I came on board."

Natt wasn't sure he could feel any more uncomfortable. He'd barely found an even keel from his Sunday afternoon and evening with the DeLord's and Marcy and now to spend six days with a bunch of Christians?

He barely held in a shudder. Maybe he could find his way back to DeLord's! If the moon was full later on, maybe walk the trail back! It had to be better than six days with seven Christians! Yeah, he'd found the Bible Isabel kept in his cabin, but still….

Turning away and starting to open his tent up, he mumbled, "Good to know."

Tony thumped him on the back. "Hey, we'll have a great time!"

After they ate the stew the ladies had put together, Ron asked, "Could we have devotions or do we need to bed down?"

Ramon looked up at the rays of the setting sun and said, "I think devotions would be great! The sun hasn't even gone down all the way. We can't get on the trail until after daylight tomorrow anyway, let's do it with devotions!" Ramon pumped his fist.

"Great!"

Everyone but Natt rummaged through his backpack and pulled out a Bible. It was still hot and there was still a lot of daylight, so no one sat around the fire, but they sat together inside the circle of tents. Natt thought about escaping, but before he could, Eric sat down beside him and said, "I'll share so you can read along, Natt."

"Yeah, okay," he mumbled. To himself he said, *Is a Bible standard equipment on a hike? Gads, why did I want to come on a hike so bad?* All the other hikers gathered around them, there was no way for Natt to escape. He squared his shoulders, he was a man; he could endure a Bible study that had to end before dark. After all, he had read that book of John like Grandad had told him.

When all the hikers had gathered and sat holding their Bibles, Ron said, "Since I'm the one to suggest this, I guess I'll be the leader tonight. All day today, as we've walked along in these magnificent hills and valleys, I couldn't help but think about Psalm 8. Can we turn there?" After some rustling pages, he said, "I'll read it, but then let's talk about it."

"'O LORD, our Lord, how majestic is your name in all the earth!
You have set your glory above the heavens.
From the lips of children and infants you have
ordained praise because of your enemies
to silence the foe and the avenger.

> When I consider your heavens, the work of your
> fingers, the moon and the stars, which
> you have set in place, what is man that you are mindful of him,
> the son of man that you care for him?
> You made him a little lower than the heavenly beings
> and crowned him with glory and honor.
> You made him ruler over the works of your hands;
> you put everything under his feet;
> all flocks and herds, and the beasts of the
> field, the birds of the air, and the
> fish of the sea, all that swim the paths of the seas.
> O LORD, our Lord, how majestic is your name in all the earth!'"

Before anyone else said anything, Natt exploded, "Really?"

"What do you mean, Natt?" Tony asked.

"Who's this Lord, you're talking about? What does it mean 'he put everything under him'? Somebody put sheep, cattle, wild beasts, fish and birds… under… man? What's that mean? Most of those animals don't even like people."

Tony looked earnestly at Natt. "That's true, but it's not so much that all those things are under man's rule, it's the fact that God made them, everything on the earth, including man. God, the LORD, made all things to honor and bring glory to Himself. He's put all things around us for us to see His majesty. As we look around, we see what He's made. Look, see the moon rising? Soon it'll be dark enough to see the stars. God put all this here for us to see His majesty."

Snapping his fingers, Natt asked, "He snapped His fingers and it just happened?"

Ron nodded. "He could have, but He was the only one here and it doesn't say He did it that way. In the first book of the Bible it says He *spoke* and it happened."

"Wow!"

Others jumped into the discussion until all the light was gone from the sky. Ramon was about to speak, when Tony, who was leaning back on his elbows exclaimed, "Hey, everybody! Look up! There's a shooting star!"

The conversation stopped and everybody threw their heads back. The brilliant star had started in the black northern sky and was now directly over the campers. Before anyone spoke, it continued racing on until it reached nearly the southern horizon. The blaze was lost in a cluster of stars. Silently, Natt wondered if that was part of the Milky Way.

"Wow!" Tony said, in awe. "This sky is incredible! It's not like this in Atlanta!"

"No, that's for sure," Ron agreed. "In fact, I think I'll try out that state park close to Seminary Church. Maybe the sky is darker in those woods and our youth groups could see the night sky. It's a thought lots of those kids rarely leave their neighborhoods."

FOURTEEN

In the morning, as they left camp, Natt decided he'd take up with Tony again, rather than with his cousin, since Ramon had him tied up with studying the maps and things he'd need to know as a guide that Natt, as a hiker didn't care about. He might like being out-of-doors, but being a hiking guide wasn't on his bucket list. As everyone moved away from the campsite and settled into their backpacks, their hiking boots and the trail, Natt moved as close as he could behind Tony, wishing the trail was wider so he could walk beside him. "So tell me why you believe that God spoke and all this stuff happened. That's not what I learned in school."

"No, it's not what teachers teach in public school. It's sad, because Evolution is only a theory, but the Bible is God's Word, He told us what really happened."

"You know that?"

Tony nodded and held up his hand, as if he was taking an oath. "I believe it with all my being, Natt! After all, what men say is just what they think happened. They weren't there, but God is eternal, He's always been, He always will be. If He said that's what happened, then I believe that's what did happen."

Natt scowled and looked around. After several minutes, he asked, "So how long did this creating stuff take? My science teachers said it took millions or even billions of years."

"Yeah, there are some scientists who want us to believe that, but tell me, if God spoke and something happened, how long do you think it could take?"

Natt thought for a few minutes, before he said, "Well, I guess it wouldn't take long at all if all He did was speak. But really? God spoke and it happened?"

Tony looked down in time to see a root sticking up in his path, so he stepped over it, but then he grinned at Natt and said, "Actually, you're right. It says in the first book of the Bible, in Genesis, that God took six days to make everything, everything we see, along with everything we don't see, right down to single celled creatures."

Natt stepped over the same root. "You mean that? He created everything in six days? Unbelievable! But the rocks, things so dense, so huge,… just got spoken into existence?"

Tony knew speaking over his shoulder wasn't how he wanted to have this discussion with Natt, it was too important, so he said, "Let's talk about this after we stop for the night and I'll show you. Deal?"

"You got it!"

"Okay, we're on for tonight around the campfire."

Skeptically, Natt said, "I'll be interested."

Tony nodded, "Yup, we'll make a believer out of you yet!"

After making camp that evening and eating their supper, everyone gathered in the circle again with their Bibles. No one had volunteered last night to have devotions, so Tony said, "If it's all right with everybody, I'd like to do devotions tonight."

Ron nodded. "Sure, go for it!"

After everyone gathered in the circle was quiet, Tony said, "Natt and I talked a bit this morning about something we started last night in our devotions. I told him we'd talk some more about it tonight. Let's open our Bibles to that all important first book, Genesis."

There was a bit of rustling and one pastor's wife, Natalie said, "That book gives me goosebumps when I read it. It's an awesome book!"

"It sure is! Okay, let's look at the very first verse.

'In the beginning God created the heavens and the earth.'

If you're with me, I'd say that says a mouthful."

"It sure does, Tony! Look around! God created all this."
"Yes, He did, Ron, out of nothing."
"Nothing?" Natt asked skeptically.
"Yeah, out of nothing," Eric agreed.
"Right. Let's move on to verses two and three:

> 'Now the earth was formless and empty, darkness was over the surface of the deep and the Spirit of God was hovering over the waters. And God said, "Let there be light," and there was light.'

He spoke those words and it happened just like that!"

"That's the sun you're talking about, right?" Natt asked, nodding toward the few faint rays on the western horizon.

Shaking his head, Tony said, "No, God is light. God didn't make the sun, moon and stars until the fourth day, but He shined His own light on the earth that first day. On the second day, He made the sky above the earth. The third day He pulled the waters together and made the oceans and the land, but He didn't leave it alone, He made the plants and trees...."

Scowling, Natt held up his hand, as if to slow Tony's forward motion and said, "Wait a minute, there's still no sun? I thought it took the sun's light and heat to make all that grow. Don't the tides and stuff like that depend on... the moon? How can that be?"

Tony grinned at the young man. "That's right, Natt, you got it! Still, those God-made objects didn't come along until the fourth day.

> 'And God said, "Let there be lights in the expanse of the sky to separate the day from the night and let them serve as signs to mark seasons and days and years and let them be lights in the expanse of the sky to give light on the earth." And it was so. God made two great lights—the greater light to govern the day and the lesser light to govern the night. He also made the stars.' (vss 14-16)

He did it all in one day."

By now, the sunlight was gone from the sky, only the few clouds in the western sky held the colors. Even those straight overhead had turned dark, but the moon and the stars were bright. Natt didn't speak, but his head tipped back and his eyes roamed the blackness above him. The moon was in the east, but bright pinpricks of light covered the sky. He shook his head, then finally brought his head down and looked around at all the dark shapes that during the day were green trees. "Amazing! I've never heard all this before."

"Yes," Tony agreed, "God truly is amazing. On the fifth day God made all the creatures in the oceans and the fresh water, along with the birds. He made them each special – the fish so they could live in water and the birds so they could fly. Then on the sixth day He made all the land creatures as well as Adam and Eve. However, He loved Adam and Eve way more than all His other creations and came and spent time with them each day."

"Really? Why, how come, He doesn't do that now!"

"No, He can't do that now, because, even though Adam and Eve were in a beautiful garden and were perfect, Satan came and tempted them. Eve listened to Satan's lie and ate the forbidden fruit then handed Adam some and he ate it so that they both sinned."

"Sinned, what does that mean?"

"Have you ever done something you know is wrong?"

"Oh, yeah, most all the time!" Natt agreed, readily. Smiling ruefully he continued, "Maybe early on, when I spit that Gerber spinach all over Mom's face."

A tiny smirk on his own face, Tony said, "Natt, that's sin. All of us sin, because Adam sinned, it's in our nature to sin and to disobey God. We are selfish, we want our own way. Because Adam and Eve sinned, God couldn't walk with them any longer. He made the first sacrifice. He killed a lamb and made coverings for Adam and Eve's bodies. He knew they were ashamed, not just because they were naked, but they knew they'd disobeyed God, they had done exactly what God had told them not to do."

"So this is all in that first book? Amazing!"

After a few moments of silence, Tony said, "Yes, it is, Natt. Even more amazing is that God loves each and every one of us, individually. But we are sinners and God can't look at or tolerate sin. That's why He made that sacrifice, killed that innocent sheep for Adam and Eve's sin, but because people have been sinning ever since then, two thousand years ago, He sent His Son to earth. His Son, Who is God and was there at the time of creation, became a human being and we know as Jesus. Jesus, Who was totally God, but totally Man at the same time, came as a substitute, because we are all sinners. We have that sin nature that is part of us because we all trace our ancestry back to Adam. However, Jesus had no sin, He did no sin, but was killed by being crucified on a cross so that He could pay our sin debt."

"So that's why people sing '*The Old Rugged Cross.*'"

Tony nodded, "Yes, Jesus died on that cross there had never been such an agonizing, brutal form of death as crucifixion ever in all of history, until the Romans brought it about, but three days later God raised Him from the dead. That's why we celebrate Easter, because Jesus rose from the dead. Today Jesus is in heaven, but He's listening to our conversation. He wants you to know He's pleading with His Father for one more person to become part of His family."

By now, the sun had totally vanished. In the darkness, the only light came from the moon and a soft glowing from the fire, Tony looked at Natt and asked, "Natt, would you like to let Jesus take your sin debt away? When you give your sin to God, He covers it with Jesus' blood. He doesn't see it anymore and He makes you one of His children. Our bodies die, but our souls live always wouldn't you want it to live with God when it leaves your body?"

Nodding thoughtfully, the young man said, "Yes, I guess I need to do that."

"Great! How about we pray right now?"

Looking around and only seeing the people from their group, their faces reflecting the glowing embers, Natt said, "I can do that here? I don't have to wait and do it in church?"

"Oh, no! God's ready to hear your prayer anywhere you want to say it."

After Tony and Natt prayed, no one spoke for several minutes. Finally, Ramon said, "Natt, welcome to God's family! Just before we left our room yesterday morning Sandy and I prayed that you would give your heart to God and let Jesus take your sin away. Praise God, He's answered our prayers." He grinned at the young man, but then said to the others, "Folks, it's time to bed down for the night. Six o'clock comes early. Believe me we have a full day of hiking ahead of us tomorrow again."

Ron's wife, Natalie groaned. "I sure hope there's no stone under my hip tonight. It was hard to get to sleep with that there last night."

Ron chuckled. "You know, my dear, I looked for that 'stone' you complained about when we took down the tent this morning." Holding up his hand and making a circle with his thumb and first finger, he said, "It was a pebble, about the size of a quarter and almost as flat. It couldn't have dug up your side like you said it did, Sweetheart."

"Ronald," she huffed, "I have very tender skin."

"Mmm, hmm, the 'Princess and the pea', I've heard about that tale."

Tossing her head, she grinned widely at him. "Of course! People may not *call* me a princess, but..."

After taking his time in the woods, but getting back before Ramon and Eric went in their tents, Natt saluted those two men then crawled into his tent. *Well*, he mused, as he shucked his boots, his belt and his jeans then crawled into his sleeping bag, *I guess I've slept in on Sunday morning for the last time.* Just before he fell asleep, another little voice pushed its way into his brain and murmured, *Umm, weren't you thinking about some pretty maid with dark hair who appeared for the first time in town only a week or so ago?*

"No! I was not!" *Umm, maybe your nose is growing, Pinocchio?* Perhaps thinking he could blot out the voice taunting him, he pulled the edge of the sleeping bag up over his head. There was no stone under Natt's hip and every bone in his body ached. He still wasn't very much in shape. He was asleep in minutes.

Sandy and Marcy had gotten so carried away with shopping and Jon had been so good, that when Sandy drove into Vansville late Friday afternoon, Marcy was sleeping in the passenger seat of the van and Sandy didn't have the heart to wake her as she passed the hardware store on the way to her home. As Sandy turned to back into the garage, she took a better look at her sister and could easily see how pale she was, she had probably over done it. Maybe she felt good right after they saw Derek, but by now, Marcy needed an early supper and her bed.

Sandy woke her when she left her place behind the wheel. Cheerfully, Sandy said, "Looks like I got two sleepyheads who need supper and bed.

One of you probably needs their pants changed, I won't mention which one that might be, though."

"Sis," Marcy hissed, "thanks for that!"

"Oh, sure, not a problem!" Sandy said as she lowered herself to the garage floor. Marcy showed how tired she was, instead of starting right in making their supper, Marcy slouched into a chair in the living room to wait for Sandy to change Jon's diaper. Then she walked the few steps into the kitchen to watch Sandy make supper.

Saturday morning, after her devotions, Marcy decided to brave the not-the-most-pleasant Brad Thomas in his hardware store to find out about land around the church for Sunday school. She wanted to have something to tell Corky on Sunday, she hadn't had anything to tell him last week, but she would tomorrow, she was determined. A slouch she was not and even though she didn't do well dealing with older men, she would get the job done.

She walked in the store and a man with thick, dirty blond hair stood up from a chair in the 'coffee drinkers nook' and with a smile, said, "Yes, Ma'am, can we help you this morning? Now you know, of course, if it's too complicated I'll have to refer you to my boss over there. He's the man in the know!"

After a minute looking at the man, Marcy shook her head and said, "That's so weird! Yesterday at my sister's breakfast table, I saw somebody I know was your twin. You think about twins as being kids, but I've never known adult twins."

Chuckling, the man said, "Ah, yes, but twins are about like other boys or girls, we have a way of growing up. So you've met my twin, but he didn't stay in town too long. Actually, you must admit, I'm the better looking twin." Still chuckling, Matt said, "Of course! And what can this twin do for you?"

Marcy smiled at the man then looked at the man behind the counter with his eyes closed and said, "Actually, I have no reason to buy anything, but I need to speak with that man behind the counter. You won't mind, will you?"

Matt winked and whispered, "I don't think he's napping, but you might tread softly until you get right there then pound your fist on the counter. I'm sure then he'll be glad to help you. Once he's had his first cup of coffee, he's pretty affable."

The man in question, grumbled, "I heard that, young fella!" Opening his eyes, he stretched a bit to look over the counter and said, "Yes, Miss, what's on your mind?"

Marcy took two steps, then leaned on the counter and said, "Mr. Thomas, I'm Marcy Bernard. Umm, I have something I need to ask you about."

Brad shrugged. "No harm in askin'."

Taking a deep breath, Marcy plunged ahead. "Actually, it was a few Sundays ago a man here in town named Corky and I were talking about how we could get a Sunday school started for the church here."

"Yeah, I think I heard about that. So you and Corky have a bee in your bonnets to start Sunday school in our town. What about it?"

"Anyway," Marcy said, the man unnerved her, his dark, beady eyes seemed to look right through her. After a moment's hesitation, she repeated, "Anyway, umm, I found out that you own the land around the church. Corky can get some portable classrooms, but there's not enough room behind the church to put something like that before the trees start."

Brad picked up his coffee mug from the counter, rested it on his belly and said, "Hmm."

For several seconds, the only sound in the store was the ticking of the battery powered clock. Since Matt wasn't involved, he'd returned to his seat in the nook. He seemed like a nice enough man, but he didn't offer Marcy any support, something she could use. She continued to lean on the counter, looking at Brad, but Brad turned his head and looked beyond Marcy, out through the glass door and across the street to the church. His expression gave nothing away.

"Yeah," Brad finally said, "I own that land. Been in my family a lotta years. Tell me about Sunday school. Why's it important?"

Taking a deep breath, Marcy said, "Mr. Thomas, I'll tell you what Sunday school means to me. My parents are good Christian people and taught me many things from the Bible as I grew up. Still, when I went to Sunday school each week I learned many more things and the teachers had different things to use to teach the classes than my parents had. The thing that bothers me the most about the church here is that there are no children or young people who come to the church except for Heidi and baby Lenny. That church needs young families coming to it so that it can grow. If only older people and middle aged couples come, the church will soon die. People need to be hooked on church from a young age. Roger's a good preacher, but where are the young people and children? They need to be there!"

Brad put the mug to his lips and took a long drink. Once he'd emptied the mug, he set it back on the counter, before he looked at Marcy. "Yes, I guess that's true. Hadn't really thought too much about it, since my kids was grown when Joyce and I moved here. Natt's here now, but there ain't nobody his age ta go there, 'cept you, and yor jes visitin'. So, old Corky can get some classrooms fer a Sunday school if ya had some land? So Missy, where you propose to get these kids yor talkin' about?"

"Yes, Corky said a school nearby wants to get rid of some portable classrooms and he can get them. I don't know where lots of kids are, but my sister has forty-nine piano students who don't come here to church. Surely some of them would be interested."

"Yeah, they jes might. Lemme think on it a bit. Ya got a good point, I give it some thought. You be at church tomorra?"

"I plan to be, Mr. Thomas."

"I'll letcha know then."

"Thank you, sir! I'll hunt you up."

Brad's lips turned up just a bit, as he said, "Yeah, I'm shore you will."

Marcy gave the old man a grin, then turned to leave and nearly fell over Matt, who had seen Brad put his empty mug on the counter and was coming to get it for a refill. "Oh, I'm sorry, I didn't see you."

"No harm done. So you're wanting to get Sunday school started here. I agree with you. Wish I'd stayed with my roots that got started early in Sunday school." He made a face. "I'd probably still be married if I'd kept on the way I was raised."

Marcy nodded, as she headed for the door. "Yes, children need all the help they can get to learn early about Jesus and His love for them."

"Yep, I guess that's so."

Sunday morning, Sandy was up at her usual time, getting Jon and herself ready for church when the phone rang. When she answered, there was a croak and then a hard cough on the other end before a voice Sandy hardly recognized, said, "Sandy, Ruth and I…" another cough shot into Sandy's ear, "we're both sick and can't go to church." Another cough ended the few words. "I'm sorry."

"Isabel! You sound miserable! Of course, stay home and get better. We'll be fine. Call me when you're feeling better, but drink lots of liquids. That'll help wash those germs out."

Isabel coughed again and whispered, "We will, bye."

Sandy replaced the receiver. "That poor dear!"

She loved going to the big church in Blairsville, but she loved the little church here in Vansville, except for the loud praise team Roger used in his Sunday morning service. That was the one thing that kept her and Ramon going to Blairsville, there they used hymnbooks and sang hymns with a piano and organ accompaniment. It was what she loved, what she'd grown up with. She loved the old hymns they had a message the newer, praise songs were often lacking. Many of the old hymns were bathed in Scripture.

Sandy looked at the clock on her bedside table. She'd answered the phone and sat thinking long enough that unless she hurried, she'd be late for church there in Blairsville. She sighed, what would be the hurt if she went with Marcy today to Roger's church? He preached a good sermon, she knew he would. She could worship her Savior even if they weren't doing the music she preferred. She heard Marcy stirring in her room, so she dressed, moved back into her chair, then dressed Jon and placed the baby on her lap. She and Marcy left their rooms together.

In the hall, Marcy asked, "Who was on the phone?"

"Isabel, the poor dear! She and Ruth are both sick and can't go to church today."

"So, since Ramon's not here will you still go by yourself to Blairsville?"

Sandy sighed, "No, I guess I'll go with you to Roger's church."

Reaching the kitchen, Marcy went straight for a cupboard door and pulled out a pan, while she said, "Sis, it's really not so bad. From what I've heard, it's not near the noise it once was. Yes, they sing a lot of choruses and songs I don't know, but in the last few weeks Roger has handouts to pick up at the back that have the words to a couple of hymns. He has a couple of verses there and we sing each one. Usually one of them comes right before his message and it helps get my mind ready to hear what he's going to say."

"Good, I'll go with you."

During breakfast, Marcy looked shyly at her sister and said, "Umm, could I ask you to do something for me?"

"Sure! You don't ask for much, what is it, Girl?"

"Last week, Roger asked me to sing something. I sorta told him I would. During my devotions each day I've been practicing *The Old Rugged Cross*, would you play it for me?"

Exasperated, Sandy said, "Marcy, of course, you know I will!" Then she grinned at her sister. "Did you give Isabel and Ruth some germ so they'd be sick today and I'd go with you to church? Is that why you told Roger you'd sing?"

"No!" she huffed. "I did not! I told him I'd sing only if you'd accompany me. We both knew that would be in an evening service. But since you're going this morning, I can do it now and get it over with."

The sisters ate their breakfast, then as they cleared the table, Sandy looked at the clock in the kitchen over the sink and said, "Okay, let's get these dishes in the dishwasher and get down there to practice a time or two."

"Okay." Marcy sighed, "You know I'm for that, I need to practice for everything."

On her way to the garage, Sandy stopped in the living room at the piano. "It's good Ed sent my hymnbook along when he gathered up all that stuff from my piano and sent it down all those months ago. You can use that for the other verses that you may not know so well."

"That's good I may draw a blank when I get up in front of all those people. At least when I sang last Christmas, I stood by the piano to sing."

"Sis, you know I could help you learn a bit about music now that you're here."

"It would help, I guess."

When they arrived at the church, only Roger and his family were there. Heidi was still outside running around, while Raylyn sat on a lawn chair in the sun with Lenny in his infant seat asleep. Roger wasn't with them, but both Sandy and Marcy were sure he was inside putting the last minute touches on his sermon.

As Sandy motored up the ramp toward the little porch, Raylyn exclaimed, "Sandy! You're here for service this morning?"

"Yes, Ramon's out with a group and Isabel and Ruth are sick, so Marcy persuaded me to come with her. Then she told me she's to sing so we came early to practice together."

"Go ahead in, the praise team isn't here yet, but Roger has the door open. Heidi needs to run off some steam, so we're out here doing that."

Sandy had the hymnbook and her Bible on her lap and Marcy carried her Bible along with the infant seat inside, then they both moved up the side aisle to where they would sit close to the piano. Sandy moved to the keyboard, while Marcy put Jon's seat on the second seat in, then took the hymnbook, stood beside the piano and found the page with the beloved hymn on it. Sandy played a beautiful introduction then nodded for Marcy to start singing. Marcy took a deep breath, she loved to sing, but in front of people was not her favorite.

Roger raised his head and listened to the music as Sandy started playing. Tears came to his eyes, as he recognized the old hymn. He'd loved it as a teen and then at Christian college, they'd sing it often in chapel, but he'd lost so much in the years following. However, he would never forget what happened that night when the same lady had played that hymn when he was at her house. Those words he'd known for years and the simple sentence she'd spoken had cut straight to his soul. His life had been changed that night and would never be the same. God had been in that house and he'd gone running, but he couldn't get away, no matter how hard he ran. Yes, he'd been the rabbit, but the hounds of heaven had had him in their sights.

When Marcy started singing, Roger whispered the words along with her. She started a second verse and Roger knew Marcy had to have a hymnbook. As he listened, he decided copying hymns onto sheets of paper for people to sing from wasn't how it should be. The next time they had a business meeting, he'd ask that money for hymnbooks be put into the budget. Not singing hymns was a part of Christian heritage that people of Vansville church were missing.

Sandy and Marcy went all the way through the hymn again, but Roger could hear others gathering in the auditorium. The praise team had arrived. He was almost sad; yes, Sandy would play in his morning service, but only for her sister. The much louder music makers would be supplying what the worshipers would be singing. Only moments after Sandy's final note faded away, a much louder sound took over. Roger sighed, wishing he could redo more than a half dozen years of his ministerial life. However, that was not to be – at least not today.

Roger put his notes in the place where he would read Scripture, closed his Bible and headed out to the auditorium. Sandy and Marcy sat very close to the door of his office, so he took two steps over and smiled at the two sisters. He looked at the piano that usually sat silent most Sundays and said, "Great to see you two sisters here together! You two sounded perfect. You will sound great as our special this morning."

"Thanks, Roger," Sandy said, "Isabel and Ruth are sick and Ramon's on a trail, so we came together. Only a few minutes ago Marcy let me in on your secret, so we came early so we could practice together."

"I'm glad. I know just the time slot where I want you to sing. How about right after the offering, Marcy? Then Sandy can be at the piano and we'll sing a hymn before I preach."

"You'll have me play for people to sing and not them?"

"Yes, usually only one instrumentalist plays the hymn before the message."

"Great! I'll be glad to do that."

Roger winked at Sandy. "I was sure you would."

"Roger, you are something else!"

After the service, many people spoke to Marcy and told her how much her singing meant to them. She thanked them, but it seemed every person who'd been in the service came to speak with her. They also thanked Sandy for playing the hymn they sang. Roger couldn't help but hear, he was glad he'd decided to get some hymnbooks. Sandy always waited for most of the people to leave, because she felt her chair hemmed people in and made them feel uncomfortable. Marcy had the baby in his seat, but Sandy moved ahead of her down the outside aisle.

Roger and Raylyn waited at the back door. After seeing the last person out and following Sandy and Marcy onto the covered porch out front, Roger said, "I see Natt didn't come with his grandparents again, but Brad's nephew came with them."

Her eyes twinkling, Sandy said, "He couldn't have come today if he'd wanted to."

"Oh, why's that?"

"Brad's other nephew is training to be a new guide. Our major requirement for a guide-in-training is that he go on two hikes with one of our guides. He took Natt along on this hike with Ramon. Let me tell you a secret! Eric, Brad's nephew, is a Christian."

"A very dedicated Christian," Marcy added.

"Praise God!" Roger exclaimed.

Chuckling, Sandy said, "Yes, but that's not all. The group Ramon was leading, that Natt's a part of, is made up of two pastors and their wives on vacation and a seminary student. There are five of them, Eric and also Ramon. I'm pretty sure Natt is outnumbered!"

Roger threw his head back and laughed so hard Heidi came running up the steps. "Daddy! Why you laughing so hard?" Raylyn was wiping her eyes, also from laughing so hard.

Roger whirled her up in the air, then snuggled her against his shoulder. "Oh, Munchkin, Miss Sandy told me something so good I had to laugh." Looking back at Sandy, still with a grin on his face and twinkles in his eyes, he said, "On that note, let's go home! That boy will be pulled, kicking and screaming into the kingdom!"

Sandy also chuckled. "That's the truth!"

Marcy hadn't said anything, she'd let Sandy tell her tale and let those three enjoy a moment. She'd walked on, but by now, she stood on the sidewalk waiting for Sandy to come with her keys to open the van door and lower the lift. She still held Jon, who slept peacefully in his seat. Both Roger and Sandy looked at each other, then down from the small porch to where Marcy stood. Marcy wasn't looking at them she stood looking across the street at the closed Thomas complex. Roger looked back at Sandy who sat watching her sister and grinning.

Raylyn had also laughed. She whispered, making sure Marcy didn't hear her. "Am I thinking what you both are thinking?"

Roger set Heidi on the walkway, then picked his son off his wife's shoulder and said, "It's a good possibility, Love. We'll just have to wait and see on that one."

The group Sandy described was on a high plateau that morning. Whenever Ramon led a group of believers on a hike that had Sunday as part of their hiking days, he always asked if they wanted to have a service. If they did, he found out if they wanted to have some time in the morning before they broke camp or if they'd wait until evening around the campfire. This group had asked to have time in the morning, so while Sandy and Marcy were practicing in Vansville church, Ramon's hikers were having their service in God's great cathedral. The only thing missing were the stained-glass windows.

Of course, Natt still had no Bible, but he eagerly sat beside Tony to read along. Ron had been picked to lead the service. "Okay, folks, let's start off by singing, *The Old Rugged Cross.*" Immediately he started singing and the others joined in.

> "On a hill far away, stood an old rugged cross,
> the emblem of suffering and shame.
> And I love that old cross where the Dearest and
> Best for a world of lost sinners was slain.
> So I'll cherish the old rugged cross, till my trophies at last I lay down;
> I will cling to the old rugged cross, and exchange it some day for a crown."

Natt, of course, didn't know the words, he had never heard the hymn before, but he listened to the words. The men harmonized with the ladies, obviously, these people were very familiar with the song. They sang it beautifully and from their hearts. They only sang one verse, of course, they had nothing with them that had other verses, but what they sang sank into Natt's heart. That cross had held his Savior, the One who had died there to take away his sins. His blood had covered his sins so that now he was God's child. As the last note faded away, tears stung Natt's eyes.

He had lots to learn, but he would. He knew where the Bible Isabel had in his cabin was he would get it out and start reading. Perhaps he and Eric could have a Bible study, since they were next door neighbors now. Of course, that would be when he wasn't leading a hike, but Natt knew there was plenty to read on his own. He'd already decided he'd have a chat with Roger there was the man with the answers. Natt smiled through his tears, he felt like a new man!

Before lunch time, Ron ended his remarks and they sang another song. Since everything was packed up and ready for the trail, the men helped their wives put on their backpacks then shouldered their own. Ramon, with Eric right behind him, started down the trail, then the two couples, with Tony and Natt bringing up the rear. Natt looked off across the wild acres. Did those colors seem brighter? Perhaps it was his new perspective, now that he was God's child!

Tony looked over his shoulder and asked, "So, did I see tears in your eyes, Man?"

Natt sighed, "Yeah, I guess you did, but it's so overwhelming! You know, that song, *The Old Rugged Cross*, I heard about that several times recently, but I didn't know it, I'd never heard it. I had no idea why it meant anything until you guys sang it today. It means so much now!"

Tony smiled. "It's meant a lot to me, too. Who's been talking about it?"

Natt looked down just in time to see a root. "Grandad told me it was the song that converted the pastor of the Vansville church."

Tony scowled. "You mean as a kid, a teenager?"

"No, I guess it was only a couple of years ago, after he'd been at that church for a while. I don't know all the particulars, since I wasn't there."

"Your grandad knows?"

"Maybe Ramon knows. From what I hear, he and the preacher are good friends."

Tony scowled and muttered under his breath, "The preacher was converted… He was already a pastor? Wow!"

"Yeah, sort of stunned me, too."

That evening, after devotions, while everyone sat around the fire to talk, Tony said, "Ramon, Natt told me something this morning that didn't quite add up. He said maybe you'd know. He said that the song, *The Old Rugged Cross* was what converted the pastor of the Vansville church. Is that so?"

Ramon sat for a few minutes, before he answered. "Maybe converted isn't quite the right word, but close enough. When my wife came to Vansville, she came as my office manager. At that time I had no use for God and didn't want to hear anything about Him. I was eager to tell her so, too."

Incredulously, Tony said, "Really?"

Ramon nodded. "One of the first questions out of her mouth, after I gave her the job was, 'Does this church here in town preach the Word?' I told her I didn't know and I didn't care."

"Uh oh," Natt whispered, but Ramon heard him.

Ramon grinned. "You got that right! From then on I knew my life as I knew it was in grave danger of being changed. I didn't know it when I hired her, but Sandy is a powerhouse for the Lord! Yes, my life was changed not too many weeks later and she was a huge reason it happened. Anyway, I suggested she play a concert in Roger's church, since she wanted to get students and her chair seemed to scare people off. Another thing, Roger's church was the largest building in town. Of course, being his church, we had to deal with him about the particulars."

Natalie scowled. "'Her chair scared people off.'?" she parroted. "A chair scared people off? What do you mean?"

"Yes, Sandy is paralyzed and sits in a motorized wheelchair. Anyway, we got it settled Roger talked with her about a program. When I came back from a hike soon after she told me that she and Isabel, her landlady, were praying for him. She wasn't sure he was truly a believer."

"Ramon, you have me totally confused!" Ron exclaimed. "First you talk about Sandy's chair scaring people, but the pastor of a church not being a true believer? My goodness! She must be something else!"

Ramon grinned again. "Well, to make a long story short, things happened on a hike and I became a Christian. After that, Sandy became my wife, she got her students, but she was still praying for Roger. You see, her landlady wouldn't go to his church because he only read from a book and didn't preach from the Word. From what he said and how he acted, they were convinced he wasn't a believer or he was a backslidden Christian."

"So where does *The Old Rugged Cross* fit in?" Tony asked.

"One day, before Thanksgiving a year and a half ago, I invited Roger to come help me paint the rooms I'd had built as our bedroom suite to accommodate Sandy's chair. He came over, helped me paint and stayed for supper. Sandy was going to play another concert, so after supper we went in the living room to listen to her practice."

"Practice! Hah!" Natt blurted out, "She doesn't need to practice she's awesome!"

"I know," Ramon said, grinning, "but she always says she has to practice. Anyway, without either Roger or me knowing what she was doing, she never raised her hands, only blended into the music *The Old Rugged Cross*. She only played the tune, never sang the words, but when she'd finished one verse, she raised her hands, turned and looked Roger in the eye and said, 'Roger, how many people have you brought to that old rugged cross?' I have never seen a man move so fast as Roger did! His coat trailed out behind him as he slammed out the front door and his Jeep squealed out of my parking lot seconds later. We never saw him until a week later, but on Thanksgiving Day he preached his first sermon in that church."

"So he was converted?"

Looking at Tony, knowing that the man presently went to seminary, Ramon said, "He's told us he was raised in a godly family and had lots of Christian influence growing up, went to a Christian college, but when he went to seminary, some of the professors pulled him away from his roots and made him a skeptic. Because of what Sandy said God did a work in his life and brought him back to those roots."

Tony nodded. "I know what you mean. I looked into a lot of schools before I picked the one I'm going to now for just that reason. It's unconscionable that seminaries are like that! Those are places where men and women are trained to bring people closer to their Savior, but they hire professors who are skeptics!"

After some moments of silence, when only the tree toads and other night sounds dominated the evening, Natalie said, "So what does your wife play?"

"She plays and teaches piano."

She looked at Ramon, as if to make sure he was being sincere, then looked at her own feet and said, "Ramon, I make an attempt to play the piano. Believe me, I wouldn't think of giving a concert! I use my foot to use the sustaining pedal and even that doesn't make it sound very professional. If she's paralyzed…in a wheelchair…"

Ramon grinned and nodded. "She's played for many years, Natalie. When she was young, she and her brother rigged up a little pouch that connects somehow into the workings of the piano. It fits over the back of her wheelchair and she works it with her back."

"Oh, my!"

"So she's good?"

"Good!" Natt exclaimed. "She's awesome! She played a concert a week ago in Roger's church. Some of what she played only a master could play!"

Humbly, Ramon said, "Yes, she's great, but she gives all glory to God. She is the most humble person I know about her playing. My step-dad got her a position as guest pianist with the Atlanta Symphony a couple of summers ago. The encores went on and on. She even had to play a solo piece before the audience let her leave the platform. It was an evening neither she nor I will ever forget."

"Amazing! We can meet her when we get back?"

"Of course. She may play you a number if you twist her arm just right," Ramon said, grinning. "In the meantime, it's getting late we'd better hit the dirt."

Natalie sighed, "Don't remind me. Dirt can be very unforgiving."

"Mmm, I know. My wife gets a grain of sand between the mattress and box springs and she's sure she's sleeping on a boulder," Ron said.

Natalie huffed, "I'm not *that* bad!"

"Close to Princess and the pea, Sweetheart."

Monday morning, at breakfast, Marcy stirred cream into her decaf coffee and said, "You know, since I sang yesterday, I forgot to talk to Brad about the land behind the church. He said he needed to think about what I asked him to do about Sunday school. I never remembered last night, either. I guess I'd better make a trip to the store and see what he decided about that land behind the church today."

Sandy grinned. "I suppose, or you could wait until, umm, Tuesday."

Giving her sister a glare, Marcy said, "Sister, dear, I will *not* wait until Tuesday! Today's the perfect day to have a talk with Brad. Besides, I need the exercise."

Sandy shrugged. "As you say…"

Soon after breakfast dishes were in the dishwasher, Marcy grabbed her purse, slung it over her shoulder and marched out the front door. The sun was out in all its glory, after all, it was July. As usual, since it was the day after the holiday weekend in north Georgia, the heat of the morning grabbed her. She blew out a big huff that lifted her bangs and decided the walk to the hardware store several blocks away was just what she needed.

As she entered the store, Matt came from the back of the store, smiled and said, "Howdy miss Marcy. You did a really good job on that hymn yesterday. That lady that played the piano for you, who is she?"

"She's my sister Sandy. Thank you for the compliment that hymn's one of my favorites. I guess Brad's here?"

Nodding, the man said, "He's in his favorite chair."

Marcy walked up to the counter and saw Brad sitting there. He'd heard the exchange, so he had his eyes open and looked at Marcy. Chucking, he said, "I was kinda waitin' fer ya. Sorta fergot yesterday, did ya?"

"Yes, I did, but that's why I'm here this morning."

FIFTEEN

"Well, ya know that land thar was my granddaddy's. Yeah, 'cept for where the church is, it's been in the family for lotsa years."

"Well…," Marcy licked her lips. She had no idea what to say.

Brad grinned at her. "Ya don't know me too well, but I used ta be a *real* grouch a couple years back, 'fore your sister came ta town."

From a chair in the coffee drinkers nook came a strangled sound, but no words.

Marcy pulled in a deep breath and blurted out, "Mr. Thomas, we… umm, really you won't have to part with the land… if there was more room around the church to put them…."

He looked for his coffee mug, but when he saw it was empty he waved his hand instead and exclaimed, "So put 'em there! No harm in that."

"But, umm, Corky said some of those trees on the back would have to be cut down."

"He got a chain saw?"

"I don't know."

"Find out, girl get your ducks all in a row. Mebe it ain't so hard as ya think."

Marcy just stared at the man. Get her ducks in a row? What was the man talking about?

"You don't know his real name? Call that Roger guy, he'd know. In fact, I know Roger got a chain saw. Tell 'im ta use it! Be about time. Come ta think on it, it be about time ta git Ms Sandy's pi-ana kids in that church fer school!" When Marcy still stood leaning in the counter with her mouth hanging open, Brad waved his hand, shooing her away and said, "Git on with it, girl. We don't got many flies here, but 'nough you could get sick if ya swallered some."

Marcy's mouth snapped shut. She swallowed again and in a tiny voice, said, "Umm, yeah, I'll get right on that. Thanks."

Looking beyond her, he raised his mug and said to his nephew, "My mug's empty, Matt, could ya do me the favor?"

Matt also swallowed, jumped from his seat and taking long strides, said, "Sure, Uncle Brad, I'll get that right now."

As Matt swung around the counter, Marcy whirled around, pushed her purse strap up farther on her shoulder and scurried from the store. She hadn't even made it to the sidewalk before she skipped once, raised her head and shouted, "***Thank You, God***!"

Marcy hurried. She knew better than try to run the five blocks from the hardware store to Sandy's house, but she did hurry. She knew Sandy would be in the office, so she cut across the parking lot to that door and burst in. She was so loud about it that Jon woke up with a start. He didn't cry, though, he was in his car seat that he loved.

"Oh! I'm sorry, Sis. I'm just so excited I forgot Jon would be sleeping."

Sandy picked up the baby, placed him on her shoulder and patted his back. Moments later, he sighed, turned his head into Sandy's neck and fell back to sleep. Sandy scowled and said, "What are you excited about? You did just go to see Brad about the land, didn't you? I guess he gave you some good news?"

"Yes! I didn't go anywhere else, either." A grin spread across her face so big it nearly split her face. "But Brad told me to call Roger to cut down some trees behind the church to put in those rooms for Sunday school! He said to be about it and get your piano kids on the stick and coming for Sunday school."

Incredulously, Sandy snapped her fingers and said, "Just like that?"

Marcy couldn't wipe the grin off her face. "Yeah, that's what he said! At first he asked if Corky had a chain saw. I told him I didn't know and I didn't know Corky's last name, so he said to call Roger for his number, but then he said he knew Roger had a chain saw and to tell him to cut down the trees!"

"We have Roger's number, but I don't know Corky's, so you'd better call Roger. Still, you'd better talk to Corky to see about those classrooms."

"I will!"

Marcy sat down at the side of the desk, found Roger's number and dialed. When Raylyn answered, Marcy said, "Hi, Raylyn, is Roger there?"

"He's here on the property, but he's out cutting trees. He's across the field and he couldn't hear me if I tried to call him. He'll be in for lunch, could he call you then?"

"That'll be great, Raylyn! We sure had fun at your place the other day. Thanks for having us and that stew you made was super!"

Raylyn chuckled. "Actually, that's Roger's specialty. When we came down for that Thanksgiving, he invited us out to the farm. He fixed that stew. I told him I was impressed with his culinary skills, but he confessed that and mac and cheese were the extent of his kitchen skills. Still, we love that stew and it always hit's the spot."

"Yes, it was good. So you'll have him call when he comes in?"

"I will. Heidi's here, she'll help me remember."

"Thanks, Raylyn, I'll talk to you again."

Sandy and Marcy were fixing sandwiches for lunch when the phone rang. Since Marcy expected Roger to call, she answered, but the voice wasn't masculine. Almost sure what the lady had called about, Marcy said, "Hi, Mom! What's on your mind? I wasn't expecting you to call, but it's good to hear your voice. Sandy and I are having a great time, we're just fixing lunch."

Without making any small-talk, Colleen asked, "When are you coming home, Marcy?" It almost sounded like an accusation. "You know Doctor wants to see you."

Not wanting to let the words give her a guilty conscience, Marcy said, "Maybe not for a while, Mom. I'm having a great time here, it's a great little town and we're about to get Sunday school up and running here in Vansville."

Colleen nearly huffed into the phone, "Marcy! You need to come home! You're doing way too much! What's the matter with your sister? She should make you rest, not do all that hard stuff! Why, if I was there...."

Marcy grinned and interrupted before Colleen could get on her crusading horse, "But you're not, Mom! Sandy let's me do whatever I feel up to. This morning I walked five blocks to the hardware store and five blocks back. It was hot, but I feel great and haven't had a heart twinge or palpitation in days. If I need to, I take a nap after lunch, but I haven't needed to since the day after I got here. Mom, I'm great!"

Like any concerned mother, Colleen asked, "Are you eating right? Do you get all the vegetables and the protein you need?"

Marcy couldn't help but chuckle. "Yes, Mom, we're fine. I need to go someone's supposed to call, so I need to get off the phone. Take care of Daddy, talk to you again." Breezily, Marcy hurriedly hung up.

The phone rang immediately. This time, it was Roger. "Marcy? You needed to talk with me? Raylyn said to call you."

"Roger thanks for calling! You won't believe this!"

"Okay, you got my undivided."

"Remember when Corky and I talked about Sunday school?"

"Vaguely, but yes."

"He and I met the next day and he said he could get some portable classrooms because the county school was going to build an addition. I said I didn't think there was enough room around the church, so he said he thought Mr. Casbah owned some land, he didn't know if it was there by the church or not."

"No, it's Brad Thomas."

"I know, when I talked with Derek, he told me. Anyway, I went to see Brad Thomas on Saturday, then again today."

"Ahh, and what did he have to say?"

Marcy chuckled. "You sound a bit leery, Roger."

"Mmm, well, I've known Brad for some time now…"

"Yeah, he told me he used to be a *real* grouch."

Roger chuckled then and said, "Okay, what else did he say?"

"He asked if Corky had a chain saw…."

"A chain saw?"

"When I told him I didn't know, he said he knew you did and that I should call you and have you get out there to cut enough trees we could put in those classrooms for Sunday school."

Totally astonished, Roger exclaimed, "You… what! He told you to tell me to bring my chain saw and cut trees behind the church so we could put in portable classrooms?"

"Yes! He didn't tell me to *ask* you, either. He told me to *tell* you to do it! He said we needed to get Ms Sandy's piano students into Sunday school."

"Wow! I am speechless! Those two things are unbelievable!"

Marcy laughed. "You mean that you're speechless and that he ordered you to cut trees?"

"That's it!"

Still laughing, Marcy said, "Well be about it, Roger!"

"Let's you, Corky and me get together and see how this can be done."

"Okay, want to call him?"

"Yes, I have his number I'll give him a buzz and call you back."

Later, Roger called back and said, "I tried to reach Corky, but then I learned he and Loretta are out of town for the holiday. Surely, this can wait until Sunday I'll call a meeting of anybody who's interested. How's that?"

"Great! You know I'll be there."

"Oh, yes, I was sure of it!"

Monday afternoon, a hot, sweaty and bedraggled bunch of hikers gathered on the parking lot at DeLord's. The last forty-five minutes they all had moved as fast as they could, because black clouds were gathering in the west and everyone could feel the humidity climbing, especially, as they came down out of the hills. Just as they reached the parking lot, the sun went behind those ominous clouds. All three of the hikes had originated at DeLord's and they all came back within minutes of each other.

They all said hasty goodbyes, lightning was jumping around in the clouds and thunder was growling as the hikers scrambled for their cars. Ramon, Eric and Natt waved to their hiking companions, as they dumped their backpacks into one trunk and hurriedly climbed into Ron's car. At the same time, Eric and Natt threw their backpacks into Eric's trunk, then yanked the front doors open and dove in as Ramon ran for the house. Only seconds later, the roar of the rain came. Fortunately, the hikes were finished and it hadn't rained during their six days on the trails. They had all had a fantastic time.

Sandy had been watching and as Ramon ran for the door, she pulled it open then moved back so her husband could run through the door uninhibited. He nearly threw his backpack at the desk, as he kicked the door closed. His arms outstretched, he exclaimed, "Darling! Thanks! We nearly ran the last half hour! We saw the clouds roiling and knew we were in for a bad one."

"Honey, I'm glad you're home!" Their lips came together in a wonderful kiss. Thunder roared outside and sheets of rain came down at the same time. Anything Ramon might have said was drowned in the noise. Fortunately, it was outside the closed door. He didn't mind rain, but if he could be inside during a storm he'd take that option, especially if that option could be in the same place as his wife and baby.

Tuesday morning, after very early devotions with Eric, Natt pulled the door closed on his cabin, made his way down the walk in front of cabin one and headed across the parking lot for the street. The rain that had chased them home yesterday was only a memory. The day was bright and beautiful. That storm had tempered the breeze and the temperature was pleasant.

Natt couldn't stifle his grin and his feet felt like they hardly touched the ground as he walked to the store. He'd had a great time on the trail! He'd made some good friends and his spirit was renewed being out-of-doors for six days, but best of all, he now had Jesus Christ as his Savior and his soul was free and alive. He knew he was not the same man, he'd never be again.

He walked onto the complex parking lot and stopped first at the Laundromat to unlock the door and turn on the lights. As he came back out, he saw Brad doing his 'constitutional' around the corner. Moments before the old man arrived at the store, Natt turned the key in the hardware store door and stepped inside.

When Brad pushed the door open, Natt was at the switch for the gas pumps and called, "Hi, Grandad, did ya miss me?"

"Boy, you know what I missed? It was that coffee you make. Nothin' like it! Git yor brew goin' so's I kin have the first cup."

Natt laughed. "I'm on it, Grandad! Didn't Matt follow my recipe?"

"Dano, but it shore didn't taste like yors!"

While Natt was filling the urn Roger's Jeep pulled around the corner and stopped beside his office door. Brad had been watching the church corner ever since Marcy had paid him a visit on Monday. He'd wondered when the preacher would get on with the task he'd given the go-ahead for.

As Roger went to the hatch on his vehicle, Brad smiled, nodded and sank into his chair behind the counter. *Mebe I won't nap quite so much taday, looks like it could get intrestin.*

When Natt brought the urn from the back and went to the nook, he looked out the big window and saw Roger's Jeep. He kept watching as he plugged the cord into the big urn and saw Roger move from his Jeep with a clipboard and what looked like a tape measure. He scowled and asked, "Grandad, what's the preacher doing over there? He's not even going into the church! Looks like he's going back to that row of trees."

"Yeah, probly is, Son."

A bit exasperated, but he should be used to his grandad's less than helpful answers, Natt asked, "But why? What's in those trees?"

"He's gonna cut 'em down."

"Cut them down?"

"Yep! They's in the way."

He and the urn let out a big wheeze together. Of course, the urn kept on wheezing, but Natt said, "Grandad! You know why he's doing that! You have a huge grin on your face. Why's he cutting down those trees?"

"'Cause I tole 'im to!"

It was almost like when his dad had pulled out a baby tooth and nearly as painful. "Grandad, why did you tell Roger to cut down those trees?"

Brad shrugged. "I didn't tell Roger nuthin', but the church needs the land and them trees're in the way. Roger's got a chain saw, so he's cuttin' 'em."

"And that would be because?"

"Corky's got some buildin's he's bringin' in purdy soon."

"Oh."

Since Natt had never been to Sunday school, he had no idea why there was a need for buildings around the church. Natt had been in the building three times, once on Christmas Eve for a service of carols, the evening service that Ramon and Sandy had brought him to and the concert where Sandy played. Two of those times he could understand why they might need to expand the auditorium, but add rooms outside? He shrugged without a clue.

"Why?"

"You never been to Sunday school, Son?"

"No-o-o-o, what's that?"

"It's where you go to class and they teach you stuff from the Bible on Sunday. You know, Sunday… school."

"Oh, I get it."

The coffee urn let out its last wheeze just as another truck pulled around and parked in front of Roger's. Corky got out and lifted out a chain saw from his truckbed. He also disappeared behind the church. Natt took Brad's mug, pushed it under the urn spigot and filled the mug to the brim. Before he moved from the nook, he saw a young woman with dark hair walking the sidewalk toward the same corner. Still holding the mug, he watched her turn the corner until he lost sight of her behind the church. The third person to appear across the street put a stop to the young man's forward motion.

"Umm, Son, you gonna bring me that mug sometime soon, 'fore it ices over?"

"Uh-h, sure, Grandad. Right away." Reluctantly, he pulled his eyes from the last spot he'd seen Marcy, turned and headed toward the counter, holding out the mug toward his grandad. He even thought to turn the handle so Brad could take the cup.

A smirk on his face, Brad asked, "So, how was that hike?"

"Awesome, Grandad!"

"Good to get out in the out-of-doors?"

"Grandad, not only that… well, I came face to face with God out there."

Brad thumped his mug down on the counter, sat up straight in the chair and said, "You mean that, Son?"

"You bet! Before Sunday I learned why *The Old Rugged Cross* did such a number on Roger! They sang it for their church Sunday morning, and… well… I knew why he'd run out of Ramon's house that night."

"So you became a Christian on the trail? Eric help ya?"

"No, it wasn't Eric, but one of the guys on the hike is going to be a preacher. We had a lot of talks. Now, when Eric's home, we'll have Bible studies together."

"That's great! I'm pleased as peanuts about that, Son. I saw that dark headed miss you was watchin', you could have Bible studies with her."

"Grandad…" Natt cautioned.

Taking a long swig of coffee, Brad grinned and said, "Jes' sayin."

"Mmm, yeah, matchmaker!"

When Corky and Loretta returned Monday evening, he saw Roger's number on his caller ID, since it wasn't late he gave the young man a call. "So Roger, what's your call about?" he asked, after Roger answered.

"Corky, hold onto your hat! Marcy got us the go ahead from Brad to cut trees out behind the church to make room for those classrooms you can get. He told Marcy to get us – you and me – on the stick!"

"Great! We'd better be about it, Pastor. The school board met last Tuesday and the classrooms gotta be outta there before the end of this month."

"Shoo! No time to waste!"

"Nope, bring your saw and meet me back there tomorra morning."

"How many buildings are we talking about?"

"We can have all of 'em. There's five."

"Wow! Five! Do we need that many?"

"Don't know, but we might as well take 'em all. They'll cluster and we can tack 'em onto the church. Maybe not at first, we won't need all five, but you'll never get this good of a deal again in a real long time."

"That's true, Corky, I'll see you tomorrow morning before it gets hot."

When Roger disconnected, he dialed Ramon's number. When Marcy came on the line, he said, "Corky and I are meeting at the church tomorrow morning early to start cutting trees…."

"Roger! I'll be there!"

Chuckling, Roger said, "I figured you would."

Brad had just returned from his lunch break and Natt was about to push the front door of the store open, when he looked across the street and saw Marcy walk to the corner, then cross to the sidewalk in front of the hardware store. Natt debated whether to walk out right then, but his stomach gave a growl loud enough that Brad chuckled from his seat.

"Better be about it, Boy, yor belly needs fillin'."

Natt sighed, "Yeah, Grandad, I'm out of here."

Chuckling, Brad said, "Yeah, knew ya would."

Intercepting her close to the Laundromat, Natt said, above the noise of the chain saws, "So, what brought you to town today?"

As Natt fell in beside her, she grinned and said, "Roger and Corky are cutting trees back there so we can bring in portable classrooms for the church to have Sunday school! Since I don't have much experience with a chainsaw, I'm going after subs at Alex's store so they can have some lunch. Are you on your lunch break, too?"

"Yup!" Just before they reached Alex's door, Natt pulled in a long breath and said, "And Marcy, I asked Jesus to be my Savior on our hike."

Marcy had to grab her purse strap, but she surely wanted to wrap her arms around the young man by her side. Instead she gave him a huge grin. "You did! Natt! Praise God!"

"Yeah, it was an awesome hike, believe me!"

Natt opened the grocery store door and let Marcy precede him inside. Both of them walked down the aisle to the refrigerator section of the grocery store. Natt opened the door, but let Marcy reach in for three different subs then Natt pulled out one. Before they headed for the checkout, Marcy picked up a six-pack of cola. After they each made their purchase, Natt followed Marcy to the door and pushed it open for her.

As she went by, he said, "Umm, would it be alright if I joined you for lunch, Marcy?"

Giving him another megawatt smile, she said, "I'd be honored, Natt!"

"Great! After you give the guys their subs we can sit on those steps and eat ours, okay?"

"Sure, I'll do that!"

After Natt left, Brad picked up his mug and went to the nook for a refill. He sat in the chair right beside the little stand and watched as one of the big trees behind the church swayed, then fell. It was a huge tree he even heard the crash from behind the closed door of the store. He had no customer at the time, so he didn't move. Only a few minutes later, he saw Natt walking Marcy down the sidewalk across the street in front of the church. They each carried a bag, probably their lunch. At the corner, they turned then disappeared behind the church.

Nodding, Brad saw what he wanted, so he stood to go to his favorite seat and muttered, "'Bout like I figgered. Them two's jes' right fer each other." A little voice in his head that sounded suspiciously like one he heard often said, *You're matchmaking, Grandad.* "Yep! Yep, that I am! Not a bit sad about it, neither!"

Ramon was home for several days, so he and Sandy talked for several minutes around the supper table. However, it was something concerning the business and didn't involve Marcy. She had been away all day, but Marcy didn't enter into the conversation, instead she seemed wrapped in her own thoughts. Marcy was like that.

Finally, when Ramon and Sandy seemed to have exhausted their topic, Sandy turned to her sister, looked her in the eye and said, "So, Sister, dear, you were gone all day, it helped your tan being out in the sun. Tell me, did Roger and Corky get all the trees cut down that they needed to for those buildings?"

"Yes, they did. I filled Corky's truck with limbs and stuff he even got up on top and jumped on them to make room for more. It was a huge pile and they're meeting back again tomorrow to cut up lots more to take back to Roger's. He asked Brad if he could have the wood for his woodstove and Brad said he could."

"So you're helping?" Ramon asked.

"No, they said it was too heavy for me to do."

"But I could go help and use my truck to haul it back to his place."

Marcy nodded. "I'm sure he'd be glad for the help."

"Good, it'll give me a break from this hiking stuff."

"Okay," Sandy said, "so why the quiet act, Sis?"

"It's nothing."

"Mmm, hmm, me thinks there is something."

Marcy sighed, *Isn't there anything I can keep from my sister?* "What do you mean?"

"Sister, dear, usually when Ramon and I are talking about something general like we were you're right there with us. You were not with us, you were off in your own little world and quiet as a mouse. What gives?"

Marcy shrugged. "I didn't think there was anything to add. I mean you two can hold a conversation by yourselves. You did before I came, I'm sure."

Ramon grinned. "Has that ever stopped you before? Sandy's right, maybe it wasn't la-la-land, but you weren't here."

Marcy let out another long sigh, glanced between the two, then looked down at her plate and mumbled, "Umm, Natt Thomas ate lunch with me."

"Oh, he did?" Sandy said, looking at Ramon.

"Yes."

"And so, the store owner took his lunch break at exactly the same time as you."

"Seems so."

Sandy moved her hand, in a 'come on' motion. "So out with the details, Sis."

Marcy shrugged. "What details? We picked up subs at the grocery, I got some for Roger and Corky, we sat on the church steps and ate, he went back to the store, I went back to picking up limbs and brush. End of story."

"Did he tell you he'd become a Christian on the hike?"

"Mmm, hmm."

"No interest, though, is that it?"

Marcy didn't blush very often, but she felt her cheeks warm. After taking a big breath, she said, "Ramon, I'm still waiting to find out what God's will is for my life, since He took away the foreign missionary nurse."

Sandy looked at her sister and said, "Marcy, He may not drop an envelope into your lap that spells it out 'this is what you must do with your life,' you know. You're working with Corky and Roger to make the Sunday school happen. Nancy asked you about doing that job at the clinic. Am I getting it right?"

Marcy's fork clattered to her plate, as she looked intently at her sister. "I know…" her next words came out in a whisper, "But Sis, I'm damaged goods… I have a weak heart, it's scarred I'm not what I once was…"

"Marcy, look at me!" Sandy's eyes flashed there was no smile on her face. Ramon also looked at his wife he'd never seen her look so fierce before.

Finally, Marcy raised her eyes to her sister. "Yes?" she whispered, as she raised her head. "Yes?" she repeated.

"Marcy, look at *me*," Sandy said, a second time. "What do you see?"

"I see…." Both Ramon and Sandy saw in Marcy's eyes the instant she realized what Sandy was asking her to see. Marcy was out of her chair that instant. "Sandy! Oh, Sandy!" Tears rushed down her cheeks as she fell into her sister, throwing her arms around her neck. Brokenly, Marcy said, "Oh, Sandy! How horrid of me!"

After the sisters embraced for several minutes, Sandy said, "Marcy, you are a woman made in God's image! He allowed you to become ill with Rheumatic Fever, but you've survived, so your heart's a bit weak. Don't you think God has a work for you that is exclusively for you to do? Do you think someone is going to snub you because of your heart problem? Don't you think you could lead someone to the Lord just because you had Rheumatic Fever and can't be a nurse or a foreign missionary?"

"Umm, well, I guess." Marcy took her time moving back to her seat at the table. "Yeah, I guess you're right."

"Of course! So what's the real problem?"

"I… well… he asked if he could take me out for the evening on Saturday…"

"And you told him?"

"I… I told him I'd go," she whispered.

Ramon held a sleeping Jon on his shoulder, but he slapped his other hand on the table and exclaimed, "That's great!"

"But… but shouldn't I tell him I had Rheumatic Fever, I have a weak heart? I'm not, umm…" waving her hand, she trailed off, not sure what else to say.

Before Marcy could speak again, Sandy said, "Nonsense! On one date he needs to know all that? Give me a break! You know, something else I think you should do is trot yourself down to the clinic real soon and see about getting that job Nancy told you about back when you first came. You haven't had any weak spells since you arrived. You took a nap that very first day after you came and the other day when we came home from Blairsville you were tired out from shopping. Back when you came you were probably worn out from the trip, or maybe it was the difference in the altitude. I know we had a big day on Saturday, I was tired out. You're doing great, Sis! I think you could give them a good job. Damaged goods! Listen to you!"

"But eight hours?"

Ramon shrugged. "So tell them you don't think you can do an eight hour shift at first, maybe you could do eight to eleven and one to four. That'd give you a good rest in the middle."

Nodding, Marcy said, "Maybe I'll go down there tomorrow."

"Yes, I think you should, Sis."

Nodding, Marcy said, "I'll pray about it when I do my devotions in the morning."

"Yes, you do that!" Sandy said.

Marcy knew that Dr. Stan only worked three days a week at the clinic, so Wednesday morning, while Ramon went to help Roger and Corky with the wood, Marcy set out for the clinic. Soon after she left DeLord's house, the sound of two chainsaws echoed through the town. Marcy sighed, she couldn't hear any birdsongs, but she was happy for the noise, because that meant classrooms for Sunday school would soon be in place. Maybe she could convince Sandy and Ramon to start attending Roger's church and be teachers.

Soon she walked past Isabel's driveway and past the imposing building that was the clinic. There were two cars parked in spots away from the door and as she turned onto the walkway, another car wheeled in and went to the back. Marcy didn't know the doctor, but Nancy had told her that he was perpetually late, so she was pretty sure that was the late Dr. Stan getting to work at his fashionably late time.

As she neared the door, his car door slammed and he called, "You needing some help?"

Marcy waited at the door. Stan walked up and she said, "Nancy said you have an opening for a phlebotomist after the Fourth, so I came to see if you've filled that position yet."

Stan reached for the door handle and said, "And you would be?"

"I'm Marcy Bernard."

Stan scowled. "Why would Nancy tell you about the position?"

Marcy let out a sigh. She didn't really want to tell her whole life story, but if she was to get a job, she needed to tell the man something. "Well, when I was in nursing school in Philadelphia I learned to start IV's and sometimes we had to get blood samples at the same time for the lab. I was never a phlebotomist, but since I got pretty good at hitting a vein for an IV, she thought I'd qualify for this job."

Marcy preceded Stan into the cool building, but he motioned her to follow him and he led her to a small room that reminded her of Jason Wright's office at General. Stan went to a file cabinet, opened a drawer and pulled out some papers, then sat down at the desk. "So if you were in nursing school in Philadelphia, you're a nurse, why are you wanting a phlebotomist job?"

Marcy shook her head and said, "I was in nurse's training, but had to drop out for health reasons and my doctor said I can't go back to finish training."

"Really? Why?"

"I became ill with Rheumatic Fever, it has injured my heart. Dr. Wright said it weakened me enough that nursing school would be too strenuous."

"Ah," Stan's face burst into a smile, "but you love working in that kind of setting, so a phlebotomist job would be right up your alley. Is that it?"

Marcy's heart was pounding in her chest, but she knew it wasn't from a weakened heart. She nodded and said, "Yes, I believe it would be. I don't think I'm quite up to par yet, but I'm sure I could do, say three hours in the morning and three in the afternoon."

Stan picked up the papers in front of him, snapped them together once on the desk and handed them to Marcy. "As a formality, I'll need you to fill these out, but as of this moment, Vansville Clinic has a phlebotomist named Marcy Bernard."

Marcy swallowed and reached for the papers. "Wow! Even babysitting the neighbor's kids was harder than that! So I should start when? What hours do you want me? What's the schedule the clinic's open?"

"You can start today. You said six hours, you tell me."

"Eight to eleven and one to four?"

"It's yours!" Stan held out his hand. "Welcome aboard! As you can imagine, Saturday's are busy, but since Nancy works every other Saturday and she's off this week, how about you work and be off on Monday. Those hours are fine will five days a week work for you? Maybe I shouldn't start you at the same pay as the man who left, since he had five years experience…" After he named a figure, he said, "We'll start at that and if all works well, we'll see after that. Will that work for you, Marcy"

Marcy smiled. "Dr. Stan, that works for me!"

"Hey, except when we have patients present, I'd just as soon be just plain Stan."

"Great! Thanks for the job. I'd like to go home for lunch, but I could be back at one o'clock, would that be okay?"

"Sure, see you after lunch."

Marcy grinned. "I'll be here!"

The chainsaws were still buzzing as Marcy turned from beside the clinic. Maybe the men would like her to get them subs again for lunch.

She looked at her watch and hurried to the church. The saws shut off just as she reached the corner, but Ramon had a huge armload of logs and was headed for his truck. He saw his sister-in-law and gave her a grin.

As she walked closer, he called, "Just in time to do lunch duty, girl! How about the job?"

"I got the job, starting after lunch! I came around to see if you guys were hungry."

Roger came along with his arms loaded with logs and said, "Girl, you're a sight for sore eyes and more than a welcome sight if you're on your way to Alex's for subs. Those you brought yesterday hit the spot." He winked. "Didn't I see you had company yourself?"

Marcy huffed. "Roger, Natt came out of the store at the same time as I went by to go to Alex's. We both went to get subs for lunch, so we came out at the same time. The store's right over there…"

"Mmm, yes, so it is."

Brad looked over the counter out the window and said to Natt, "Say, that dark-haired girl's over there gettin' sub orders agin today, better hurry on out."

"Grandad, you usually go first for lunch," Natt chided.

"Not taday, you're first. Joyce's lunch'll still be there when you're back. Git on out there, 'fore she's gone!"

Natt sighed, so much for small town Georgia. Marcy crossed the street just as Natt pushed the door open. As they approached each other, he said, "So you're on sub duty again?"

"Seems so, and you're on lunch break." She grinned. "What a coincidence!" She wasn't about to tell a soul that her heart was palpitating.

"Yup, I think we got some helpers."

"Mmm, I know we do."

Again at Alex's he held the door for her then followed her to the refrigerator. They picked out the subs, Marcy got four this time, but Natt only got one. Marcy picked up another six pack of cola, but Natt waited and let Marcy go ahead of him at the cash register. Again today, they went around the corner to the side of the church, but Natt waited by the side steps while Marcy took the subs to the back of the church to the men, then came back.

As Natt and Marcy sat down on the church steps, she said, "I got a job at the clinic!"

"Really? Doing what?"

"I'm going to be their phlebotomist! I start at one o'clock!"

"Umm, what's a phlebotomist?"

She giggled and her cheeks turned a little pink. "Since most people don't know what that word means and are too chicken to ask, it's a glorified word for somebody who draws blood for tests in a clinic or doctor's office."

Natt shrugged. "Well, I guess you can tell I'm not too chicken to ask if I don't know."

"Nope, I guess that's the newspaper man in you."

"Must be."

As they wadded up their empty sub wrappers, he asked, "So are we still on for Saturday evening, Marcy?"

She gave him her megawatt smile. "I'm planning on it!"

"Great! I'll throw away your wrapper now and see you then."

"Thanks, Natt, I'm really looking forward to it."

It was four fifty-five Saturday afternoon. Natt pulled the plug on the big coffee maker then picked it up and as nonchalantly as possible left the coffee drinker's nook for the back room to dump out what was left and clean the huge pot for the first splash of water on Monday morning. In between, those two points, the sly old man sat in his chair behind the counter with his eyes closed, but Natt knew he wasn't sleeping.

Brad confirmed his thought only seconds later, when he said, "So, you be in a hurry to close up taday?"

"Yeah, Grandad, it's Saturday, we're out of here for a whole day!"

"Uh huh, and that's the only reason you be in a hurry."

From the back room, water splashed into the big sink, but Natt said, over the noise, "If you must know, Grandad, this man has a date!"

Brad chuckled to himself, but he said, "Ah, so, year makin' yer move on that dark haired beauty tonight?"

A loud chuckle ended with, "You could say that, Grandad!"

"Good fer you, Son, good fer you! I'm downright pleased with yer choice. Seems like a good one ta me!"

"Yeah, I think it's pretty cool myself!"

Marcy looked at the big clock on the wall behind the receptionist's desk. It was two minutes to five. There was no one in the clinic, dare she grab her purse and rush out to her car before the hour, since it was Saturday and nobody was seeing a professional? It had been the longest afternoon she could remember living through since high school. Just to think she wasn't at General, she'd have Sunday off!

The gal behind the desk opened the bottom drawer, grabbed out a purse and flung it on the desk, as she reached for another and said, "Get out of here, girl! I'm about to lock the door and you wanna be on the other side of it when I do! Go break a leg!"

Laughing, Marcy grabbed her purse and as she flung it over her shoulder, she headed for the door to the parking lot. "I will! See you!"

"Yup, and I expect a minute by minute!" came the voice after her.

Minutes later, Marcy flung her purse on the passenger seat as she quickly slid behind the wheel of her car. She usually didn't drive to work, in fact, she'd only gone back to DeLord's to get her car after lunch with Natt, but tonight was a first. A handsome young man was coming for her in forty-five minutes to take her to Blairsville for dinner and a date! She would be ready and not be late! Walking several blocks in Georgia heat was not how to do that.

Marcy still stood looking in the mirror fussing with her hair when there was a knock on the front door. Sandy called, "Come in, Natt, the door's open!"

Natt stepped in the cool house and said, "Hi, Sandy, I guess Marcy's about ready?"

Stuffing her comb in her purse, Marcy appeared in the hallway into the living room and said, a bit breathlessly, "Yes, I'm ready... oh my! You look great, Natt!"

Natt took a step toward Marcy, a grin covering his face. "Wow! I'd say you're spectacular, Marcy! Thanks for going with me."

Marcy looked at her sister for a second, but Sandy had the biggest smile on her face and gave her sister a nod. "Go break a leg, little sis and have a great time!"

Marcy wasn't sure her feet were touching the floor as she moved across to where Natt waited for her. "Thanks, I'm sure we will!" Both of them grinning, Natt held the door and Marcy walked through.

Sandy did the unthinkable! She wheeled herself to the big window in the living room and looked out. Natt had his hand on Marcy's waist! "I love it when a plan comes together!"

Later that evening, the phone rang. Ramon reached back from his seat at the kitchen table and grabbed the handset from the wall unit. "Hello, DeLord's!"

"Ramon, is Marcy there?" Colleen asked.

A grin on his face, he looked at Sandy and said, "No, Mom, she's out on a date, wanna talk to her sister?"

Before Ramon could hand off the set to Sandy, they both heard the explosion from the phone. "WHAT!! What did you say?"

Ramon pulled the set back and said, "Oh, Mom, I think you heard me. Marcy's out on a date with the store owner. I do believe they went to Blairsville for dinner. Here's Sandy."

Sandy made a face at her husband. Before she brought the set to her face, she whispered, "Thanks a lot!" Ramon grinned and put Jon on his shoulder, but stayed to listen to Sandy's side of the coming conversation. "Hi, Mom…."

"You let your sister go on a date?" Colleen accused.

"Sure, Mom, she's over twenty-one. I have no say if she goes out. Oh, she felt fine after her full day at the clinic…"

"Sandra! What all are you throwing at me!" Colleen cried. "Marcy's been sick, but you're letting her go on a date? What was she doing at the clinic? She… she's on a date after she was at the clinic?"

"Sure, Mom, she worked her six hour shift today. When she came home she rushed in and took a shower. She was ready to go when Natt arrived to take her out."

"But… but, Sandy…" Colleen whispered. "She was so sick! Her heart's weak. Dr. Wright wants to see her soon. She needs to come home."

"Mom, listen to me. Dr. Wright said for her to have a good life, to do whatever she felt she could. She's doing that. Yes, she *was* sick, but she's not now, she feels fine. She's working in the clinic, she loves being around people who need care. I think the next time you see her will be when we all come back for Ed's wedding in October. Mom, get used to the idea that neither Marcy nor I need you to take care of us anymore."

"Well!" the phone went dead in Sandy's ear.

Sandy sighed and said to Ramon, "That went well."

Snow was falling lazily. There was a thin layer of white on the ramp up to the Vansville Community Church the last day of January. The clouds looked like their cheeks were puffed out, nearly bursting to let go of the wind and snow they were holding back. However, the church was warm, beautiful music floated through the sanctuary and outside as the door opened again and again to let more people in. The chairs were quickly filling up and some of the men of the assembly were unfolding chairs along the sides. Two young people from the community were getting married today. It was to be the wedding of the year! It wasn't every day the store owner and the clinic phlebotomist were getting married!

Sandy began to play the Mother's March. Ramon escorted Eleanor, with Nathan following close behind them to their seat on the front row. He went to the back, but then Ed brought his mom down the aisle. Everyone who knew her hoped she would allow herself to be happy today for the marriage of her second daughter, her youngest child.

As soon as Colleen was seated, Sandy pushed a key on the piano, then turned toward the audience and began to sing. The song was based on a Bible verse from the book of Ruth.

> "Don't urge me to leave you or to turn back from you.
> Where you go I will go, and where you stay I will stay.
> Your people will be my people and your God my God.
> Where you die I will die, and there I will be buried.
> May the LORD deal with me, be it ever so severely,
> if anything but death separates you and me." (1: 16,17)